Trees in Britain

For Elsie Phillips

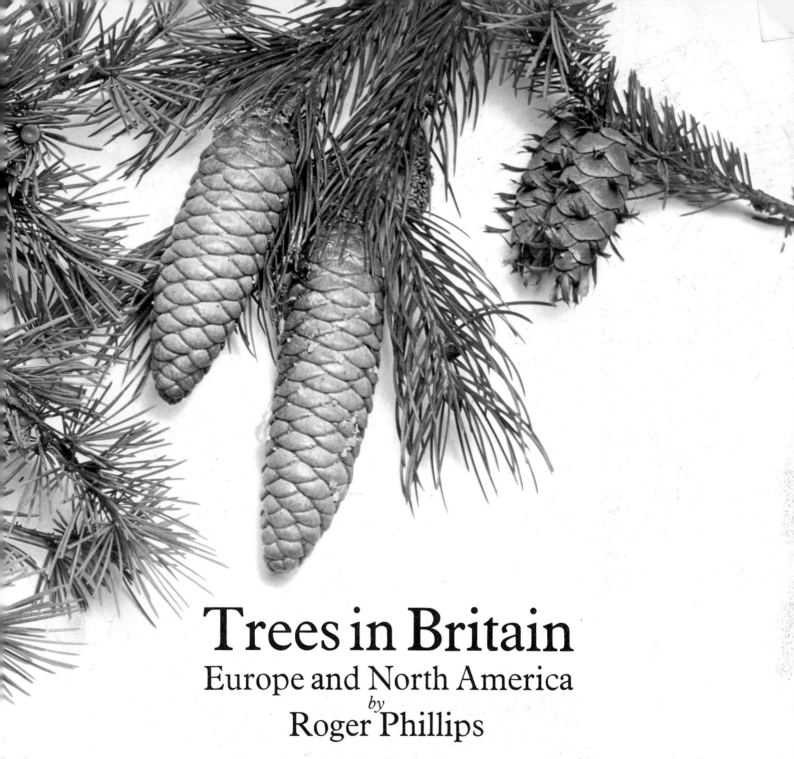

Trees in Britain
Europe and North America
by
Roger Phillips

assisted by Sheila Grant
edited by Tom Wellsted
line drawings by John White

A PAN ORIGINAL

Acknowledgements

It was only possible to consider doing this book when I had been offered help and cooperation by the organizations in charge of our wonderful arboreta. I would particularly like to thank the following:

The Royal Botanic Gardens, Kew.
The Forestry Commission at:
    Alice Holt Lodge, Surrey;
    Bedgebury National Pinetum, Kent;
    Westonbirt Arboretum, Gloucestershire.
The Royal Horticultural Society, Wisley.
Hillier Arboretum, Hampshire.
University of Cambridge Botanic Garden, Cambridge.
United States National Arboretum, Washington D.C.
English Eucalyptus Garden Centre, Kent.

I am indebted to a great many people for the work they have done in identification, specimen collection, tree climbing, typing, tracing and all the other tasks needed to complete the work. Thank you: John Albers, Peter Barnes, Beverley Clark, Jenny Deakin, Nicky Foy, Hatton Gardner, Sally Jellis, John Jobling, Jim Keesing, Clive King, Isobyl & Eric Lacroix, Roy Lancaster, Gus Macartney Filgate, Ruth Messom, Lindsey Mitchel, Sam Phillips, Martyn Rix, Malcolm Scott, Beverley Stokes, Lucy Su, Tim the Tree climber, Uncles and Summers, V. A. Waldren, Alf Westall, John White, R. M. Wickham, Felicity Youett.

In addition I would especially like to thank Alf Westall and Malcolm Scott for their work in checking the text and photographs of the conifer entries.

First published 1978 by Pan Books Ltd,
Cavaye Place, London SW10 9PG
9
Text © Roger Phillips 1978
Illustrations © Roger Phillips 1978
ISBN 0 330 25480 4
Printed and bound in Singapore
by Toppan Printing Co., (Singapore) Pte., Ltd.

Four colour origination by
City Engraving (Hull) Limited

Contents

Introduction

Of all the flowering plants I have come to know from doing my wild flower book, the ones I have become most fond of and intrigued by are the trees. But I soon found that though there are many fine textbooks none was designed to help people like myself, who have no academic training, to make accurate identification of trees. Having arrived at a clear analysis of what it was I myself needed, I set about actually producing it. The first thing I have done is establish a leaf index. Traditionally a tree book begins with a key that requires the reader to make yes/no decisions about the characteristics of leaves, flowers and other aspects of the tree. The problem with this method is that it involves learning and understanding the specialized vocabulary which botanists have evolved to describe the minute and precise differences between leaves. My innovation is to do visually what they have done verbally: if you can see the leaf you do not need to know whether it is lanceolate or oblong lanceolate, you just look at it and compare it with the photograph, and if it is too broad or too narrow you pass on to the next leaf or page of leaves. Then check with the text. Bear in mind that I have illustrated a selection of over 500 of the most common and important trees that can be found in temperate climatic regions. If the leaf fits none of those shown you may have come up with a species or variety that I have not been able to include in the book.

I have used the word 'index' to describe what would traditionally, I suppose, be called a 'key' because all you have to do is turn the pages looking for the leaf that matches the one of the tree you wish to identify.

The second thing I have set out to do is consistently illustrate three aspects of each of the main trees in the book with the following: a photograph of the flowers; a photograph of the fruit; and a drawing of the adult tree shape. I have retained this formula for two reasons. First, it is very frustrating to use a book which is inconsistent in the information given entry by entry and secondly, it has enabled me to show many aspects of trees which have not been adequately illustrated in photography before.

How to use the book

The book is in two main sections, first the fifty page leaf index and then the larger section with the trees arranged alphabetically by Latin name.

The Leaf Index

512 leaves and foliage samples have been grouped according to shape. The following table shows the thinking behind the layout.

10–23:	**Conifers**
10–11:	Scale-like leaves, including cypresses.
11–12:	Needle-like leaves at all angles round the stem, including junipers.
13–18:	Needle-like leaves in 2 rows; silver firs, spruces, hemlocks, etc.
19–20:	Needle-like leaves in bunches of 2; pines.
21:	Needle-like leaves in bunches of 3; pines.
21–22:	Needle-like leaves in bunches of 5; pines.
23:	Needle-like leaves in bunches of more than 5; cedars and larches.
24–49:	**Broad-leaves (Simple)**
24–42:	Narrow leaves (willows), grading to broad (magnolias and cherries) to heart-shaped (limes).
43–47:	Palmately lobed; including maples.
47–49:	Pinnately lobed, including oaks.
50–59:	**Broad-leaves (Compound)**
50:	3 leaflets.
51–52:	Palmate; horse chestnuts.
53–58:	Pinnate; including ashes.
59:	Bipinnate.

Each leaf has its Latin botanical name, common name(s) and the page number for the main text. The leaves in this section were all photographed from mid July to mid August. Each page carries a scale, the circle represents a diameter of 1 centimetre and the horizontal line represents 1 inch.

If you wish to make an identification of a tree you have found, whether in the wild or planted in a street, park or garden, compare the leaf with those shown in the leaf index and note which trees it closely resembles, and then look them up and compare details of shape, height, environment, flowers, fruit and bark. Do take into account that leaves can vary a great deal; they develop and grow and change colour during the year, often the leaves from suckers are much larger than those on the main branches of the same tree, and they may also vary from tree to tree.

The text photographs

In the majority of cases the photograph on the left shows the flower and that on the right the fruit. In cases where one or other has been unavailable or insignificant we have shown a detail of the bark as a further aid. Do not forget to observe the leaves on these photographs, often the flower photograph will show the young spring leaves and the fruit photograph the mature autumnal leaves. In addition to the general photographs there are two spreads of autumn leaves; pages 76, 77, 188, 189 and a small section of bark pages 216 to 220 inclusive.

The drawings

John White of the Forestry Commission has done simple line drawings of each tree, designed to show you first whether it is evergreen; drawn with a full canopy of leaves, semi-evergreen; drawn with a partial covering of leaves; or deciduous, drawn without leaves. But the main function of the drawings is to give an indication of the shape of the mature tree. Remember when comparing your tree to the drawing to consider the conditions under which it is growing; the drawings below are to remind you how the shape and size of a tree may be altered by age and position. All the drawings are based on live specimens.

Scots Pine *Pinus sylvestris* left an old tree, centre a fairly mature middle aged tree, right a young specimen.

Oak *Quercus* three examples of a tree roughly one hundred years old, on the left a tree growing in normal woodland, tall and thin because it is competing for light, centre a tree grown in the open without undue exposure to wind, right a tree grown in the open but in a position very exposed to strong winds.

Family Name

The family name is included after the botanical name of the first member of a genus. In the case of a large or more important genus it has been included in the short general description which precedes the detailed text.

Common Names

I have included a full selection of common or vernacular names in the text, the main authorities being *Trees and Shrubs Hardy in the British Isles* W. J. Bean vols I, II, III; *Manual of the Trees of North America* by Charles Sprague Sargent; *A Field Guide to the Trees of Britain and Northern Europe* by Alan Mitchell; *The Manual of Cultivated Plants* by L. H. Bailey.

Botanical Names

The botanical or Latin names are set in italics. They have been drawn from the same books as the common names above except for in one or two cases where I have had to make reference to *Flora Europaea*. Occasionally, when there has been a recent name change or where there is some dispute as to which is the correct name to use, I have included a synonym. The botanical name is followed by an initial, a group of initials or an abbreviated name, which refers to the botanist responsible for giving it that name.

Origin

I have started the text with the details of the country of origin of the tree.

Height

The height given is that of a normal mature specimen. When comparing a tree, take into consideration the factors which control its growth: its age, the quality of the soil, whether or not it is exposed to high winds, the altitude, and whether or not it has had to reach up for light in a wooded position.

Flowering time

The dates when the tree is likely to flower will vary and those given are average; if you are far north or south allowance must therefore be made.

Fruiting time

This is a more vague figure as the fruit forms and ripens over a period and in many cases stay on the tree for a considerable time; some pine cones for instance may stay on the trees for many years.

Scale

Although the leaf index photographs have a scale indication, no scale is included on the main text photographs but relevant measurements are stated in centimetres and (inches) in the text.

The photographs

The photographs in the leaf index were taken on 5 x 4″ size, Daylight Ektachrome E6 using a De Vere camera and a 210mm lens, with aperture f.64 The small photographs in the text that were taken in the studio – that is those on plain backgrounds – were taken on a Pentax 6 x 7cm camera using close-up lenses, with an aperture of f.22. The film stock was Kodak either E.P. 120 (E3 processing) or E.P.R. 120 (E6 processing). The bark photographs were taken on a Nickormat using Kodak E.P.D. 135. In the studio the light source was a 2 x 3ft Fish Fryer head and strobe boxes with an output up to 13,000 Joules.

Glossary

Alternate Of leaves, arranged successively up the stem or branch, neither OPPOSITE, nor in WHORLS.
Annual A plant which completes its life-cycle within one year.
Anther The part of the flower on the STAMEN which produces POLLEN.
Berry Fleshy fruit, usually containing many seeds.
Bipinnate A leaf which has PINNATE divisions.
Bract A leaf, or modified leaf which bears a flower in its axil.
Capsule A dry fruit which consists of more than one CARPEL and splits to release its seeds.
Carpel A modified leaf, one or more of which make up the female parts of a plant.
Catkin A hanging spike of small, usually rather insignificant flowers.
Chimaera A plant formed from the tissues of 2 different forms or species, usually originating at the point where one form has been grafted onto the other, and showing parts of each parent. A graft-hybrid.
Clone A group of identical plants derived asexually from a single plant.
Compound Made up of several similar parts; a leaf made up of several LEAFLETS.
Coniferous Cone-bearing.
Coppicing Cutting back a tree to a stump to encourage growth of slender sprouts which have traditionally been used in basket and fence making.
Cultivar A cultivated plant distinct from others in any of its characteristics and which remains distinct when reproduced.
Deciduous A tree which sheds all its leaves annually.
Entire Referring to leaf margins, means not toothed or lobed.
Evergreen A tree which is in leaf throughout the year. Semi-evergreen—A tree which loses some of its leaves in autumn retaining some until new leaves form in the spring.
Glabrous Hairless.
Graft-hybrid See CHIMAERA.
Hardy Able to withstand cold.
Hermaphrodite Containing both sexes, i.e. functional OVARY and STAMENS.
Husk The thin dry covering on some fruits and seeds.
Hybrid A plant originating from the fertilization of one species by another.
Kernel A seed within a hard shell or the edible part of a nut.
Leaflet One of the divisions of a COMPOUND leaf.
Lenticel A warty or corky mark on the surface of branches or stems which provides a pore for air to reach the tissues beneath the bark layer.
Native Not known to be introduced.
Nut A hard dry fruit.
Nutlet A small dry one-seeded fruit: the stone of a fleshy one.
Opposite Of leaves; arising at the same point on either side of a stem or branch.
Ovary The part of the flower which encloses the OVULES.
Ovule The female part which, on fertilization, forms the seed.
Palmate Having lobes or leaflets arising from one point in a hand shape.
Panicle A branched flowerhead.
Pinnate Referring to a COMPOUND leaf with 2 rows of LEAFLETS on either side of a central stem.
Pistil The female parts of a flower.
Pollen The fertilizing (male cells) powder formed in the ANTHERS.
Pubescent Covered with soft, short hairs.
Receptacle The enlarged end of a stem which bears the parts of a flower. Also the fleshy part which encloses the OVARIES in some types of plant.
Semi-evergreen See EVERGREEN.
Sessile Unstalked.
Simple Not COMPOUND.
Shrub A woody plant, much branched and smaller than TREES. (Often taken as less than 4.5m (15 ft) tall).
Sucker A shoot arising from roots eventually forming a new plant.
Tree A large plant with a single woody trunk. (Often taken as taller than 4.5 m (15 ft)).
Whorls Leaves or flowers arranged at the same level around the branch or stem.

Abbreviations used in the text:

cv.   cultivar
var.   variety
X   denotes a hybrid
+   denotes a graft-hybrid or a bigeneric-hybrid

Further Reading

Trees & Shrubs Hardy in the British Isles Vols I-III, by W. J. Bean (John Murray, eighth edition)

A Field Guide to the Trees of Britain and Northern Europe, by Alan Mitchell (Collins)

Manual of the Trees of North America Vols I, II, by Charles Sprague Sargent (Dover)

The Manual of Cultivated Plants, by L. H. Bailey

Trees of North America, by C. Frank Brockman (Golden Press)

Hilliers' Manual of Trees & Shrubs. Fourth edition

Conifers in the British Isles, by A. F. Mitchell (Forestry Commission Booklet No. 33)

Trees for Your Garden, by Roy Lancaster (Floraprint Ltd.)

Field Recognition of British Elms, by J. Jobling and A. F. Mitchell (Forestry Commission Booklet No. 42)

Trees and Bushes of Europe, by Oleg Polunin and Barbara Everard (Oxford)

The International Book of Trees, by Hugh Johnson (Mitchell Beazley)

The Oxford Book of Trees, by B. E. Nicholson and A. R. Clapham (Oxford)

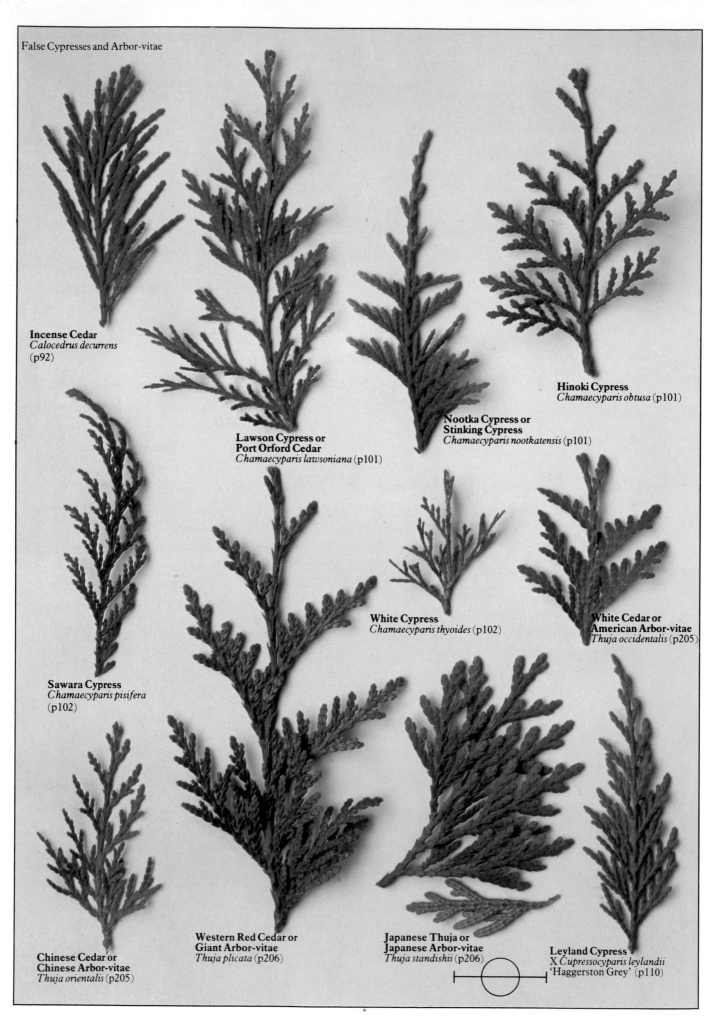

False Cypresses and Arbor-vitae

Incense Cedar
Calocedrus decurrens
(p92)

**Lawson Cypress or
Port Orford Cedar**
Chamaecyparis lawsoniana (p101)

**Nootka Cypress or
Stinking Cypress**
Chamaecyparis nootkatensis (p101)

Hinoki Cypress
Chamaecyparis obtusa (p101)

Sawara Cypress
Chamaecyparis pisifera
(p102)

White Cypress
Chamaecyparis thyoides (p102)

**White Cedar or
American Arbor-vitae**
Thuja occidentalis (p205)

**Chinese Cedar or
Chinese Arbor-vitae**
Thuja orientalis (p205)

**Western Red Cedar or
Giant Arbor-vitae**
Thuja plicata (p206)

**Japanese Thuja or
Japanese Arbor-vitae**
Thuja standishii (p206)

Leyland Cypress
X *Cupressocyparis leylandii*
'Haggerston Grey' (p110)

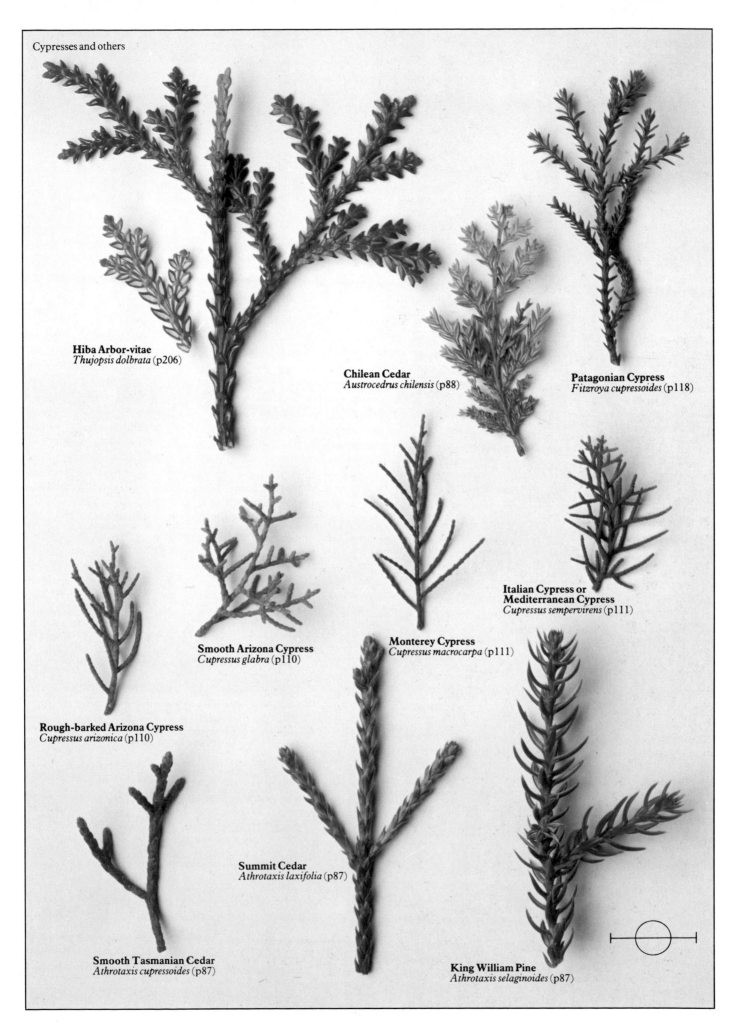

Hiba Arbor-vitae
Thujopsis dolbrata (p206)

Chilean Cedar
Austrocedrus chilensis (p88)

Patagonian Cypress
Fitzroya cupressoides (p118)

**Italian Cypress or
Mediterranean Cypress**
Cupressus sempervirens (p111)

Smooth Arizona Cypress
Cupressus glabra (p110)

Monterey Cypress
Cupressus macrocarpa (p111)

Rough-barked Arizona Cypress
Cupressus arizonica (p110)

Summit Cedar
Athrotaxis laxifolia (p87)

Smooth Tasmanian Cedar
Athrotaxis cupressoides (p87)

King William Pine
Athrotaxis selaginoides (p87)

Mostly Junipers

Chinese Juniper
Juniperus chinensis (p125)

Taiwania cryptomerioides (p203)

Wellingtonia or California Big Tree
Sequoiadendron giganteum (p197)

Japanese Cedar
Cryptomeria japonica (p109)

Common Juniper
Juniperus communis (p126)

Syrian Juniper
Juniperus drupacea (p126)

Mexican Juniper
Juniperus flaccida (p126)

One-seed Juniper or Cherrystone Juniper
Juniperus monosperma (p126)

Drooping Juniper or Himalayan Juniper
Juniperus recurva (p127)

Temple Juniper or Needle Juniper
Juniperus rigida (p127)

Pencil Cedar or Eastern Redcedar
Juniperus virginiana (p127)

Nutmegs, Redwoods and others

Japanese Nutmeg
Torreya nucifera (p209)

California Nutmeg
Torreya californica (p209)

Monkey Puzzle or Chile Pine
Araucaria araucana (p85)

Cephalotaxus harringtonia (p100)

Chinese Fir
Cunninghamia lanceolata (p109)

Cow's Tail Pine or Japanese Plum Yew
Cephalotaxus harringtonia var. *drupacea* (p100)

Chinese Plum Yew
Cephalotaxus fortunei (p99)

Coast Redwood
Sequoia sempervirens (p196)

Dawn Redwood
Metasequoia glyptostroboides (p140)

Swamp Cypress or Bald Cypress
Taxodium distichum (p203)

Plum-fruited Yew or Chilean Yew
Podocarpus andinus (p165)

Prince Albert's Yew
Saxegothaea conspicua (p196)

Golden Irish Yew
Taxus baccata
cv. 'Fastigiata
Aureomarginata' (p204)

Chinese Yew
Taxus celebica (p204)

**Common Yew or
English Yew**
Taxus baccata (p204)

**Pacific Yew or
Western Yew**
Taxus brevifolia (p204)

**Eastern Hemlock or
Canadian Hemlock**
Tsuga canadensis (p209)

Chinese Hemlock
Tsuga chinensis (p210)

Japanese Yew
Taxus cuspidata (p204)

Carolina Hemlock
Tsuga caroliniana (p210)

Western Hemlock
Tsuga heterophylla (p211)

Southern Japanese Hemlock
Tsuga sieboldii (p211)

Northern Japanese Hemlock
Tsuga diversifolia (p210)

Mountain Hemlock
Tsuga mertensiana (p211)

**European Silver Fir or
Common Silver Fir**
Abies alba (p60)

**Red Silver Fir or
Pacific Silver Fir**
Abies amabilis (p60)

Santa Lucia Fir
Abies bracteata (p60)

Greek Fir
Abies cephalonica (p61)

**Colorado Fir or
White Fir**
Abies concolor (p61)

Delavay's Silver Fir
Abies delavayi var. *georgei* (p61)

**Momi Fir or
Japanese Fir**
Abies firma (p62)

**Grand Fir or
Giant Fir**
Abies grandis (p62)

Nikko Fir
Abies homolepis (p62)

Alpine Fir
Abies lasiocarpa (p63)

Red Fir
Abies magnifica (p63)

Caucasian Fir
Abies nordmanniana (p64)

Algerian Fir
Abies numidica (p64)

Noble Fir
Abies procera (p64)

Veitch's Silver Fir
Abies veitchii (p65)

Blue Douglas Fir
Pseudotsuga menziesii var. *glauca* (p178)

Large-coned Douglas Fir
Pseudotsuga macrocarpa (p177)

Douglas Fir or Green Douglas Fir
Pseudotsuga menziesii (p177)

Norway Spruce
Picea abies (p145)

Dragon Spruce
Picea asperata (p145)

Sargent Spruce
Picea brachytyla (p145)

Blue Engelmann Spruce
Picea engelmannii glauca (p146)

White Spruce
Picea glauca (p146)

Koyama's Spruce
Picea koyamai (p147)

Brewer's Weeping Spruce
Picea breweriana (p146)

Hondo Spruce
Picea jezoensis var. *hondoensis* (p147)

Likiang Spruce
Picea likiangensis (p147)

Black Spruce
Picea mariana (p148)

Siberian Spruce
Picea obovata (p148)

Serbian Spruce
Picea omorika (p148)

**Oriental Spruce or
Caucasian Spruce**
Picea orientalis (p149)

Tiger-tail Spruce
Picea polita (p149)

Colorado Spruce
Picea pungens (p149)

Blue Spruce
Picea pungens glauca (p150)

Red Spruce
Picea rubens (p150)

Sitka Spruce
Picea sitchensis (p150)

**Sikkin Spruce or
East Himalayan Spruce**
Picea spinulosa (p151)

Picea wilsonii (p151)

**Morinda Spruce or
West Himalayan Spruce**
Picea smithiana (p151)

Umbrella Pine
Sciadopitys verticillata (p196)

Two-needled Pines

Jack Pine
Pinus banksiana (p154)

**Shore Pine or
Beach Pine**
Pinus contorta (p155)

Lodgepole Pine
Pinus contorta var. *latifolia* (p155)

Aleppo Pine
Pinus halepensis (p156)

Bosnian Pine
Pinus heldreichii var. *leucodermis* (p157)

Bishop Pine
Pinus muricata (p158)

Austrian Pine
Pinus nigra (p158)

Crimean Pine
Pinus nigra var. *caramanica* (p159)

Corsican Pine
Pinus nigra var. *maritima* (p159)

**Maritime Pine or
Cluster Pine**
Pinus pinaster (p160)

Stone Pine or Italian Stone Pine
Pinus pinea (p160)

Red Pine
Pinus resinosa (p161)

Chinese Pine
Pinus tabuliformis (p163)

Scots Pine
Pinus sylvestris (p162)

Japanese Black Pine or Kuro–matsu
Pinus thunbergii (p163)

Mountain Pine
Pinus uncinata (p163)

Scrub Pine
Pinus virginiana (p164)

Three-needled Pines

Lacebark Pine
Pinus bungeana (p154)

Knobcone Pine
Pinus attenuata (p153)

Big-cone Pine
Pinus coulteri (p156)

**Pinyon,
Mexican Nut Pine or
Mexican Stone Pine**
Pinus cembroides (p155)

Jeffrey Pine
Pinus jeffreyi (p157)

Western Yellow Pine
Pinus ponderosa (p161)

Monterey Pine
Pinus radiata (p161)

Five-needled Pines

Whitebark Pine
Pinus albicaulis (p152)

Bristle-cone Pine
Pinus aristata (p152)

Northern Pitch Pine
Pinus rigida (p162)

21

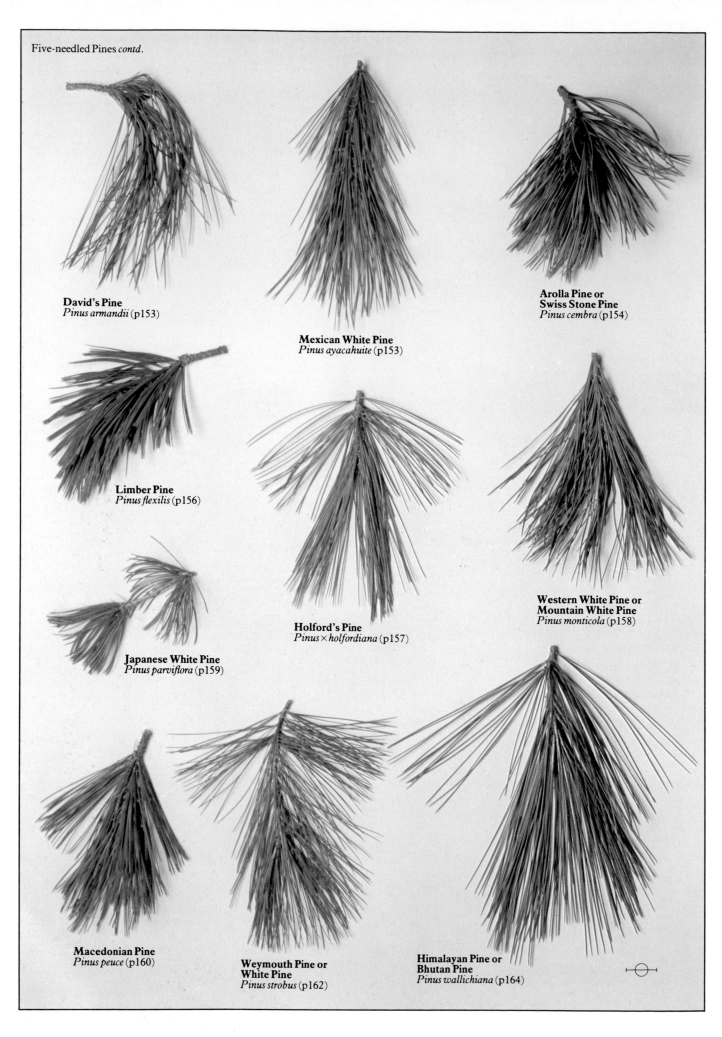

David's Pine
Pinus armandii (p153)

Mexican White Pine
Pinus ayacahuite (p153)

**Arolla Pine or
Swiss Stone Pine**
Pinus cembra (p154)

Limber Pine
Pinus flexilis (p156)

Holford's Pine
Pinus × holfordiana (p157)

**Western White Pine or
Mountain White Pine**
Pinus monticola (p158)

Japanese White Pine
Pinus parviflora (p159)

Macedonian Pine
Pinus peuce (p160)

**Weymouth Pine or
White Pine**
Pinus strobus (p162)

**Himalayan Pine or
Bhutan Pine**
Pinus wallichiana (p164)

Blue Cedar
Cedrus atlantica
var. *glauca* (p97)

Cyprus Cedar
Cedrus libani var.
brevifolia (p98)

Atlas Cedar
Cedrus atlantica (p97)

Deodar
Cedrus deodara (p97)

**European Larch or
Common Larch**
Larix decidua (p129)

Dunkeld Larch
Larix × eurolepis (p130)

Dahurian Larch
Larix gmelinii (p130)

Cedar of Lebanon
Cedrus libani (p98)

**Tamarack,
American Larch or
Hackmatack**
Larix laricina (p131)

**Western Larch or
West American Larch**
Larix occidentalis (p131)

Tibetan Larch
Larix potaninii (p131)

Japanese Larch
Larix kaempferi (p130)

Very Narrow Leaves

Osier
Salix viminalis (p195)

Oleaster
Eleagnus angustifolia (p113)

Willow-leaved Pear
Pyrus salicifolia (p180)

Willow-leaved Magnolia
Magnolia salicifolia (p135)

**Canyon Live Oak or
Maul Oak**
Quercus chrysolepis (p182)

Golden Chestnut
Chrysolepis chrysophylla (p102)

Laurel Oak
Quercus laurifolia (p184)

Chilean Fire Bush
Embothrium coccineum (p114)

Willow Oak
Quercus phellos (p186)

Winter's Bark
Drimys winteri (p113)

Spinning Gum
Eucalyptus perriniana (p115)

Snow Gum
Eucalyptus niphophila (p114)

Cider Gum
Eucalyptus gunnii (p114)

Mostly Willows

White Willow
Salix alba (p193)

Contorted Willow
Salix matsudana 'Tortuosa' (p194)

Golden Weeping Willow
Salix × chrysocoma (p194)

**Crack Willow or
Brittle Willow**
Salix fragilis (p194)

**Almond-leaved Willow or
French Willow**
Salix triandra (p195)

Grey Sallow
Salix cinerea (p194)

**Bay Willow or
Laurel-leaved Willow**
Salix pentandra (p195)

Southern Nettle-tree
Celtis australis (p98)

**Pin Cherry or
Wild Red Cherry**
Prunus pensylvanica (p173)

Peach
Prunus persica (p173)

Tibetan Cherry
Prunus serrula (p174)

Japanese Stewartia or Deciduous Stewartia
Stewartia pseudocamellia (p202)

Chinese Stewartia
Stewartia sinensis (p202)

Portugal Laurel
Prunus lusitanica (p172)

Hornbeam Maple
Acer carpinifolium (p66)

Mountain Snowdrop Tree or Silver Bell
Halesia monticola (p121)

Medlar
Mespilus germanica (p140)

Hybrid Strawberry Tree
Arbutus × andrachnoides (p85)

Bamboo-leaved Oak
Quercus myrsinifolia (p185)

Cherry Laurel
Prunus laurocerasus (p172)

Strawberry Tree
Arbutus unedo (p86)

Sweet Chestnut or Spanish Chestnut
Castanea sativa (p95)

Lebanon Oak
Quercus libani (p184)

Tanbark Oak
Lithocarpus densiflorus (p133)

Chestnut-leaved Oak
Quercus castaneifolia (p181)

Date Plum
Diospyros lotus (p112)

Common Persimmon
Diospyros virginiana (p112)

**Evergreen Magnolia,
Southern Magnolia or
Bull Bay**
Magnolia grandiflora (p135)

Kohuhu
Pittosporum tenuifolium (p164)

Madrona
Arbutus menziesii (p86)

**Cyprus Strawberry Tree or
Eastern Strawberry Tree**
Arbutus andrachne (p85)

**Sorrel Tree or
Sour Wood**
Oxydendrum arboreum (p143)

**Sugarberry or
Mississippi Hackberry**
Celtis laevigata (p99)

Wilson's Magnolia
Magnolia wilsonii (p136)

Northern Japanese Magnolia
Magnolia kobus (p135)

Magnolia × soulangiana (p135)

27

Japanese Big-leaf Magnolia
Magnolia hypoleuca (p135)

Cucumber Tree
Magnolia acuminata (p134)

Umbrella Tree
Magnolia tripetala (p136)

Shingle Oak
Quercus imbricaria (p183)

Veitch's Hybrid Magnolia
Magnolia × veitchii (p136)

Papaw
Asimina triloba (p86)

**Fraser Magnolia or
Ear-leaved Umbrella Tree**
Magnolia fraseri (p134)

Campbell's Magnolia
Magnolia campbellii (p134)

Californian Live Oak or Encina
Quercus agrifolia (p180)

Hackberry or Nettle-tree
Celtis occidentalis (p99)

Roblé Beech
Nothofagus obliqua (p142)

Cork Oak
Quercus suber (p190)

Dombey's Southern Beech or Coigüe
Nothofagus dombeyi (p141)

Antarctic Beech or Nirre
Nothofagus antarctica (p141)

Raoul or Rauli
Nothofagus procera (p142)

Holm Oak or Holly Oak
Quercus ilex (p183)

Pontine Oak or Armenian Oak
Quercus pontica (p186)

Caucasian Elm
Zelkova carpinifolia (p215)

English Elm
Ulmus procera (p213)

Wych Elm or Scotch Elm
Ulmus glabra (p212)

Keaki or Japanese Zelkova
Zelkova serrata (p215)

Prunus 'Shirofugen' (p175)

Prunus 'Hokusai' (p174)

Great White Cherry
Prunus 'Tai-Haku' (p176)

Prunus 'Pink Perfection' (p175)

Prunus 'Shirotae' (p175)

Prunus 'Amanogawa' (p174)

Prunus 'Kanzan' (p175)

Prunus 'Ukon' (p176)

Prunus 'Accolade' (*Prunus sargentii* × *P. subhirtella*) (p170)

Prunus 'Mikurama-gaeshi' (p175)

Yoshino Cherry
Prunus × *yedoensis* (p177)

Other Cherries

Cherry Plum or Myrobalan
Prunus cerasifera (p171)

Pissard Plum Purple-leaved Plum
Prunus cerasifera 'Pissardii' (p171)

Sloe or Blackthorn
Prunus spinosa (p176)

American Red Plum
Prunus americana (p170)

Manchurian Cherry
Prunus maackii (p172)

St Lucie Cherry
Prunus mahaleb (p172)

Black Cherry or Rum Cherry
Prunus serotina (p174)

Spring Cherry or Rosebud Cherry
Prunus subhirtella (p176)

Choke Cherry
Prunus virginiana (p176)

Bird Cherry
Prunus padus (p173)

Sargent Cherry
Prunus sargentii (p173)

Prunus 'Hillieri' (p171)

Gean, Wild Cherry or Mazzard
Prunus avium (p170)

Quince
Cydonia oblonga (p111)

Persian Ironwood or Iron Tree
Parrotia persica (p144)

American Smoketree
Cotinus obovatus (p105)

Box
Buxus sempervirens (p92)

Balearic Box
Buxus balearica (p92)

Tree Privet or Glossy Privet
Ligustrum lucidum (p132)

Himalayan Tree-cotoneaster
Cotoneaster frigidus (p105)

Bay or Laurel
Laurus nobilis (p132)

Californian Laurel, California Bay or Headache Tree
Umbellularia californica (p214)

Yellow Cucumber Tree
Magnolia cordata (p134)

Magnolia × loebneri 'Leonard Messel' (p135)

Goat Willow or Pussy Willow
Salix caprea (p193)

Common Beech or European Beech
Fagus sylvatica (p116)

Purple Beech
Fagus sylvatica purpurea (p117)

Oriental Beech
Fagus orientalis (p116)

Eucommia ulmoides (p115)

American Elm, White Elm or Water Elm
Ulmus americana (p212)

Rock Elm or Cork Elm
Ulmus thomasii (p214)

Single-leaved Ash
Fraxinus excelsior diversifolia (p119)

American Hornbeam or Blue Beech
Carpinus caroliniana (p93)

European Hop Hornbeam
Ostrya carpinifolia (p143)

Eastern Hop Hornbeam or Ironwood
Ostrya virginiana (p143)

European Hornbeam or Common Hornbeam
Carpinus betulus (p93)

Japanese Hornbeam
Carpinus japonica (p93)

Smooth-leaved Elm
Ulmus minor (p213)

Wych Elm or Scotch Elm
Ulmus glabra (p212)

European White Elm or Fluttering Elm
Ulmus laevis (p213)

Huntingdon Elm or Chichester Elm
Ulmus × hollandica 'Vegeta' (p212)

Dutch Elm
Ulmus × hollandica 'Hollandica' (p212)

Whitebeam
Sorbus aria (p197)

Red Alder or Oregon Alder
Alnus rubra (p84)

Sorbus 'Wilfred Fox' (p202)

Grey Alder or European Alder
Alnus incana (p83)

Père David's Maple
Acer davidii 'George Forrest' (p68)

Père David's Maple
Acer davidii 'Ernest Wilson' (p68)

Table Dogwood
Cornus controversa (p103)

Cornelian Cherry
Cornus mas (p104)

**Nuttall's Dogwood or
Pacific Dogwood**
Cornus nuttalli (p104)

Flowering Dogwood
Cornus florida (p103)

**Alternate-leaf Dogwood or
Pagoda Dogwood**
Cornus alternifolia (p103)

Snowbell Tree
Styrax japonica (p203)

Osage Orange
Maclura pomifera (p133)

**Tupelo,
Black Gum or
Pepperidge**
Nyssa sylvatica (p142)

Sweet Bay
Magnolia virginiana
(p136)

Holly-leaved Cherry
Prunus ilicifolia (p171)

American Holly
Ilex opaca (p124)

Perny's Holly
Ilex pernyi (p124)

Hedgehog Holly
Ilex aquifolium 'Ferox' (p123)

Ilex aquifolium
'Recurva' (p123)

**Common Holly or
English Holly**
Ilex aquifolium (p122)

Ilex aquifolium
'Aurea Marginata' (p123)

Ilex aquifolium
'Argentea Marginata' (p123)

Ilex × altaclarensis
'Wilsonii' (p122)

Ilex × altaclarensis
'Golden King' (p122)

Ilex × altaclarensis
'Hendersonii' (p122)

Ilex × altaclarensis
'Hodginsii' (p122)

Ilex × altaclarensis
'Camelliifolia' (p121)

Himalayan Holly
Ilex dipyrena (p124)

**Snowy Mespilus or
Allegheny Serviceberry**
Amelanchier laevis (p84)

Siberian Crab
Malus baccata (p136)

Magdeburg Crab
Malus 'Magdeburgensis' (p138)

Common Pear
Pyrus communis (p179)

Japanese Crab
Malus floribunda (p137)

**Crab Apple or
Wild Crab**
Malus sylvestris (p139)

Oregon Crab
Malus fusca (p138)

Purple Crab
Malus × purpurea (p139)

Hybrid Cockspur Thorn
Crataegus × lavallei (p108)

**Broad-leaved Cockspur Thorn or
Frosted Hawthorn**
Crataegus × prunifolia (p109)

Cockspur Thorn
Crataegus crus-gallii (p106)

Prairie Crab Apple
Malus ioensis (p138)

**Sweet Crab Apple or
Garland Tree**
Malus coronaria (p137)

Black Hawthorn
Crataegus douglasii (p106)

Scarlet Hawthorn
Crataegus pedicellata (p108)

Western Birch
Betula occidentalis (p89)

Himalayan Birch
Betula utilis (p91)

**River Birch or
Red Birch**
Betula nigra (p89)

Yellow Birch
Betula lutea (p89)

Downy Hawthorn
Crataegus mollis (p108)

**Silver Birch or
European White Birch**
Betula pendula (p90)

Downy Birch
Betula pubescens (p91)

**Grey Birch or
White Birch**
Betula populifolia (p90)

Blue Birch
Betula coerulea-grandis (p88)

Hawthorn-leafed Maple
Acer crataegifolium (p67)

**Cherry Birch,
Sweet Birch or
Black Birch**
Betula lenta (p88)

**Paper Birch or
Canoe Birch**
Betula papyrifera (p90)

Common Hazel or Cobnut
Corylus avellana (p104)

Turkish Hazel
Corylus colurna (p105)

Lime-leafed Maple
Acer distylum (p68)

Tartar Maple
Acer tataricum (p78)

Italian Alder
Alnus cordata (p83)

Common Alder or Black Alder
Alnus glutinosa (p83)

Big Leaf Storax
Styrax obassia (p203)

Judas Tree
Cercis siliquastrum (p100)

Katsura Tree
Cercidiphyllum japonicum (p100)

Paper Mulberry
Broussonetia papyrifera (p91)

White Mulberry
Morus alba (p140)

Common Mulberry or Black Mulberry
Morus nigra (p141)

**Downy Black Poplar or
Manchester Poplar**
Populus nigra var. *betulifolia*
(p168)

Lombardy Poplar
Populus nigra 'Italica' (p168)

**Cottonwood or
Necklace Poplar**
Populus deltoides (p167)

Hybrid Black Poplar
Populus × canadensis
'Robusta' (p167)

**Hybrid Black Poplar or
Railway Poplar**
Populus × canadensis
'Regenerata' (p166)

**Balsam Poplar or
Tacamahac**
Populus balsamifera (p166)

**American Aspen or
Quaking Aspen**
Populus tremuloides
(p169)

**Western Balsam Poplar or
Black Cottonwood**
Populus trichocarpa (p169)

Big-toothed Aspen
Populus grandidentata (p167)

Grey Poplar
Populus canescens (p167)

**Aspen or
European Aspen**
Populus tremula (p169)

**Dove Tree or
Handkerchief Tree**
Davidia involucrata (p112)

**Silver Lime or
White Lime**
Tilia tomentosa (p209)

**American Lime,
American Linden or
Basswood**
Tilia americana (p207)

Oliver's Lime
Tilia oliveri (p208)

**Weeping Silver Lime or
Weeping White Linden**
Tilia petiolaris (p208)

**Caucasian Lime or
Crimean Linden**
Tilia × euchlora (p207)

Large-leaved Lime
Tilia platyphyllos (p208)

Small-leaved Lime
Tilia cordata (p207)

**Common Lime or
European Linden**
Tilia × europea (p208)

Yellow Catalpa
Catalpa ovata (p96)

Foxglove-tree
Paulownia tomentosa (p144)

Chinese Necklace Poplar
Populus lasiocarpa (p168)

Western Catalpa
Catalpa speciosa (p97)

Hybrid Catalpa
Catalpa × erubescens (p96)

**Indian Bean or
Southern Catalpa**
Catalpa bignonioides (p96)

Spur Leaf
Tetracentron sinense (p205)

**Moose-bark,
Moosewood or
Striped Maple**
Acer pensylvanicum
(p74)

**Grey-budded
Snake-bark Maple**
Acer rufinerve (p75)

Red Snake-bark Maple
Acer capillipes (p66)

Hers's Maple
Acer grosseri
var. *hersii* (p70)

**Red Maple or
Scarlet Maple**
Acer rubrum (p75)

Montpelier Maple
Acer monspessulanum
(p72)

Forrest's Maple
Acer forrestii (p68)

Cretan Maple
Acer sempervirens
(p78)

Amur Maple
Acer ginnala (p69)

**Tulip Tree or
Whitewood**
Liriodendron tulipifera
(p133)

Chinese Tulip Tree
Liriodendron chinense
(p133)

Maidenhair Tree
Gingko biloba (p120)

Black Maple
Acer nigrum (p72)

Cappadocian Maple
Acer cappadocicum
(p66)

**Rock Maple or
Dwarf Maple**
Acer glabrum (p69)

Miyabe's Maple
Acer miyabei (p71)

Chalk Maple
Acer leucoderme (p71)

Italian Maple
Acer opalus
(p73)

Fig
Ficus carica
(p117)

Sweet Gum
Liquidamber styraciflua
(p132)

Prickly Castor-oil Tree
Kalopanax pictus var. *maximowiczii*
(p128)

Oriental Sweet Gum
Liquidamber orientalis (p132)

Five-lobed Maples

Sugar Maple
Acer saccharum (p78)

Oregon Maple
Acer macrophyllum (p71)

Mountain Maple
Acer spicatum (p78)

Miyabe's Maple
Acer miyabei (p71)

Heldreich's Maple
Acer heldreichii (p70)

Balkan Maple
Acer hyrcanum (p70)

**Sycamore or
Sycamore Maple**
Acer pseudoplatanus (p74)

Acer pseudoplatanus
'Atropurpureum' (p74)

**Van Volxem's
Maple**
Acer velutinum var.
vanvolxemii (p79)

**Field Maple or
Hedge Maple**
Acer campestre (p65)

Zoeschen Maple
Acer × zoeschense (p79)

Norway Maple
Acer platanoides (p74)

Acer platanoides
'Goldsworth Purple' (p74)

Acer platanoides
'Schwedleri' (p74)

Japanese Maple
Acer palmatum (p73)

Acer palmatum
'Atropurpureum (p73)

Silver Maple
Acer saccharinum (p75)

London Plane
Platanus acerifolia (p165)

Oriental Plane
Platanus orientalis (p165)

Bigtooth Maple
Acer grandidentatum
(p69)

**Downy Japanese Maple or
Fullmoon Maple**
Acer japonicum (p70)

Vine Maple
Acer circinatum (p67)

Cut-leaved Beech or Fern-leaved Beech
Fagus sylvatica 'Asplenifolia' (p117)

Pyrenean Whitebeam
Sorbus mougeottii (p200)

Hawthorn-leaved Crab Apple
Malus florentina (p137)

Service Tree of Fontainebleau
Sorbus latifolia (p200)

Midland Hawthorn, May or English Hawthorn
Crataegus laevigata (p107)

Common Hawthorn
Crataegus monogyna (p108)

Wild Service Tree
Sorbus torminalis (p201)

Bastard Service Tree
Sorbus × thuringiaca (p201)

Oriental Thorn
Crataegus laciniata (p107)

Swedish Whitebeam
Sorbus intermedia (p199)

Sassafras
Sassafras albidum (p196)

White Poplar or Abele
Populus alba (p166)

Sessile Oak or Durmast Oak
Quercus petraea (p186)

English Oak or Pedunculate Oak
Quercus robur (p187)

Lucombe Oak
Quercus × hispanica 'Lucombeana' (p183)

Cut-leaved Oak
Quercus robur 'Filicifolia' (p187)

Purple English Oak
Quercus robur purpurascens (p187)

Downy Oak
Quercus pubescens (p187)
(Specimens not typical; should be more deeply lobed)

Pyrenean Oak
Quercus pyrenaica (p187)

Black Oak or Quercitron Oak
Quercus velutina (p191)
(Specimen not typical; should be symmetrical and more deeply lobed)

Red Oak
Quercus rubra (p190)

Ludwig's Oak
Quercus × ludoviciana (p184)

White Oak
Quercus alba (p180)

Scarlet Oak
Quercus coccinea (p182)

Shumard Oak
Quercus shumardii (p190)

Pin Oak
Quercus palustris (p185)

Californian Black Oak
Quercus kelloggii (p184)

Caucasian Oak
Quercus macranthera (p185)

Mirbeck's Oak or Algerian Oak
Quercus canariensis (p181)

Daimio Oak
Quercus dentata (p182)

Macedonian Oak
Quercus trojana (p191)

Turkey Oak
Quercus cerris (p181)

Basket Oak or Chestnut Oak
Quercus prinus (p186)

Mirbeck's Oak or Algerian Oak
Quercus canariensis (p181)

Turner's Oak
Querus × turneri (p191)

Swamp White Oak
Quercus bicolor (p181)

Black Jack Oak
Quercus marilandica (p185)

Hungarian Oak
Quercus frainetto (p182)

Lea's Hybrid Oak
Quercus × leana (p184)

Burr Oak or Mossy Cup Oak
Quercus macrocarpa (p185)

Nikko Maple
Acer nikoense (p72)

Paperbark Maple
Acer griseum (p69)

Vine-leaved Maple
Acer cissifolium (p67)

Adam's Laburnum
+*Laburnocytisus adamii* (p128)

**Hop Tree or
Stinking Ash**
Ptelea trifoliata (p178)

Nymans Hybrid Eucryphia
Eucryphia×nymansensis (p115)

**Common Laburnum or
Golden Chain**
Laburnum anagyroides (p129)

Voss's Laburnum
Laburnum×watereri
'Vossii' (p129)

Scotch Laburnum
Laburnum alpinum (p129)

**Yellow Buckeye or
Sweet Buckeye**
Aesculus flava (p80)

California Buckeye
Aesculus californica (p79)

Ohio Buckeye
Aesculus glabra (p80)

Red Horse Chestnut
Aesculus × carnea (p80)

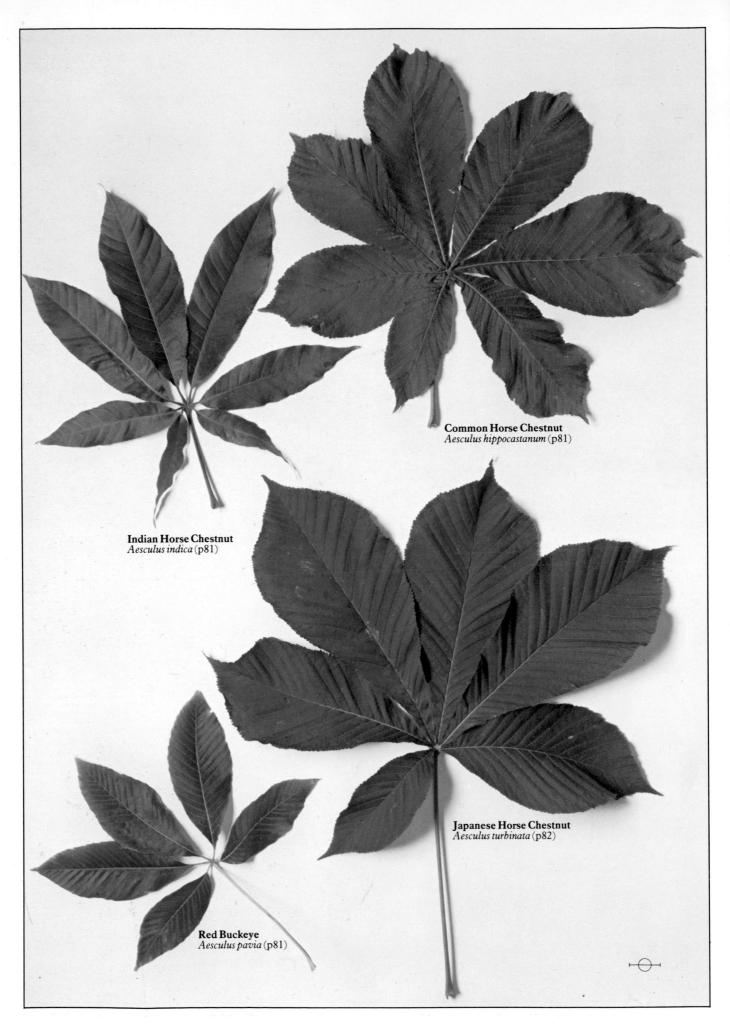

Common Horse Chestnut
Aesculus hippocastanum (p81)

Indian Horse Chestnut
Aesculus indica (p81)

Japanese Horse Chestnut
Aesculus turbinata (p82)

Red Buckeye
Aesculus pavia (p81)

52

Pignut Hickory
Carya glabra (p94)

**Velvet Ash or
Arizona Ash**
Fraxinus velutina (p120)

**Manna Ash or
Flowering Ash**
Fraxinus ornus (p119)

Box Elder
Acer negundo (p72)

White Ash
Fraxinus americana (p118)

**Shagbark Hickory or
Little Shellbark Hickory**
Carya ovata (p95)

Yellow Wood
Cladrastis lutea (p103)

Elder
Sambucus nigra
(p195)

Oregon Ash
Fraxinus latifolia (p119)

**Red Ash or
Green Ash**
Fraxinus pennsylvanica (p120)

Korean Euodia
Euodia daniellii (p116)

**Mockernut,
Big Bud Hickory or
White Heart Hickory**
Carya tomentosa (p95)

**Big Shellbark Hickory,
Bottom Shellbark
Hickory or King-nut**
Carya laciniosa (p94)

White Ash
Fraxinus americana
(p118)

**Bitternut or
Swamp Hickory**
Carya cordiformis (p94)

**English Walnut or
Persian Walnut**
Juglans regia (p125)

Caucasian Wing-nut
Pterocarya fraxinifolia (p178)

Oregon Ash
Fraxinus latifolia (p119)

Hybrid Wing-nut
Pterocarya × rehderiana
(p179)

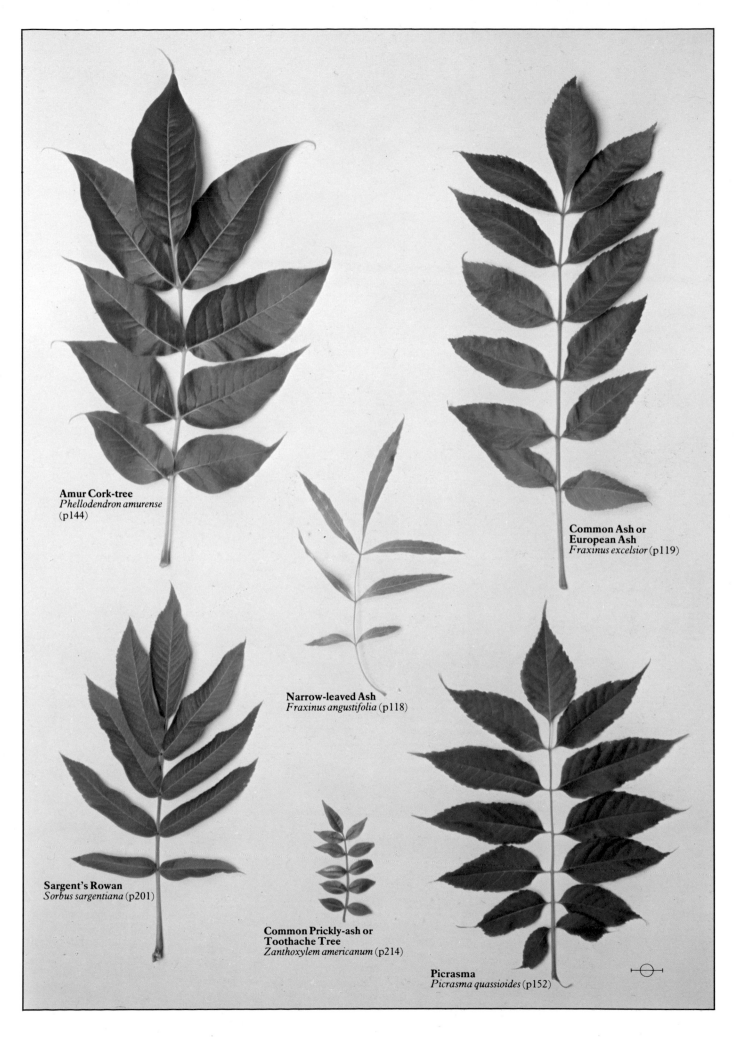

Amur Cork-tree
Phellodendron amurense
(p144)

**Common Ash or
European Ash**
Fraxinus excelsior (p119)

Narrow-leaved Ash
Fraxinus angustifolia (p118)

Sargent's Rowan
Sorbus sargentiana (p201)

**Common Prickly-ash or
Toothache Tree**
Zanthoxylem americanum (p214)

Picrasma
Picrasma quassioides (p152)

Japanese Rowan
Sorbus commixta (p198)

Chinese Scarlet Rowan
Sorbus 'Embley' (p199)

Service Tree
Sorbus domestica (p198)

Sorbus
'Joseph Rock' (p200)

Honey Locust
Gleditsia triacanthos (p121)

Hupeh Rowan
Sorbus hupehensis (p199)

**American Rowan or
American Mountain Ash**
Sorbus americana (p197)

**Rowan,
Mountain Ash or
European Mountain Ash**
Sorbus aucuparia (p198)

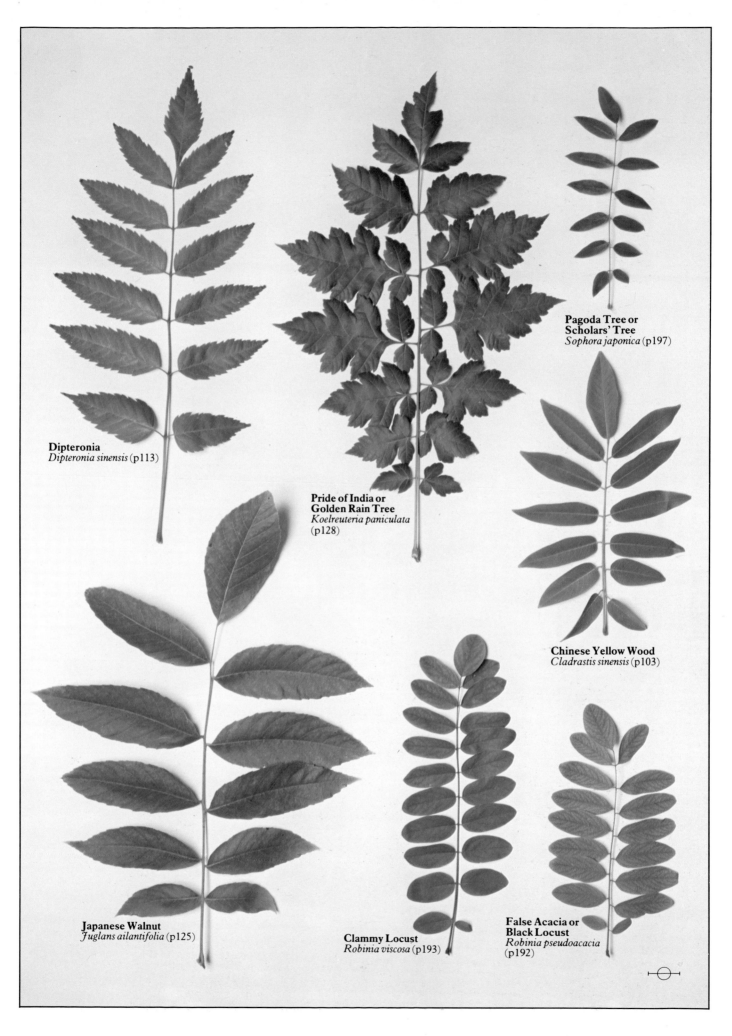

Dipteronia
Dipteronia sinensis (p113)

**Pride of India or
Golden Rain Tree**
Koelreuteria paniculata
(p128)

**Pagoda Tree or
Scholars' Tree**
Sophora japonica (p197)

Chinese Yellow Wood
Cladrastis sinensis (p103)

Japanese Walnut
Juglans ailantifolia (p125)

Clammy Locust
Robinia viscosa (p193)

**False Acacia or
Black Locust**
Robinia pseudoacacia
(p192)

Chinese Cedar
Cedrela sinensis (p97)

Stag's Horn Sumac
Rhus typhina (p192)

Varnish Tree
Rhus verniciflua (p192)

Tree of Heaven
Ailanthus altissima (p82)

**Butternut or
White Walnut**
Juglans cinerea (p125)

Black Walnut
Juglans nigra (p125)

Kentucky Coffee-tree
Gymnocladus dioica (p121)

**Devil's Walkingstick,
Hercules' Club or
Angelica Tree**
Aralia spinosa (p84)

**Mimosa or
Silver Wattle**
Acacia dealbata (p65)

Abies family Pinaceae, **Silver Fir.** A group of evergreen conifers with single needles and flowers of both sexes on the same tree. Topmost branches bear the solid cylindrical cones which break up when ripe, or are demolished by squirrels in search of the seeds, leaving the central spike on the tree.

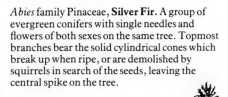

**European Silver Fir or
Common Silver Fir**

Abies alba Mill.
Native to central European mountains 800–1800m (2600–6000ft) altitude. Cultivated for timber but easily damaged by early frosts and greenfly attack. Grows slowly for first 6 years, then rapidly, gaining as much as 1m (3ft) in a year, to a height of 45m (150ft) and girth of 5m (18ft). Male flowers are grouped below previous years growth, shedding pollen in April. Females are green at first, developing into cones 12cm × 3cm (4½in × 1½in) red-brown when ripe with down curved toothed bracts (far left). Needles (p15) are white backed and notched at the tip. Bark (near left) is dark greyish and cracked into small square plates on old trees.

**Red Silver Fir or
Pacific Silver Fir**

Abies amabilis Doug. ex Forbes
Native to mountains of S.E. Alaska to Vancouver Island, Oregon and Washington. Sometimes grown as an ornamental tree outside its native environment, but usually found only in collections. Height may reach 75m (250ft) in the north of its range but is usually more modest elsewhere. Numerous, globular male flowers grow on undersides of shoots, drying to shed pollen in April. Female flowers start red developing into deep purple cones, 10–15cm (4–6in) long and 5–6cm (2–2½in) wide (far left). When crushed, the foliage (p15) gives off a strong smell of tangerines. The bark (near left) is grey with white patches.

Santa Lucia Fir

Abies bracteata (D.Don) Nutt.
Native to the canyons and rocky mountain tops of the Santa Lucia Mountains, California at altitudes around 900m (3000ft). Grown as an ornamental tree elsewhere, notably N. Italy. Height to 45m (150ft). Male flowers are 2–3cm (1in) long clustered on undersides of leaves, shedding pollen at the end of May, females solitary 2–3cm (1in) long (far left) developing into unmistakable cones 10cm (4in) long (near left). The tree is also easily distinguished by its long, 5cm (2in), sharp pointed needles (p15) and chestnut brown pointed buds, which look similar to the buds of beech trees.

Greek Fir

Abies cephalonica Loud.
Native to mountains of southern Greece and planted for ornament in large gardens. Height to 49m (130ft). Male and female flowers (far left) open in April; males red, turning yellow, females green, about 2·5cm (1in) long. Cones (near left) may be 10cm (4in) long. Foliage (p15) is distinct since the needles radiate from all sides of the twigs. This, combined with the resinous buds and bracts on the cones, makes the Greek Fir unmistakable. Bark (p216) is dark brown, breaking into small plates.

Colorado Fir or White Fir

Abies concolor (Gord.) Hildebrand
Native to Colorado, Arizona, southern California, Utah and Mexico. Grown in collections and gardens but rare, the variety *lowiana* being more common (see below). Height to about 30m (100ft) in the wild. Flowers (far left) open in late April, males round and yellow, females yellow-green, about 2·5cm (1in) long. Cones (near left) are 7·5–12·5cm (3–5in) long, and may be dark purple or bright yellow-green. Leaves (p15) are rather long, and produce a strong lemon smell when crushed. (Drawing above left.)

A. concolor var. *lowiana* (Gord.) Lemm. **Low's Fir**
Generally taller than the type, and considered to come from coastal regions from Oregon to Sierra Nevada. Two forms have been described: the northern form, with needles flat in 2 rows each side of the shoot, and the southern form with leaves curved upwards in a U shape. Trees grade between these two extremes in its range. (Drawing above right.)

Abies delavayi Franch, **Delavay's Silver Fir**
Native to western China, and rare in cultivation. Flowers and cones are similar to those shown for var. *georgii* (below) but the deep purple cones have smaller spine-like bracts showing. Foliage is also similar with leaves bluntly rounded and usually notched.

Forrest's Silver Fir

A. delavayi var. *forrestii* (Rogers) Jacks
Native to Yunnan and Szechuan provinces of China, probably the most commonly cultivated variety. Similar to the var. *georgii* but leaves are longer and deeply notched, and cones have shorter narrower bracts. (Drawing above left.)
A. delavayi var. *georgii* (Orr) Melville
Flowers (far left) open in late April. The dark purple cones (near left) are about 6–10cm (2½–4in) long, with distinctively long bracts. Foliage is shown on p15; leaves are notched, with two white bands underneath, and usually bluish in first year. (Drawing above right.)

61

**Momi Fir or
Japanese Fir**

Abies firma Sieb. & Zucc.
Native to south Japan, grown in collections and
for ornament in large gardens. Height may reach
24–30m (80–100ft). Male flowers shed pollen at
the end of April, females are 2·5cm (1in) long (far
left), developing into 8cm (3½in) cones (near
left). Foliage (p15) is bright green above, silvery
below and has a distinct leathery feel to it. The
needles are dark green and conspicuously
tapering towards the base, with 2 sharp points at
their tips. Bark is pinkish-grey.

**Grand Fir or
Giant Fir**

Abies grandis Lindl.
Native to Vancouver Island, British Columbia
south to California, now widely used as a forestry
tree, due to its remarkably fast growth rate and
tolerance to soil conditions. May reach 16m
(55ft) in 20 years and trees of 90m (300ft) have
been recorded in native environment. Male
flowers (far left) are smaller than other silver firs
and are produced only in upper part of the tree
and shed pollen in April. The cones are 7–8cm
(3in) ripening to dark brown in October (near
left) from a lovely bright green. Foliage (p15) has
a strong tangerine smell when crushed and
needles have two bright white bands on
undersides.

Nikko Fir

Abies homolepis Sieb. & Zucc.
Native to central Japan, cultivated for ornament
in large gardens. Grows to 24–27m (80–90ft),
tolerating pollution, so does better in or near
cities and towns than most other silver firs. Male
flowers are bright, light green, 2·5cm (1in) long,
shedding pollen in late April. Females (far left)
are 3·7cm (1½in) long, turning deep purple-blue
through the summer and ripening dark purple
brown (near left) in October, 8cm (3½in) long.
Foliage (p15) is composed of needles 1·5–3·7cm
(½–1½in) long, green above with two white
bands below. Bark (p216) is pinkish grey or
purplish grey eventually breaking up into small
flakes.

Korean Fir

Abies koreana Wils.
Native to Korea, often grown in gardens since it is generally rather small and bushy and produces cones freely from a young age, making a very decorative small tree. Height to 9m (30ft) in cultivation. Both male and female flowers (far left) are produced in May, males on shoots all over the tree, and females 2–5cm (1–2in) on upper branches. Ripe cones (near left) are 5–7·5cm (2–3in) long and usually covered with white resin. Leaves are shorter than most silver firs, 1–2·5cm (½–1in) with blunt, notched tips and bright white undersides. Bark is dark, covered with lenticels or pores.

Alpine Fir

Abies lasiocarpa (Hook.) Nutt.
Found on mountain tops in Alaska, British Columbia and Alberta south to Washington and Oregon. Has never done well in cultivation but occasionally grown for ornament in northern parts of America and in collections elsewhere. May reach 40m (130ft) in native environment. Male flowers (far left) shed pollen in April, females develop into dark purple cones ripening to brown (near left) 15cm (6in) which break up in October. Foliage (p16) is waxy, blue-green with shorter needles on upper branches and when crushed gives off a strong balsam smell.

Red Fir

Abies magnifica Murr.
Native to Oregon and California at altitudes of 1500–1800m (5000–6000ft) but grown as an ornamental tree in other parts of America and in Europe, as it develops into a large, beautifully symmetrical tree. An old tree may reach 65m (220ft). Flowers (far left) are produced in May and cones (near left) are sparse but large; 20cm (8in) long. They are golden green or purplish when young, ripening to brown in the autumn. Foliage (p16) is made up of curved needles which become almost four-sided with age. Bark is grey and corky and on old trees in California turns red.

Caucasian Fir

Abies nordmanniana (Stev.) Spach.
Native to the Caucasus, grown in collections and gardens for ornament. Growth may be slow but the tree can reach 50–60m (165–195ft) in its native environment. Flowers (far left) are produced in late April, males on branches all over crown, females only at the top. Cones (near left) are 15cm (6in), green and resinous through the summer, ripening to brown in October. Needles (p16) form 2 rows, the upper ones being shorter, often producing dense, luxurious looking foliage. Bark is grey and smooth, eventually splitting into square plates.

Algerian Fir

Abies numidica De Lannoy ex Carr.
Native to mountains in a small part of Algeria, planted in gardens for ornament and grows better in cities and towns than most silver firs. Growth can be rapid once established reaching 25m (85ft). Flowers (far left) appear in April, the females developing narrow cones 13cm (5in) (near left) ripening brown and covered in resin. Foliage (p16) is distinct in having needles set all round the twigs and all pointing upwards, dark bluish green above sometimes with a triangular patch of grey near the rounded tip. Two white bands beneath. Bark is pale pink-grey to orange, splitting to form plates when older.

Noble Fir

Abies procera Rehd.
Native to Washington and Oregon at altitudes of 600–1500m (2000–5000ft) cultivated elsewhere for its timber which is close grained and useful in building. Also valuable as an ornamental tree. Growth is rapid after a few years, reaching 45–60m (150–200ft) in its native environment, though rather less in cultivation. Male flowers (far left) shed pollen in May and females form distinctive cones (near left), 20–25cm (9–10in) long, with toothed downward pointing bracts, which almost cover the cone. Cones may be produced on relatively small trees, 5m (15ft). Foliage (p16) is bluish and strongly parted on undersides of twigs, the needles sweeping upwards. Bark is pale grey or purplish and splits into long deep cracks with age.

Veitch's Silver Fir

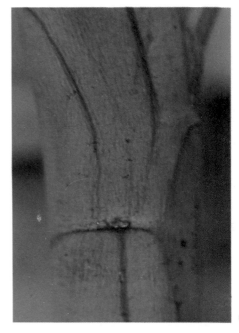

Abies veitchii Lindl.
Native to central Japan, planted for ornament in gardens, tolerant to town conditions. Growth is quite fast, even in first few years, but trees tend to be short lived. Grows to 22m (75ft). Flowers (far left) appear in April. Females develop from 2–3cm (1in) into blue-purple cones (near left) 6–8cm (2½–3in) and which ripen to brown in October. Foliage (p16) is similar to *A. nordmanniana* but is much softer. Needles are notched at the tip, glossy green above with bands of silver beneath. Bark is dark grey with horizontal lines, and sometimes has white patches.

Mimosa or Silver Wattle

Acacia dealbata Link, family Leguminosae.
An evergreen, native to New South Wales and Tasmania, now widely grown in central and southern Europe for its fragrant yellow blossom which is sold in city florists in early spring. Distribution is limited by its sensitivity to frost, but in its native environment it may reach 24m (80ft) with a girth of 3m (10ft). Individual flowers are about 0·5cm (¼in) in diameter and appear in January through March (near right). Seed pods, not shown, are bluish white, 5–7cm (2–3in) long and 1cm (½in) wide. Leaves (p59) are made up of tiny leaflets 2cm (1–2in) long. Bark is bright green-grey on young trees (far right), but sadly, turns brown then almost black with age. Persian Acacia (*Albizia julibrissen*) has similar shaped leaves.

Acer family Aceraceae, **Maple**. Deciduous trees and shrubs, with opposite, usually lobed, leaves and unusual winged fruits, or 'keys', similar to ash fruits (*Fraxinus*) but in pairs.

Field Maple or Hedge Maple

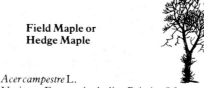

Acer campestre L.
Native to Europe, including Britain. Often found in hedges and the timber is used for turning and carving since it is usually in short lengths. Height to 4·5–9m (15–30ft) sometimes much larger. Flowers are hermaphrodite (far left) clustered in upright heads of 10 or so, appearing in late April or early May and developing into the hanging fruits (near left). The leaves (p45) turn golden yellow to red in autumn (p76). Field Maple hybridizes with the Montpelier (*A. monspessulanum*) and Cretan (*A. sempervirens*) Maples in south Europe, where confusion may arise over identification. A milky sap exuded from the leaves distinguishes the Field Maple.

Red Snake-bark Maple

Acer capillipes Maxim.
Native to Japan, grown in large gardens and becoming popular in small gardens for its attractive appearance. Height may reach 9–14m (30–45ft). Flowers (far left) open in May, about 25 in a curved flowerhead. Fruits (near left) in the same long drooping bunches, have keys 1–2cm (½–¾in) long with wings spread at an angle of 120–180°. Leaves (p43) are similar to those of Moose-bark (*A. pensylvanicum*) and Grey-budded Snake-bark Maple (*A. rufinerve*) but do not have rusty hairs on undersides, and usually have bright red stems. They turn orange and red in autumn (near left) making a stunning display in a small garden. The green and silver striped bark (p216) gives the name Snake-bark.

Cappadocian Maple

Acer cappadocicum Gleditsch
Native tree of the Caucasus, the Himalayas and China, now grown in large gardens and collections, and as a street tree in Europe. Fast-growing, reaching a height of 25m (80ft) with a girth of 2·5m (8ft). Flowers (far left) open in May, are 5–8mm (¼–⅓in) with five pale yellow petals, 15 or so forming an upright cluster. Keys (near left) have widely spread wings about 7cm (2¾in) long. Leaves (p44) have tufts of hair in the axils underneath and turn bright golden yellow in autumn (p76).
A. cappadocicum cv. 'Aureum' has yellow unfolding leaves turning green in summer and back to yellow in autumn.
A. cappadocicum cv. 'Rubrum' is distinguished by having red unfolding leaves.

Hornbeam Maple

Acer carpinifolium Sieb. & Zucc.
Native to Japan, cultivated in some collections. Grows to 15m (50ft) in Japan but hardly ever reaches more than 10m (33ft) elsewhere. Flowers (far left) open in late April, early May in clusters 10–12cm (4–4¾in) long. Fruit (near left) have down curved wings about 1·5cm (⅝in) long. Leaves (p26) are unlike any other maple being more akin to a hornbeam leaf, though are opposite rather than alternate as on hornbeams. They turn rich shades of brown and yellow in autumn.

Vine Maple

Acer circinatum Pursh
Native to west N. America, growing on stream banks on British Columbia coasts southwards to Sacramento River, California. The wood is heavy and close-grained and was once used by the Indians of the northwest for making fishing net frames. The tree is now becoming popular in small gardens in Europe. It may grow to 10–12m (33–40ft) and has a stout trunk but in its native state is usually prostrate and bushy with branches rooting where they touch the ground. The flowers (far left) are unusually bright for a maple and have male and female parts in separate flowers in the same cluster. Keys (near left) have wings 3·7cm (1½in) long and are bright red when young. Leaves (p46) are bright red and orange in the autumn (p76).

Vine-leaved Maple

Acer cissifolium (Sieb. & Zucc.) K. Koch
Native of Japan, cultivated in large gardens and collections. Grows to 9m (30ft) with a girth of 1m (3ft). Male and female flowers (far left) are produced on the same tree in May, forming pairs of flowerheads 10–12cm (4–4¾in) long. Keys (near left) have red wings, 2–3cm (1in) long, diverging at an angle of 60° or less. Leaves (p50) have 3 leaflets. Compare with Box Elder (*A. negundo*) and Nikko Maple (*A. nikoense*). They turn pale yellow and red in autumn.

Hawthorn-leaved Maple

Acer crataegifolium Sieb. & Zucc.
Another snake-bark maple, native to Japan. Grown in large gardens and collections. Usually reaches about 9m (30ft). Flowers (far left) are produced in April in upright clusters, 3–5cm (1–2in) long. Keys (near left) have red wings 2–2·5cm (¾–1in) long, spread at 180°. Leaves (p38) are smaller than other snake-barks, have red stems and remain faintly pink throughout the summer. Bark is green with vertical white stripes most pronounced on young shoots.

Père David's Maple

Acer davidii Franch.
Named after the French missionary who discovered this tree in its native China. Now a rather confused species since it has several forms and has often been wrongly labelled and confounded with other snake-bark maples. It is thought that there are at least 4 types in cultivation, 2 of which are:
A. davidii 'George Forrest'. A narrow open tree, 14m (48ft) (drawing above left). Young shoots are purple or dark red, and leaves (p34) are flat, larger and broader than other types with little autumn colour.
A. davidii 'Ernest Wilson' is smaller, with a more rounded habit (drawing above right), narrower leaves (p34) which are folded along the middle. They colour orange in autumn.
Flowers (far left) open in May, in spikes about 7·5–10cm (3–4in) long. Those shown are from the Wilson type. Keys (near left) have wings 2·5–3·7cm (1–1½in) long. This specimen is of the Forrest type. Bark is green with white stripes.

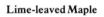

Lime-leaved Maple

Acer distylum Sieb. & Zucc.
Native to Japan and found elsewhere only in larger collections. Has grown to 9m (30ft) in cultivation, though may reach 15m (50ft) in the wild. Flowers (far left) are produced in May in upright clusters 7·5–10cm (3–4in) long. Fruits (near left) form upright spikes (most maple fruit clusters droop). The keys have wings about 2·5cm (1in) long diverging at 100°. The leaves (p39) look rather like lime leaves, but are narrower, and the stem may be pink or red. Bark is green with orange stripes.

Forrest's Maple

Acer forrestii Diels.
Native to China, where it was discovered by George Forrest early this century. May grow to 12m (40ft) in its native environment. Flowers (far left) are open in May forming arched spikes up to 10cm (4in) long. The keys (near left) have wings 2·5cm (1in) long spread almost horizontally. Leaves (p43) have red stems, tufts of hair in axils beneath, and remain green in autumn. Bark is similar to other snake-barks, green with vertical white stripes.

Amur Maple

Acer ginnala Maxim.
Native to China, Japan and Manchuria, now becoming popular for small gardens. A rather small tree reaching 9m (30ft) often forming a bushy shrub. Flowers (far left) open in May in dense upright clusters, 3·7cm (1½in) across. Fruit clusters droop (near left) and have wings 2·5cm (1in) long, almost parallel with each other. Leaves (p43) have a red stalk, and usually have a red main vein. They turn bright crimson red early in the autumn.

Rock Maple or Dwarf Maple

Acer glabrum Torr.
Native to western N. America, where it is found by mountain streams at altitudes of 1500–1800m (5000–6000ft). Grows to 9–12m (30–40ft) but is often rather smaller and shrubby in cultivation. Flowers (far left) open in late April, male and female flowers usually on separate trees. Fruits (near left) have down curved wings 2·5cm (1in) long. Leaves (p44) are 3- or 5-lobed and may even by split into 3 leaflets.

Bigtooth Maple

Acer grandidentatum Nutt.
Native to western N. America, where it grows by mountain rivers. Closely related to Sugar Maple (*A. saccharum*) which it replaces on the western side of America. Height to 9–12m (30–40ft). Male and female parts are in separate flowers, though may be on the same drooping cluster, produced in May. Keys have wings 1–2cm (½–¾in) long, turning from pink to green at maturity. Leaves (p46) turn yellow and red in autumn. Bark is dark brown and scaly.

Paper-bark Maple

Acer griseum (Franch.) Pax
Native to China, often cultivated in gardens for its ornamental bark (p216). Grows to 14m (45ft). Flowers (far left) open in May in bunches of three or five. Fruits (near left) are unusually large, having wings 3·7cm (1½in) downcurved and almost parallel. Leaves (p50) have 3 leaflets, and turn bright clear red and orange in autumn. Bark (p216) is orange, peeling in papery strips.

Hers's Maple

Acer grosseri Pax var. *hersii* (Rehd.) Rehd.
Native to the Honan Province of China, now
much planted in parks and gardens in England
and N. America. Height to 14m (45ft). Flowers
appear in May, 10–15 in a long spike (far left).
Keys have large 5cm (2in) green wings which are
almost horizontal (near left). Leaves (p43) turn
yellow, orange and red in autumn (p189) and the
bark is green with silver stripes as on other snake-
bark maples.

Heldreich's Maple

Acer heldreichii Orph.
Native to the Balkans and Greece, cultivated in
collections. Height to 19m (65ft) with a girth of
2m (7ft). Flowers are yellow and open in late May
in erect clusters. Keys have downcurved wings
2·5–5cm (1–2in). Leaves (p45) are distinctly
deeply cut and often likened to Virginia Creeper
leaves. They have brown hairs on the veins
underneath and turn yellow, sometimes red, in
the autumn.

Balkan Maple

Acer hyrcanum Fisch. & Mey.
Native to south-east Europe, cultivated in some
collections. Grows slowly to 6–15m (20–50ft)
tall. Flowers (far left) are produced in April in
bunches of 20 or so. Keys (near left) have wings
1·2cm (½in) long downcurved and almost
parallel. Leaves (p45) are similar to Italian Maple
(*A. opalus*) but are more deeply lobed and have
long 10cm (4in) narrow yellow or pink stalks.

Downy Japanese Maple
or
Fullmoon Maple

Acer japonicum Thunb.
Native to Japan, grown in large gardens. Height
to 9m (30ft). Flowers brightly coloured (far left)
open in mid April. Keys (near left) are slightly
downy at first, with widely spreading wings
2·5cm (1in) long, with red stems. Leaves (p46)
are almost circular, with 7–11 lobes, more than
most other maples, and remain green in autumn.
A. japonicum cv. 'Aconitifolium', **Fernleaf
Maple**, has deeply cut leaves with toothed lobes
turning dark red in autumn (p76). Height
reaches about 3m (10ft) though usually bushy.
A. japonicum cv. 'Vitifolium' is similar to the
species but is larger, to 13m (42ft) with larger
leaves which turn glorious reds and orange in
autumn (p76).

Chalk Maple

Acer leucoderme Small
Native to south-eastern United States, particularly Georgia and Alabama, and similar to the Sugar Maple (*A. saccharum*). Sometimes used as a street tree in some eastern American towns. Height to 6–7·5m (20–25ft). Flowers (far left) open at the end of April, male and female in the same bunch. Keys (near left) are slightly hairy when young and have spreading wings 1–2cm (½–¾in) long. Leaves (p44) are 3–5-lobed, often turning red in autumn.

Oregon Maple

Acer macrophyllum Pursh
Native to west coast of N. America from California to Alaska, sometimes grown in parks and in collections. Large tree to 30m (100ft). Flowers (far left) form a long spike 25cm (10in) opening in April. The keys have wings 5cm (2in) long joined at about 90°. Leaves (p45) are unusually large, 15–30cm (6–12in) across. A small specimen is shown. They display bright orange colours in autumn in their natural habitat, but are often less spectacular elsewhere.

Miyabe's Maple

Acer miyabei Maxim.
Native to Japan, but rather similar to the European Norway Maple (*A. platanoides*) though smaller, to 15m (50ft). Flowers (far left) open in May in spikes 5–7·5cm (2–3in) long. Fruits (near left) have downy nutlets and wide spreading wings 1–2cm (½–¾in) long. Leaves (p44) usually turn yellow with a red stalk in autumn.

Montpelier Maple

Acer monspessulanum L.
Native to south Europe and west Asia, where it grows on dry rocky ground. Cultivated in small gardens and parks, and often as a hedge in south Europe. May grow to about 15m (50ft) but is usually much less and often shrubby in form. Flowers (far left) open in June developing into a mass of usually red keys, with downcurved wings about 2·5cm (1in) long (near left). Leaves (p43) are similar to those of Cretan Maple (*A. sempervirens*), but fall earlier. Bark is dark, almost black with vertical cracks.

Box Elder or Ash-leaved Maple

Acer negundo L.
Native to a large area of east and central N. America, where it grows on swamp and streamsides. Box Elder has provided a source of sugar, or maple syrup, in the past but it is now more important as an ornamental tree both in Europe and in western N. America. Height to 12–15m (40–50ft). Male and female flowers (far left) are produced on different trees in April. Males are the dense red tassels, females the drooping green clusters. Keys (near left) have wings 3–3·7cm (1¼–1½in) long. Leaves (p53) have 5 leaflets, arranged like an ash leaf, but may have only 3 leaflets. Autumn colour is clear yellow (p77).
A. negundo cv. 'Variegatum'. A female clone, with white and green variegated leaves and fruit, making an attractive ornamental tree for streets and gardens.

Black Maple

Acer nigrum Michx. f.
Native to north-east N. America. A similar tree to the Sugar Maple (*A. saccharum*). Height to 24m (80ft). Tassels of pale green flowers are produced in April and keys are similar in shape to those of Sugar Maple (p78). Leaves (p44) are pale green and downy on the undersides and colour clear yellow in autumn.

Nikko Maple

Acer nikoense Maxim.
Native of Japan and central China where it may grow to about 15m (50ft) tall, with a trunk girth of 30–45cm (12–18in). In cultivation it is usually smaller and sometimes rather shrubby, making it useful in small gardens. Flowers (far left) are produced in May in bunches of three. Keys (near left) are downy, 3·7–5cm (1½–2in) long on hairy stalks. Leaves (p50) are also hairy, borne on hairy stalks, turning bright reds and yellows in autumn (p77).

Italian Maple

Acer opalus Mill.
Native to central and southern Europe, cultivated for ornament in large gardens. Grows to 9–19m (30–65ft) tall, though may sometimes be small and shrubby. Flowers (far left) are produced in April and make a spectacular display in their bright yellow hanging bunches with yellow opening leaves. Fruit (near left) have downcurved wings 2·5cm (1in) long, pinkish-green. Nuts turn red when ripe. Leaves (p44) are fairly similar to Sycamore (*A. pseudoplatanus*) but are smaller and have only three deeply-cut lobes. The base is usually more heart-shaped than is shown.

Japanese Maple

Acer palmatum Thunb.
A small maple, native to Japan, China and Korea, much grown in small and large gardens. Height to 6m (20ft) in cultivation but can grow much larger in its native environment. Flowers (far left) are small, 0·6–0·8cm (¼–⅓in) opening in early April in erect clusters. Fruits (near left) are also in erect bunches, though may be hanging in some of the many cultivated types. Leaves (p46) are 5–7-lobed, deeply cut, and turn red and purple in the autumn (p76). A huge number of cultivated varieties have been produced, the more common ones are briefly described below.

Acer palmatum cv. 'Atropurpureum' **Purple Japanese Maple**.
A cultivar of the Japanese Maple (above) popular in gardens of all sizes. Grows to 10m (33ft). Flowers (far left) open in April and fruits (near left) soon follow. The leaves are the most notable feature, being deep red purple throughout the year, similar in shape to Japanese Maple.
A. palmatum cv. 'Dissectum' has very deeply cut green leaves with 7–11 lobes, giving a fern-like appearance.
A. palmatum cv. 'Dissectum Atropurpureum' is similar to *A. palmatum* 'Dissectum' but has reddish purple leaves.
A. palmatum heptalobum cv. 'Osakazuki' has 7-lobed leaves, deeply cut, green through the summer turning brilliant red in October.
A. palmatum cv. 'Senkaki' **Coral-bark Maple** has deeply lobed yellowish green leaves, turning orange in October. Winter shoots are brilliant coral-red.

Moose-bark, Moosewood or Striped Maple

Acer pensylvanicum L.
A snake-bark native to north-east N. America, around New England, Quebec and Wisconsin, south to Georgia, often forming the undergrowth of forests. Cultivated for ornament in other northern states and also in Europe, as its striped bark and pretty fruits make it a most decorative tree. Height to 9–12m (30–40ft) though usually smaller in cultivation. Flowers (far left) are abundant, opening in May on long drooping spikes 15cm (6in) long. Fruit (near left) have wings 2·5cm (1in) long. Leaves p43) are large and variable but always with 3 forward-pointing lobes and bright green when young, turning red in autumn (near left). Leaf-stalks are usually pinkish, rather than red. Bark is green when young, reddish brown when mature, with vertical white stripes.

Norway Maple

Acer platanoides L.
Native to Europe from Norway southwards, but not to Britain. Cultivated in streets, parks, gardens and shelterbelts in Europe and N. America. Grows to about 18–21m (60–70ft). Flowers (far left) open in late March or early April. Fruits (near left) have wings almost horizontal, ripening from green to brown, often persisting on the tree through winter. Leaves (p45) have finely pointed, almost thread-like, lobes and the stems exude a milky sap when broken. They turn clear deep yellow in autumn (p189).
A. platanoides cv. 'Goldsworth Purple' has larger deep purple leaves (p45).
A. platanoides cv. 'Schwedleri' has unfolding leaves dark reddish purple, fading to green with a purple tinge in the summer (p45) and turning bright orange red and purple in the autumn.

Sycamore or Sycamore Maple

Acer pseudoplatanus L.
Native to central and southern Europe, cultivated as a shelter tree in town streets and parks, and for its timber which is used to make many small items from violins to wooden spoons, and as a veneer. Height to 30m (100ft). Flowers (far left) open in April in hanging spikes 6–12cm (2¼–4½in) long. Fruit (near left) have wings 2·5cm (1in) long which often turn bright red during the summer. Leaves (p45) may be only 3-lobed on some older fruiting trees. Leaf-stalks may be red or pinkish yellow.
A. pseudoplatanus cv. 'Atropurpureum' has leaves dark green above and dark purple beneath (p45).

Red Maple or Scarlet Maple

Acer rubrum L.
A large tree, native to eastern N. America, cultivated in Europe for its autumn colours, and used in America in furniture manufacture. Height to 36m (120ft) though often smaller in cultivation. Flowers (far left) open in late March or early April and often have male and female flowers on separate trees. The dense red clusters give the leafless tree a beautiful red glow. Fruit are also red on longer stalks than the flowers with wings 1cm (½in), spread at an angle of 60°. Leaves (p43) are similar to Silver Maple (*A. saccharinum*) but are less deeply lobed. They are most spectacular in autumn (near left).

Grey-budded Snake-bark Maple

Acer rufinerve Sieb. & Zucc.
A native of Japan, frequently cultivated for its ornamental bark and autumn colours. Distinguished from other snake-barks by its grey, downy young shoots. Height to about 13m (42ft) with a girth of 1m (3ft) and relatively short-lived. Flowers (far left) are 0·8cm (⅓in) produced in mid-April with the unfolding leaves in upright bunches 7·5cm (3in) long. Keys (near left) have red down on the nutlets at first and drop from June onwards. The leaves (p43) are about 10cm (4in) long, colouring orange to rich crimson in autumn (p77). The young bark is green with white stripes and as it matures loses the white becoming dull rough grey brown.

Silver Maple

Acer saccharinum L.
A handsome tree, native to eastern N. America from Quebec south to Florida, cultivated for ornament in Europe, particularly in Britain where it is often grown in parks, on roadsides and in gardens. Height to about 27–36m (90–120ft). Flowers (far left) open in March before the leaves unfold. Fruits have stalks 3·7–5cm (1½–2in) long and twisted wings spread widely. Since they form early, seed can germinate and produce several leaves before the end of the season, but in Britain seed is rarely set. Leaves (p46) have a silver underside and colour yellow and red in autumn (near left). Bark is smooth and grey and often covered with shoots and suckers.
A. saccharinum forma. *laciniatum* (Carr.) Rehd. has weeping branches and deeply cut narrowly lobed leaves.

Japanese Maple
Acer palmatum (p73)

Field Maple or Hedge Maple
Acer campestre (p65)

Acer japonicum 'Vitifolium' (p70)

Cappadocian Maple
Acer cappadocicum (p66)

Fernleaf Maple
Acer japonicum 'Aconitifolium' (p70)

Vine Maple
Acer circinatum (p67)

**Paper Birch or
Canoe Birch**
Betula papyrifera (p90)

Nikko Maple
Acer nikoense (p72)

Beech
Fagus sylvatica
(p116)

**Tupelo,
Black Gum or
Pepperidge**
Nyssa sylvatica (p142)

**Box Elder or
Ash-leaved Maple**
Acer negundo (p72)

**Grey-budded
Snake-bark Maple**
Acer rufinerve (p75)

Sugar Maple

Acer saccharum Marsh.
Native to eastern N. America. Cultivated as an ornamental or shade tree, but perhaps best known as the major source of maple sugar in N. America. Height to 30–36m (100–120ft). Flowers (far left) open in April on slender stalks 5cm (2in) long. Keys (near left) have wings about 2·5cm (1in) long. Leaves (p45) are similar to Norway Maple (*A. platanoides*) but the liquid in the stem is clear rather than milky. Leaf base is usually less heart-shaped than is shown. The autumn colours are considered the most spectacular of all American maples, turning crimson, orange and yellow in huge masses.

Acer sempervirens L. **Cretan Maple**
Native to the east Mediterranean, and grown in collections. Height to 9–10·5m (30–35ft) often shrubby. Flowers are yellow green in clusters 2·5cm (1in) long, opening in April. Keys have wings 1cm (½in) long at an angle of 60° or nearly parallel. Leaves (p43) may be unlobed and remain on the tree well into winter.

Mountain Maple

Acer spicatum Lam.
A small, sometimes bushy, maple native to east N. America, and sometimes cultivated in parks for ornament. Height to 7·5m (25ft). Flowers (far left) open in June in an erect spike, 7·5–15cm (3–6in) with male flowers at top and female lower down. The keys (near left) have wings about 1cm (½in) long, red and yellow, going brown in the autumn. Leaves (p45) are usually 3-, but sometimes 5-lobed, downy on the underside, and usually less heart-shaped at the base than is shown. They colour orange, yellow and red in autumn. Bark is smooth and reddish brown.

Tartar Maple

Acer tataricum L.
Native to south-east Europe and west Asia, cultivated in collections. Height to 9m (30ft) and may be bushy. Flowers (far left) open in erect bunches in late May developing into red keys (near left) with wings 2·5cm (1in) long. Leaves (p39) have 3 or 5 shallow lobes but often unlobed on mature trees, with down on the veins underneath. They colour yellow in autumn and fall early.

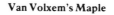

Van Volxem's Maple

Acer velutinum Boiss. var. *vanvolxemii* (Mast.)
Rehd.
A native of the Caucasus, cultivated in
collections. Height to 22m (75ft). Flowers (far
left) open in late May in erect clusters 7·5–10cm
(3–4in) long. Keys (near left) are downy. Leaves
(p45) are similar to Sycamore (*A. pseudoplatanus*)
but are larger, up to 20cm (8in) and have a longer
stalk, which may be 27cm (11in) long. The veins
have brown hairs underneath. Bark is smooth
and grey, with rings formed by branch scars.

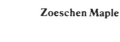

Zoeschen Maple

Acer × zoeschense Pax
A garden hybrid between Field Maple
(*A. campestre*) and either Lobel's Maple
(*A. lobelii*) or Cappadocian Maple
(*A. cappadocicum*). Height to 15m (50ft).
Flowers (far left) open in May in erect clusters
about 5cm (2in) across. Keys (near left) have
wings often tinged pink 2cm (¾in) long, a similar
shape to Field Maple keys. Leaves (p45) are
bright green and shiny with tufts of hair in the
vein axils beneath and red stems.

Aesculus family Hippocastanaceae, **Horse
Chestnut and Buckeye.** Deciduous trees with
leaves made up of leaflets radiating from one
point, and flowers in dense erect columns or
'candles'.

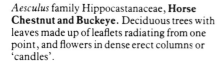

California Buckeye

Aesculus californica (Spach) Nutt.
Native to California and cultivated for ornament
in western N. America and in parts of Europe.
Height to 6–9m (20–30ft). Pale pink or white
fragrant flowers (near right) open from June to
August in clusters 15–20cm (6–8in) tall. The
stamens protrude about 1cm (½in) from each
flower giving a delicate shaggy appearance. The
lopsided fruits 5–7·5cm (2–3in) (far right) ripen
in October, splitting to release shiny brown nuts.
Leaves (p51) usually have 5 leaflets on stalks
1–2·5cm (½–1in) long, but sometimes 7. They
are smaller than other horse chestnuts and fall
early, without autumn colour.

Red Horse Chestnut

Aesculus×carnea Hayne
A hybrid arising from the Common Horse
Chestnut (*A. hippocastanum*) and Red Buckeye.
(*A. pavia*) Cultivated all over Europe as a shade
tree, in avenues, parks and gardens. Height to
18–25m (60–80ft) in continental Europe but
frequently much less. The red flowers (near
right) open in May in clusters 12–20cm (5–8in)
long developing into the fruit (far right) smaller
than Common Horse Chestnut and less spiny, if
at all. They split in October to release 2 or 3
brown nuts. The leaves (p51) are dark green and
often crinkly, with 5 or sometimes 7 almost
sessile leaflets.
Aesculus×carnea cv. 'Briottii' is a cultivar of the
Red Horse Chestnut (*A.×carnea*) above. It has
brighter heads of flowers (near right below) 15cm
(6in) long. Leaves are darker glossy green.

Yellow Buckeye or Sweet Buckeye

Aesculus flava Soland., synonym *A. octandra*
Marsh.
Native to south-east United States where it grows
on river banks and mountainsides. Height to
15–27m (50–90ft). Its wood has been put to use
as paper pulp and in manufacture of artificial
limbs. Grown in parks and gardens in Europe
and eastern states of America. Flowers (far right)
are produced in May and June, usually yellow,
but sometimes pink, in narrow clusters 10–15cm
(4–6in) tall. Fruit is spherical and smooth,
5–6cm (2–2½in) usually containing 2 brown
nuts. Leaves (p51) have 5 or 7 leaflets and colour
yellow in autumn (p188).

Ohio Buckeye

Aesculus glabra Willd.
Native to south-east and central United States,
grown in collections and gardens in eastern
N. America and in Europe. May grow to 21m
(70ft) but usually half this size. Flowers open in
April and May and are comparatively drab,
spikes 10–18cm (4–7in) long. These are not
illustrated but similar to *A. glabra* var. *sargentii*
flowers (near right). Fruits are 2·5–5cm (1–2in)
long with prickles on outside, usually containing
2 brown seeds. Leaves (p51) have short stalks on
the 5 leaflets. Bark (far right) is rough, dark grey
and scaly. It is the only American horse chestnut
with prickly fruit.
A. glabra var. *sargentii* Rehd. is found in
Missouri, Kansas, Ohio and Mississippi. It
differs from the type in having more leaflets
which are narrower and more tapering, with
more jagged edges (see flower photograph near
right).

Common Horse Chestnut

Aesculus hippocastanum L.
Native to north Greece and Albania and long
cultivated in other parts of Europe in parks,
gardens, streets and greens, where children
gather the nuts, or conkers, to play their game of
'conqueror'. May grow to more than 30m
(100ft). Flowers are white with a yellow turning
to red patch on the petal bases and form clusters
up to 30cm (12in) tall (near right). Fruits (far
right) have hard spines, are about 6cm (2¼in)
across, and split in October to release one or two
of the familiar shiny brown conkers. Leaves
(p52) usually have 7, sometimes 5, broad
stalkless leaflets. Bark (p216) is dark reddish or
greyish brown and splits into large plates.
A. hippocastanum cv. 'Baumannii' is a cultivar
having double, longer-lasting flowers which do
not produce nuts. A popular horse chestnut for
gardens.

Indian Horse Chestnut

Aesculus indica (Camb.) Hook.
Native to north-west Himalaya, cultivated in
parks and gardens since it is a highly decorative
tree. Grows to 30m (100ft). Flowers (near right)
open in June and July in panicles about 10–15cm
(4–6in) tall, though may be two or three times as
large. Stamens protrude from the flowers which
may be pink or with upper pair of petals flushed
yellow or red. Fruit (far right) has thin smooth
skin enclosing 2 or 3 wrinkled brown seeds.
Leaves (p52) have 7, sometimes 5 or 9, stalked
leaflets. Bark is smooth reddish grey on old trees,
greenish grey on young trees.
A. indica cv. 'Sydney Pearce' has darker green
leaves and larger flowers 2·5cm (1in) across and
flowerheads 30cm (12in) tall. Each flower is pale
pink or white dotted with yellow and red.

Red Buckeye

Aesculus pavia L.
A small horse chestnut, native to south-east
United States, best known as a parent of the Red
Horse Chestnut (*A.×carnea*). May often be
shrubby but as a tree reaches 6m (20ft). Flowers
(near right) open in June on spikes 15cm (6in)
tall. Fruit is smooth and egg-shaped, containing
one–two seeds which ripen in August. The leaves
(p52) are composed of 5–7 short-stalked leaflets
and colour red in autumn (far right).

Japanese Horse Chestnut

Aesculus turbinata Blume
A large tree, native to Japan and similar in appearance to the Common Horse Chestnut (*A. hippocastanum*) but more slow growing, has larger leaves and rough, but not spiny, egg- or pear-shaped fruit (far right). Flowers (near right) open 2–3 weeks after the Common Horse Chestnut in late May or early June. Leaves (p52) have 7 unstalked leaflets with tufts of orange down in vein axils underneath. They colour bright orange, then brown, and drop early in autumn. Bark is smooth with some wide cracks. On young trees it has white fissures.

Tree of Heaven

Ailanthus altissima (Mill.) Swingle, family Simaroubaceae.
Native to China, now widely planted in Europe and Central America as an ornamental, especially useful in cities. It produces many suckers and seedlings and is often considered something of a weed. Height to 30m (100ft). Male and female flowers open in late July on separate trees and look similar from a distance. Male flowers are shown far left. Female trees produce large bunches of fruits (near left) which ripen during August and September. Each winged seed is about 3·7cm (1½in) wide and the bunches often 30cm (12in) across. Leaves (p58) can be enormous, up to 1m (3ft) on young vigorous trees. Each leaflet usually has only 1–3 teeth on each side.

Persian Acacia, Silk Tree or Pink Siris

Albizia julibrissin (Willd.) Durazz., family Leguminosae.
A native to western Asia now commonly planted as a shade tree in Europe and China, in areas where it can be unaffected by severe frost. In Britain it is most commonly planted as an annual bedding plant, being destroyed or taken into a greenhouse in winter. Height may reach 12m (40ft). The brightly coloured flowers (shown right) open in July and August, their long pink stamens giving the appearance of a soft brush. The seed pod is 7·5–15cm (3–6in) long constricted between each seed.

Alnus family Betulaceae, **Alder.** Deciduous trees and shrubs. Male and female parts are separate on the same tree. Males are in long hanging catkins produced in early winter, expanding the following spring to release pollen. Females are tiny erect catkins produced in spring at shoot tips and ripen to form green then woody 'cones'.

Italian Alder

Alnus cordata Desf.
Native to south Italy and Corsica, cultivated in parks and gardens. Height to 15m (50ft). Male catkins extend to about 7·5–10cm (3–4in) and shed their pollen between February and April (far left) when tiny red females are produced. Fruit (near left) is 2·5cm (1in) long, much longer than other alders. The ripened cone, after shedding its seed, is shown with the flowers. The leaves have 5–6 pairs of veins, are shallowly toothed and dark glossy green with tufts of down in vein axils beneath (p39). Bark is smooth, grey, covered with lenticels and some short vertical cracks.

Common Alder or Black Alder

Alnus glutinosa (L.) Gaertn.
Native to Europe (including Britain), west Asia and north Africa. Grows wild in damp boggy ground and riversides, and its timber was used to make clogs in north England and Normandy. Little cultivated but sometimes planted as an ornamental in N. America. Height may reach 19m (65ft) or more. Male catkins (far left) shed pollen in early March, when they are 5–10cm (2–4in) long. Females (also far left) are about 0·5cm (¼in) long. Fruit (near left) is 1–2cm (½–¾in). They turn woody through winter as shown with flowers. Leaves (p39) are rounded with an indented tip and 7 pairs of veins, each with long tufts of hair in axils underneath. Bark (p216) is dark brown, soon splitting into thick plates.
A. glutinosa cv. 'Imperialis' is one of the many cut-leaved forms, having deeply and narrowly lobed leaves. Grown in gardens where it never attains a large size.

Grey Alder or European Alder

Alnus incana (L.) Moench
Native to Europe and the Caucasus, easily distinguished from the Common Alder (*A. glutinosa*) by its grey pointed leaves. Flowers (far left) are open in late February, the males 5–10cm (2–4in) long, females much smaller, developing into green fruits (near left) 1cm (½in) long. Ripe woody fruit is shown with flowers. Leaves (p34) have 9–12 pairs of downy veins, and are rather grey on underside. Bark is dark grey covered with pores and a few long cracks.

Red Alder or Oregon Alder

Alnus rubra Bong.
Native to western N. America, from Alaska south to California and Idaho. Alaskan Indians hollowed out trunks to make canoes and the timber is used in furniture and paper manufacture. Height to about 12–15m (40–50ft). Male catkins are 10–15cm (4–6in) long when they shed pollen in April (far left). Females develop into fruits 1–2cm (½–¾in) long (near left). Leaves (p34) have 10–15 pairs of veins which are often covered by orange down on underside. Bark is silver-grey in its home environment, but usually dark grey in cultivation.

Snowy Mespilus or Allegheny Serviceberry

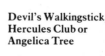

Amelanchier laevis Wieg., family Rosaceae.
A small deciduous tree, native to eastern N. America. Grows to 12m (40ft), producing delicate white fragrant blossom in late April, early May (near right) among pink unfolding leaves. Fruits (far right) ripen in July and August, through red to dark purple, 0·5cm (¼in) in diameter. Leaves (p37) colour bright red in autumn.

Devil's Walkingstick, Hercules Club or Angelica Tree

Aralia spinosa L., family Araliaceae.
An unusual tree, native to south-east United States, rarely cultivated. Height may reach 9m (30ft). Flowers are small, white, and open in August in round clusters grouped into a huge panicle, sometimes about 1–1·2m (3–4ft) long. Fruit are small, round, black and fleshy, ripening in October. Leaf (p59) is unlike any other, 1–1·2m (3–4ft) long, 0·7m (2½ft) wide. Each leaflet has a tiny stalk, but other *Aralia* species have sessile leaflets. The twigs bear stout prickles (see left). The berries and bark of roots contain a stimulant which has been used in medicine.

Monkey Puzzle or Chile Pine

Araucaria araucana (Mol.) K. Koch, family Araucariaceae.
Evergreen conifer, native to Chile and Argentina, grown as an ornamental in Europe and N. America. Height to 30m (100ft). Male and female flowers (near right) are produced on separate trees, and only on topmost branches. Males are about 10cm (4in) long and shed pollen in July; females are solitary, erect and green. They develop into cones about 10–17cm (4–7in) long, ripening from green to brown in their second autumn. The seeds used to be eaten as dessert nuts in South America, and Archibald Menzies first brought the Monkey Puzzle into cultivation by slipping some nuts from a Chilean banquet into his pocket. Foliage (p13) is composed of large thick dark green prickly leaf-like scales. Bark (p216) is grey and wrinkled, and marked with rings formed by old branch scars.

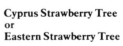

Arbutus family Ericaceae, **Strawberry Tree**.
Evergreen trees, bearing dark green shiny leaves and clusters of bell-shaped flowers.

Cyprus Strawberry Tree or Eastern Strawberry Tree

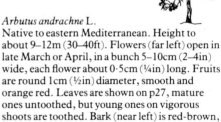

Arbutus andrachne L.
Native to eastern Mediterranean. Height to about 9–12m (30–40ft). Flowers (far left) open in late March or April, in a bunch 5–10cm (2–4in) wide, each flower about 0·5cm (¼in) long. Fruits are round 1cm (½in) diameter, smooth and orange red. Leaves are shown on p27, mature ones untoothed, but young ones on vigorous shoots are toothed. Bark (near left) is red-brown, peeling.

Hybrid Strawberry Tree

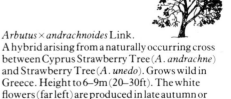

Arbutus × andrachnoides Link.
A hybrid arising from a naturally occurring cross between Cyprus Strawberry Tree (*A. andrachne*) and Strawberry Tree (*A. unedo*). Grows wild in Greece. Height to 6–9m (20–30ft). The white flowers (far left) are produced in late autumn or in March in spiked clusters 7cm (2¾in) long, developing into the fruit. Leaves (p26) are toothed and have dark red stalks. Bark (near left) can be quite spectacular, dark red, brown peeling off in thin scales leaving paler areas underneath.

Madrona

Arbutus menziesii Pursh.
Native to western N. America from British Columbia south to California and named after its first discoverer Archibald Menzies who described it in 1792. Grown in gardens in western and southern Europe. Height may reach 30m (100ft) in native environment, but usually 6–9m (20–30ft) in cultivation. Flowers (far left) open in May in an upright cluster from 7·5–23cm (3–9in) long, each flower about 0·5cm (¼in). Fruits are about 1cm (½in) across, orange-red and produced in bunches of 12–15. Leaves are toothed on young vigorous growth, but leaves from mature growth (p27) are untoothed. Bark (near left) peels to expose smooth clean pink-orange wood and has been used in tanning leather.

Strawberry Tree

Arbutus unedo L.
Native to south-west Ireland, and to south and south-west Europe. May grow to about 4·5–9m (15–30ft) high. Flowers (far left) and fruit (near left) from previous years flowers are both produced in the autumn, the fruit ripening and falling in October. These round strawberry-like fruits give the tree its English name. Flowers are 0·5cm (¼in) long and may be pinkish, forming hanging clusters 5cm (2in) long. Fruit are 2cm (¾in) across. Leaves are toothed (p26). Bark is less attractive than other species, becoming covered with muddy brown scales.

Papaw

Asimina triloba (L.) Dun., family Annonaceae. A deciduous small tree, sometimes shrubby, native to eastern United States. Although the name Papaw has long been used for this tree it is not the one which bears the fruit named Pawpaw (*Carica papaya*). Height to 10·5–12m (35–40ft). Flowers (right) are produced before leaves in early June, and are 2·5–3·7cm (1–1½in) across when fully open. Fruit, rarely produced in Britain, is cylindrical, 7·5–15cm (3–6in) long, unevenly shaped, ripening in September and October to dark brown, and containing a sweet, orange edible flesh. Leaves are shown on p28.

Athrotaxis family Taxodiaceae, **Tasmanian Cedar**. Primitive, evergreen conifers with scale-like leaves. Male and female parts in separate flowers on the same tree, fruit are small cones.

Smooth Tasmanian Cedar

Athrotaxis cupressoides D. Don
Native to western Tasmania at altitudes of 900–1200m (30000–4000ft), cultivated in botanical collections and large gardens. Height to 6–15m (20–50ft). Male and female flowers appear in March (far left), males shedding pollen, females developing into green cones (near left) about 1cm (½in) across, turning orange-brown in October and November. Foliage (p11) is made up of smooth scale-like leaves closely pressed to the stems, diamond shaped, about 0·3cm (⅛in) across. Compare with the cypresses (*Cupressus*).

Summit Cedar

Athrotaxis laxifolia Hook.
Native to western Tasmania, with foliage intermediate in appearance to the other 2 Tasmanian Cedars, and grows better in cultivation. Height to 12–21m (40–70ft), though smaller in the wild. Flowers (far left) open in March, the tiny males clustered at tips of branches, females clustered or solitary developing into bright yellow green spiky cones (near left) which ripen orange brown in October, 2cm (¾in) across. Foliage (p11) is composed of leaves 0·4–0·6cm (/.–¼in) spreading slightly from the stem, which are sharp pointed. Bark is dark orange brown, split and peeling into flakes.

King William Pine

Athrotaxis selaginoides D. Don
The largest of the Tasmanian Cedars, also native to western Tasmania, where it is of great importance as a forestry tree, producing a strong dark timber similar to redwood. Height to 27m (90ft). Flowers (far left) open in March, males shedding pollen. The tiny female flowers develop into pairs of orange brown cones, 2·5cm (1in) across (near left). Foliage (p11) consists of sharply pointed leaves 1·2cm (½in) long, bright green with two bands of white on inner surface. Bark is dark orange red, splitting and peeling, often soft and fibrous like the Wellingtonia (*Sequoiadendron giganteum*).

Chilean Incense Cedar

Austrocedrus chilensis (D. Don) Florin &
Boutelje, synonym *Libocedrus chilensis* (D. Don)
Endl., family Cupressaceae
An evergreen, native to Chile and Argentina,
grown in botanical collections. Height to 24m
(80ft). Male and female flowers are produced on
the same tree, males (near right) 0·3cm (⅛in)
shedding pollen in March. Females develop into
green ripening to brown cones (far right), 0·8cm
(⅓in) long, consisting of 4 scales. Foliage (p11) is
very distinct, flattened pairs of leaves or scales
with bright white bands beneath. Bark is dark
brown splitting into curled plates.

Betula family Betulaceae, **Birch**. Deciduous
trees and shrubs, with male and female catkins
on same tree, males being produced in late
autumn and expanding the following spring to
release their pollen, forming 'lambs' tails'.
Female catkins are smaller and more slender,
produced in a cluster above the males.

Blue Birch

Betula coerulea-grandis Blanch.
Native to eastern N. America from Nova Scotia
south to Vermont. In native environment it often
forms a shrub, but may grow to 9m (30ft) or
twice that in cultivation. Flowers (far left) are
open in May, male catkins 3–5cm (1¼–2in) long,
females about 0·8cm (⅓in). Fruit are clustered
into a cylinder (near left) about 2·5cm (1in) long
which looks similar to a catkin but which breaks
up in September, releasing the winged nuts.
Leaves (p38) are bluish green, hence English
name. Bark (p216) is pinkish white and does not
peel.

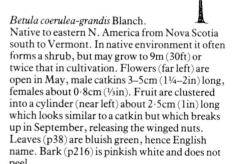

**Cherry Birch,
Sweet Birch or
Black Birch**

Betula lenta L.
A large birch, native to eastern N. America,
where it is used in forestry, yielding a strong
timber used for flooring, furniture and
sometimes boatbuilding. A sweet oil similar to
Oil of Wintergreen is distilled from the bark and
timber. This gives twigs and bark a sweet
aromatic smell when crushed. Height to 21–24m
(70–80ft). Flowers (far left) are open in May,
males 5–7·5cm (2–3in) long when shedding
pollen, females about 0·8cm (⅓in), expanding to
ripe unstalked, erect fruiting catkins (near left)
about 2·5cm (1in) long and 1·2cm (½in) wide.
These break up in September and October. Bark
is very dark and flaky but does not peel. Leaves
(p38) have tufts of hairs in vein axils underneath.

Yellow Birch

Betula lutea Michx.
A large tree, native to north-eastern N. America, where the timber is used for flooring, furniture and boxes. Twigs have a smell and taste of wintergreen. Height to 30m (100ft) in the wild. Flowers (far left) open in May, the male catkins 7 5–10cm (3–4in) long, females 1·2–2cm (½–¾in) long, developing into unstalked, erect fruiting catkins (near left) 2·5–3·7cm (1–1½in) long which differ from those of *B. lenta* by being fatter and downy. Leaves (p38) have tufts of hairs in vein axils underneath and turn clear yellow in autumn. Bark is light golden brown, outer layers peeling back.

River Birch or Red Birch

Betula nigra L., synonym *B. rubra* Michx.
Native to the eastern United States, where it grows in wet ground near rivers. Cultivated as an ornamental in northern states. Height to 24–27m (80–90ft), usually with the trunk split low down into 2 or 3 stems. Flowers open in late April, male catkins 5–7·5cm (2–3in) long, females 0·8cm (⅓in). Fruiting catkins are downy, 2·5–3·7cm (1–1½in) long, erect and have short stems. They ripen and break up early in the year in June. This allows seeds to germinate on river banks, when the water level is at its lowest. Leaves (p38) are doubly toothed, almost lobed and downy on veins underneath. Bark (near left) is distinctly dark and flaking.

Western Birch

Betula occidentalis Hook.
Native to western N. America, where it tends to be rather shrubby forming dense thickets along streamsides. Height to 6–7·5m (20–25ft) but may be shrubby in cultivation. Flowers (far left) open in April, male catkins 5cm (2in) long, females about 0·8cm (⅓in), ripening to erect, stalkless fruiting catkins 2·5–3·7cm (1–1½in) long, only slightly downy. These shed seeds in September. Leaves (p38) are dark green with only 3–5 pairs of veins and no hairs underneath with rounded or slightly heart-shaped bases. Young leaves and twigs are rather sticky. Bark (near left) is shiny dark brown, almost black, and does not peel into layers.

Paper Birch or Canoe Birch

Betula papyrifera Marsh.
Native across northern part of N. America, where its waterproof bark was used in making canoes by Indians. Its wood was used in turnery, and as fuel. A decorative tree, often planted for ornament. Height to 18–21m (60–70ft). Flowers (far left) open in March and April, the male catkins 10cm (4in) long, females 2·5–3cm (1–1¼in). Fruiting catkins are about 3·7cm (1½in) long hanging on slender stalks. Bark (near left) is shiny creamy white, peeling off in thin papery layers exposing pale orangey young bark underneath. On old trees it becomes much darker, cracked and scaley. Leaves (p38) are hairy, with black gladular dots on veins underneath, and colour yellow in autumn (p77).

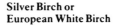

Silver Birch or European White Birch

Betula pendula Roth
Native to Europe, including Britain, and Asia Minor, planted in gardens in Europe and N. America for its graceful, pendulous form. Its timber is used in making plywood, and the tree is often planted to protect other young trees in forestry plantations. Height to 12–18m (40–60ft), but sometimes much larger. Catkins (far left) open in late March and April, males 3cm (1¼in) long, females 1·2–2cm (½–¾in) long, ripening to hanging fruiting catkins (near left) 2·5–3cm (1–1¼in) long, breaking up in late autumn and winter. Leaves (p38) are not downy and have wedge-shaped bases. Bark is white with thin horizontal lines and large dark diamond-shaped cracks and on older trees dark ridges and cracks at the base. Young twigs have no down, which distinguishes this from other birches.

Grey Birch or White Birch

Betula populifolia Marsh.
Native to eastern N. America, often used for reseeding abandoned farmland and areas devastated by fire, providing protection to other species arriving later. Height to 6–12cm (20–40ft). Catkins (far left) open in early April, males 6–10cm (2½–4in), females about 1·2cm (½in) on short stalk. Fruiting catkins (near left) are downy and hanging, about 2cm (¾in) long. Leaves (p38) turn pale yellow in autumn. Bark is creamy white, similar to Paper Birch (*B. papyrifera*), but does not peel so readily. Dark triangular marks and cracks cover the stem.

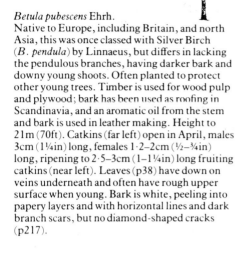

Betula pubescens Ehrh.
Native to Europe, including Britain, and north Asia, this was once classed with Silver Birch (*B. pendula*) by Linnaeus, but differs in lacking the pendulous branches, having darker bark and downy young shoots. Often planted to protect other young trees. Timber is used for wood pulp and plywood; bark has been used as roofing in Scandinavia, and an aromatic oil from the stem and bark is used in leather making. Height to 21m (70ft). Catkins (far left) open in April, males 3cm (1¼in) long, females 1·2–2cm (½–¾in) long, ripening to 2·5–3cm (1–1¼in) long fruiting catkins (near left). Leaves (p38) have down on veins underneath and often have rough upper surface when young. Bark is white, peeling into papery layers and with horizontal lines and dark branch scars, but no diamond-shaped cracks (p217).

Himalayan Birch

Betula utilis D. Don
Native to the Himalayas and China, cultivated in botanical collections and other gardens. Height to 18m (60ft) but may be almost twice as large. Catkins (far left) are open in late April, males about 5cm (2in) long, females 1·2cm (½in) on stalks the same length, ripening to fruiting catkins 3·7cm (1½in) long. Leaves (p38) have downy stems and usually 9–12 pairs of downy veins. Bark may be white with grey patches or orange brown and peeling (near left).

Paper Mulberry

Broussonetia papyrifera L.) Vent., family Moraceae.
A native of China and Japan, now widely cultivated in the east where its bark is used in papermaking. A fibre is also yielded and woven into a fine cloth, which Captain Cook saw being worn by the principal inhabitants of Otaheite. It is planted as an ornamental tree in east Asia, Europe and in eastern N. America, where it can also be found growing wild. Height to 15m (50ft), often a rounded shrub. Flowers (near right) open in June, male and female on separate trees. Male catkins are 3·7–7·5cm (1½–3in) long, furry and often curled. Females are spherical, about 1·2cm (½in) across. Fruit (far right) about 2·5cm (1in) across, falls in October. Leaves (p39) are rough and woolly. Compare with the true mulberries (*Morus*).

Buxus family Buxaceae, **Box.** Evergreen trees and shrubs with opposite leathery leaves. Male and female flowers on same plant, clustered in small bunches.

Balearic Box

Buxus balearica Lam.
Native to the Balearic Islands and south-west Spain, grown in gardens in south Europe, occasionally elsewhere. Height to 10m (30ft) in the wild but often small and shrubby. Flowers (far left) open in May about 1·2cm (½in), males clustered around females, which are therefore difficult to see. Fruits (near left) have 3 two-horned cells and are about 1·2cm (½in), green to start with, becoming brown and woody. They fall from the trees in August/September and split open from the centre to release their seeds. Leaves (p32) larger and brighter green and more even than Common Box (*B. sempervirens*).

Common Box

Buxus sempervirens L.
Native to Europe, N. Africa and west Asia. Often planted in gardens, its many cultivars providing ideal plants for hedges, winter cover and topiary. The wood is good for engraving, carving and marquetry, since it is extremely hard and can be highly polished. An extract used medicinally as a blood purifier. Height to 4·5–6m (15–20ft), occasionally larger, but most commonly rather bushy. Flowers (far left) open in April, males clustered around the females. Fruit capsules (near left) are about 0·8cm (⅓in) long, with 3 double horns. They split open and fall from the tree in September. Leaves (p32) are darker green than Balearic Box, notched at the tip. The many garden cultivated varieties differ from the type in their leaf shapes and sizes, as well as growth habits.

Incense Cedar

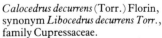

Calocedrus decurrens (Torr.) Florin, synonym *Libocedrus decurrens Torr.*, family Cupressaceae.
Native to California and Oregon, planted for ornament in Europe and middle and eastern United States. Height may reach 30m (100ft) in home range with spreading branches but may reach 45m (150ft) or more in cultivation in Britain where the shape is usually columnar. Flowers (near right) appear in January, the males 0·6cm (¼in), colouring the top half of the tree golden yellow. Females are less conspicuous, looking much like extensions of the foliage. They develop into bright golden yellow fruits (far right) about 2–2·5cm (¾–1in) long, splitting to release seed in September/October. Foliage (p10) is composed of tiny scale-like leaves closely pressed to stems. Bark is red brown, ridged and covered with scales.

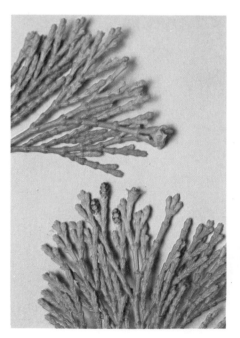

Carpinus family Carpinaceae, **Hornbeam**.
Deciduous trees, with male and female flowers in
separate catkins on same tree. Unlike *Betula* and
Alnus, the male catkins remain in bud through
the winter, emerging in the spring. The fruits are
small nuts with large conspicuous bracts.

**European Hornbeam
or
Common Hornbeam**

Carpinus betulus L.
Native to Asia Minor and Europe, including
south-east England. Cultivated in Europe and
N. America as a hedge, park or street tree and for
its hard, fine-grained timber which is used to
make, among other things, mallets, skittles and
some of the moving parts inside pianos. Height
to 19m (65ft). Flowers (far left) open in March,
the male catkins 3·7cm (1½in) long, the females
smaller emerging from the tips of growing
shoots. Fruiting catkins (near left) may be 7·5cm
(3in) long and turn brown in November. Leaves
(p33) colour bright yellow in the autumn. Bark
(p217) is grey striped brown and vertically ridged
or fluted.

**American
Hornbeam
or Blue Beech**

Carpinus caroliniana Walt.
Native to western N. America and Central
America. Its wood is used for small items, such as
tool handles. Height to 12m (40ft). Flowers (far
left) emerge in April, male catkins 2·5–3·7cm
(1–1½in) long, females 1·2–2cm (½–¾in) at
growing tips. Fruiting catkins (near left) may be
12·5cm (5in) long, composed of nutlets 0·8cm
(⅓in) surrounded by bracts which turn papery
brown and fall from the tree in the autumn.
Leaves (p33) are more tapered at the tip than
European Hornbeam (*C. betulus*) and turn
orange and red in the autumn. Bark is smooth
grey and fluted.

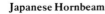

Japanese Hornbeam

Carpinus japonica Blume
Native to Japan, cultivated as an ornamental and
in botanical collections. Height to 12–15m
(40–50ft). Flowers (far left) open in April, male
catkins 2·5–5cm (1–2in) long, females at tips of
shoots 1·2cm (½in) long. Fruiting catkins (near
left), 5–6cm (2–2½in) long with toothed inward-
curving bracts, colour from green to pink-
tinged, then crimson in autumn. The leaves
(p33) have numerous strong veins, and are longer
and darker than European Hornbeam
(*C. betulus*). Bark is smooth pinkish grey or dark
with lighter stripes.

Carya family Juglandaceae, **Hickory**.
Large deciduous trees, with male and female
flowers on same tree, males in three-branched
catkins, females in few flowered clusters. Fruit is
a nut enclosed by a husk, hardening as it ripens.
Leaves have leaflets arranged in pairs, the lowest
pair being shorter than the others.

**Bitternut or
Swamp Hickory**

Carya cordiformis (Wangenh.) K. Koch
Native to eastern N. America, cultivated in
Europe in botanical collections and large
gardens. Distinguished from other hickories by
its yellow winter buds. Height to 30m (100ft).
Male catkins (near right) expand to 6–7·5cm
(2½–3in), shedding pollen in late May, or early
June. The female flowers are also shown, but are
inconspicuous between leaves at tips of growing
shoots. Fruit (far right) has 4 ridges on the top
half. Leaves (p54) have 7 or 9 leaflets.

Pignut Hickory

Carya glabra (Mill.) Sweet
Native to eastern N. America, from Ontario
south to Alabama. Cultivated in botanical
collections. Height to 18–27m (60–90ft). Male
catkins (near right) expand to 7·5–12·5cm
(3–5in), shedding their pollen in late May when
the females appear at the tips of growing shoots
(just visible in the photograph). Fruit (far right)
may be pear-shaped or rounded, about 2·5cm
(1in) long. The husk is thin, sometimes splitting
in autumn to expose an unridged nut. Leaves
(p53) usually have 5 leaflets, and turn yellow and
orange in the autumn.

**Big Shellbark Hickory,
Bottom Shellbark
Hickory or
King-nut**

Carya laciniosa (Michx. f.) Loud.
Native to eastern United States where its sweet
nuts are harvested and sold. Cultivated in
Europe in gardens and botanical collections.
Height to 36m (120ft). Male catkins (near right)
expand to as much as 12·5cm (5in) and shed
pollen in June. Female flowers open at the same
time, at the tips of shoots (also shown near right).
Fruit (far right) may be spherical or oval,
4·5–6·5cm (1¾–2½in). The husk has 4 or 6
ridges and is orange tinted, ripening to brown.
Leaves (p54) usually have 7, sometimes 5 or 9
leaflets, downy underneath on a slightly downy
stalk. The end leaflet has a short stalk of its own.
Bark is grey and splits into long 1–1·2m (3–4ft)
plates, which remain hanging on the trunk.

Shagbark Hickory or Little Shellbark Hickory

Carya ovata (Mill.) K. Koch
Native to eastern United States where its edible nuts, hickory nuts, are a valuable crop. Cultivated for ornament in gardens and botanical collections in Europe. Grows to 21–27m (70–90ft) tall, occasionally larger. Male flowers (near right) expand to 7·5–12·5cm (3–5in) and shed their pollen in June. Females are single or in pairs in tip of growing shoot (also shown near right). Fruit (far right) is 2·5–5cm (1–2in) long, ripening to dark brown, when it splits to release the 4-angled nut, white when first exposed. Leaves (p53) are made up of 5 leaflets, the end one on a short stalk of its own. A rather large specimen is shown. The bark is grey and shaggy, splitting from the trunk in 30cm (1ft) or more long flakes.

Mockernut, Big Bud Hickory or White Heart Hickory

Carya tomentosa (Poir.) Nutt.
Native to eastern N. America, cultivated in Europe in botanical collections. Height to 30m (100ft). Male catkins (near right) expand to shed pollén in June, when the female flowers also appear at the tip of growing shoot (not shown but looks similar to other hickories). Fruit (far right) is 3·7–5cm (1½–2in) long and splits along its grooves to release an extremely hard shelled nut, which contains an edible kernel. Leaves (p54) are aromatic when touched, and the winter buds are larger 1·2–2cm (½–¾in) than on any other hickory. Young shoots are covered with woolly down. Bark is dark grey, ridged and covered with small scales.

Sweet Chestnut or Spanish Chestnut

Castanea sativa Mill., family Fagaceae.
Native to south Europe, north Africa and Asia Minor. Cultivated in Europe for its edible nuts and for ornament in parks and gardens, and in N. America as an ornamental. Height to 30m (100ft) with broad trunk, as much as 9–12m (30–40ft) in girth. Flowers (far left) are open in late June and July when the male catkins, about 15–25cm (6–10in) long shed their pollen. Female flowers (centre of photograph far left) are in clusters of 5–6 at the base of a short unopened male catkin. Fruit (near left) ripens in one season, some trees producing 1–2 round nuts, some producing 3–4 flat nuts which are not good enough to eat. Leaves (p26) turn yellow then dark brown in October. Bark (p217) is dark brown and ridged, often spirally.

Catalpa family Bignoniaceae.
Deciduous trees and shrubs with large, opposite heart-shaped leaves and large loose groups of flowers. Fruit are long thin pods. *Catalpa* is a name used by the Cherokee Indians for the Indian Bean (see below).

Indian Bean or Southern Catalpa

Catalpa bignonioides Walt.
Native to south-eastern United States, cultivated in parks and gardens in eastern States and in west, central and south Europe, including Britain. Height to 7·5–15m (25–50ft). Flowers (near right) open in June and July, each about 5cm (2in) across in a bunch about 15–20cm (6–8in) tall. Fruit (far right) are 15–37cm (6–15in) long, hanging, and turn brown in the autumn splitting the following spring to release white papery seeds about 2·5cm (1in) long. Leaves (p42) are downy underneath and may be shallowly lobed. They do not unfurl till late June and turn black before falling in autumn. Bark is pinkish brown or grey and flaky or ridged.

Hybrid Catalpa

Catalpa × erubescens Carr., synonym *C. hybrida* Spaeth
A group of cultivated hybrids arising from the Indian Bean (*C. bignonioides*) and the Yellow Catalpa (*C. ovata*). *C. × erubescens* 'J. C. Teas' first raised in Indiana is the best known form of this hybrid. Height to about 14m (45ft), occasionally taller. Fragrant flowers (near right) open in July and August, similar to but smaller than *C. bignonioides*, though the bunch may contain more flowers. Fruit (far right) are pods to 40cm (16in) long, but contain no seed. Leaves (p42) unfold purple, soon turning bright green, with 5 points or shallow lobes. They are slightly downy above and have hairs along veins underneath. Bark is dark grey covered with ridges and cracks.

Yellow Catalpa

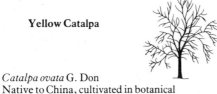

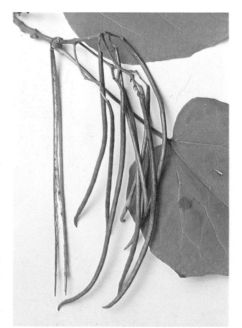

Catalpa ovata G. Don
Native to China, cultivated in botanical collections. Height to 6–9m (20–30ft). Flowers (near right) are distinctively coloured. They open in July and August in bunches 10–25cm (4–10in) high, each flower about 2·5cm (1in) across. Fruit (far right) is a pod about 30cm (12in). Leaves (p42) are darker green and more definitely 3-lobed than the American *Catalpa* species.

Western Catalpa

Catalpa speciosa Engelm.
Native to central United States, cultivated in Mississippi for timber and for ornament in eastern States and Europe. Height to 36m (120ft). Flowers (near right) open in June and July, each 6cm (2¼in) across 7–10 in a bunch 12·5–15cm (5–6in) tall. Fruits (far right) are 20–50cm (8–20in) long and split in early spring to release 2·5cm (1in) long brown seeds. Leaves (p42) are dark green with down underneath, and often have 3 shallow lobes. Bark is light reddish brown covered with thin scales.

Cedrela sinensis Juss., **Chinese Cedar** family Meliaceae.
Deciduous, native of China. Height to 21m (70ft). Flowers in June, white, in clusters 30cm (1ft) long. Fruit about 2·5cm (1in) long, with winged seeds. Leaves (p58) have 5–12 pairs of leaflets.

Cedrus family Pineaceae, **Cedar**. Evergreen conifers, with needles in bunches. Male flowers in dense clusters appearing in early summer shedding pollen in the autumn. Females, small and solitary, appear on the same tree, as males shed pollen. Cones take at least 2 years to ripen and remain on the tree after releasing the winged seed.

Atlas Cedar

Cedrus atlantica Manetti
Native to Atlas Mountains of Algeria and Morocco. Most commonly cultivated as the blue form. Foliage is green (p23).
Cedrus atlantica Manetti forma *glauca* Beissn.
Blue Cedar.
Blue form of the Atlas Cedar. Cultivated for ornament in parks and gardens in Europe and N. America. Height to 36m (120ft). Male flowers (far left) shed pollen in late September, 2·5–5cm (1–2in) long, females (also far left) develop into a green cylindrical, flat-topped cones about 8cm (3¼in) long, 3·7–5cm (1½–2in) wide, ripening to dark woody brown (near left). Foliage (p23) is blue green. Bark is paler grey than Atlas Cedar.

Deodar

Cedrus deodara (Roxb.) G. Don
Native to Himalaya, planted for ornament in parks, gardens and churchyards in Europe and N. America, also occasionally for timber in southern Europe. Height to 75m (250ft). Male flowers are pale green, 2–3cm (¾–1¼in) appearing during the summer, and expanding to about 8cm (3¼in) to shed pollen (far left) in early November. Females (also far left) are not always produced and are often rather high in the crown. Cone (near left) is about 10cm (4in) tall, remains green for 2 years when it turns brown and woody, releasing seed. Foliage (p23) consists of needles rather longer 2·5–5cm (1–2in) than on other cedars. Small branches hang down distinctively and young twigs are downy.

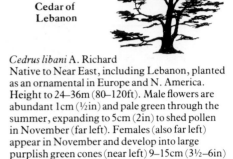

Cedar of Lebanon

Cedrus libani A. Richard
Native to Near East, including Lebanon, planted as an ornamental in Europe and N. America. Height to 24–36m (80–120ft). Male flowers are abundant 1cm (½in) and pale green through the summer, expanding to 5cm (2in) to shed pollen in November (far left). Females (also far left) appear in November and develop into large purplish green cones (near left) 9–15cm (3½–6in) which taper to the top. Foliage (p23) is made up of dark green needles up to 2cm (¾in) long. Young twigs are almost hairless.

Cyprus Cedar

Cedrus libani var. *brevifolia* Hook f.
Native to mountains of Cyprus where height is about 12m (40ft). May grow larger in cultivation. Flowers (far left) similar to other cedars, males expanding to about 6cm (2¼in) and shedding pollen in early November, females appearing at that time. Cones (near left) are smaller than of Cedar of Lebanon (*C. libani*), about 12·5cm (5in). Foliage (p23) is the most distinctive feature, being very short, about 1·2cm (½in).

Southern Nettle-tree

Celtis australis L., family Ulmaceae.
Native to south Europe and south-west Asia. Planted for shade at roadsides in south Europe and occasionally for ornament elsewhere, though may be damaged by frost. The wood has been used to make small items, for joinery and charcoal, and the bark yields a yellow dye. Height to 15–21m (50–70ft). Flowers (near right) open in May, male and female on same tree, females developing into the fruit (far right) which are about 1·2cm (½in) across and ripen to reddish brown in September. These are edible but rather tiny. Leaves (p25) are rough to the touch above, downy beneath. Bark is smooth and grey, not unlike a beech tree.

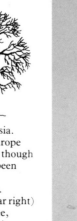

Sugarberry or Mississippi Hackberry

Celtis laevigata Willd.
Native to south-east United States, where it is often planted as a shade tree. Height to 18–24m (60–80ft). Flowers (near right) open in May, male and female separate on the same tree. Fruit is 0·6cm (¼in) and ripens from orange or yellow to dark purple. Leaves (p27) are distinctively untoothed. Bark (far right) often covered with projecting growths.

Hackberry or Nettle Tree

Celtis occidentalis L.
Native to eastern N. America, planted as a shade or ornamental tree in Mississippi, eastern States and Europe. Height to 9–12m (30–40ft). Flowers (near right) open in May, the females developing into fruit (far right) which is about 0·8cm (⅓in) across similar to fruit of *C. laevigata*, orange red ripening to dark purple. Leaves (p29) are downy on the main vein beneath. Bark is grey brown with distinctive warty growths.

Cephalotaxus family Cephalotaxaceae, **Plum Yew**. Evergreen shrubs and small trees. Male and female flowers occur on separate plants. Fruits are oval and fleshy, containing one seed. Foliage is similar to *Torreya* but much softer.

Chinese Plum Yew

Cephalotaxus fortunei Hook
Native to central China, cultivated in collections and gardens in Europe. Height to 6m (20ft) in cultivation and often low and bushy. Male flowers (far left) are produced in heads 0·6cm (¼in) across along the underside of young shoots and shed pollen in April and May. Females (also far left) are in pairs, stalked and also open at the same time. Fruit (near left) ripens the same year, about 3cm (1¼in) long, colouring brown. Foliage (p13) has long slender needles, about 5cm (2in).

Cephalotaxus harringtonia (Forbes) K. Koch
Thought to have been a Japanese garden plant
originating from central China. Height to
2·7–5m (9–18ft) as a small tree but usually
shrubby. Flowers open in May and look similar
to those of *C. harringtonia* var. *drupacea* but male
heads have longer stalks, about 2cm (¾in). Fruit
(near left) is 2·5cm (1in) long, ripening from
green to brown. Foliage (p13) has needles shorter
than *C. fortunei*.
C. harringtonia var. *drupacea* (Sieb. & Zucc.)
Koidzumi **Cow's Tail Pine or Japanese Plum
Yew.** The wild type native to Japan and Korea.
Flowers (far left) open in May, males in larger
clusters with stalks only 0·6cm (¼in) long. Fruits
look similar to those of *C. harringtonia*, but leaves
(p13) are more regular, set in two almost vertical
rows.

Katsura Tree

Cercidiphyllum japonicum Sieb. & Zucc., family
Cercidiphyllaceae.
A deciduous tree, native to Japan and China,
where it yields a valuable light timber. Grown for
ornament throughout Europe but is sensitive to
late spring frost. Height to 30m (100ft) in the
wild often with several stems. Male and female
flowers (far right) are on separate trees and open in
April before the leaves unfold. Males have
bunches of 15–20 red stamens about 0·8cm (⅓in)
long, females have bunches of 3–5 twisted red
styles about 0·6cm (¼in) long, elongating during
the summer to form fruit pods (near right)
1·5–5cm (½–2in). Leaves (p39) are bright red at
first, green through summer, then yellow,
orange, red and purple in October.

Judas-tree

Cercis siliquastrum L., family Leguminosae.
Deciduous tree, native to east Mediterranean
and south Europe, planted for ornament in
gardens of all sizes in other parts of Europe.
Height up to 12m (40ft) but usually lower with
more than one stem. Flowers (far left) open in
May and appear from old joints on branches
including the trunk. Fruit (near left) may be
about 10cm (4in) long and are often bright rosy
purple in the summer. Leaves (p39) are similar in
shape to those of Katsura Tree (*Cercidiphyllum
japonicum*) but are arranged alternately along the
shoots.

Chamaecyparis family Cupressaceae, **False Cypress.** Evergreen coniferous trees, with scale-like leaves on flattened twigs. Male and female flowers are on same tree, and cones are smaller than on true cypresses (*Cupressus*).

Lawson Cypress or Port Orford Cedar

Chamaecyparis lawsoniana (A. Murr.) Parl. Native to California and Oregon, planted with its many cultivated forms in gardens and parks in Europe and N. America. Also grown for timber in N. America and occasionally in Europe. Height may reach 60m (200ft) in the wild though usually half this in cultivation. Male flowers (near right) are produced all over the tree and shed pollen in March. Females (also near right) are tiny and green and open at the same time. Cones (far right) are about 0·8cm (⅓in) with 8 scales turning brown when ripe. Foliage (p10) usually has scale leaves closely pressed to twigs as in flower photograph. The cultivated varieties have distinctive tree shapes and foliage colours.

Nootka Cypress or Stinking Cypress

Chamaecyparis nootkatensis (D. Don) Spach A native to western N. America, from Alaska to Oregon, yielding a valuable fragrant timber. Cultivated for ornament in western States and western and central Europe. Height to 36m (120ft). Male flowers (near right) shed pollen in March and are yellow rather than red as on *C. lawsoniana*. Female flowers (also near right) which open at the same time are produced on upper branches. Cones (far right) are about 1·2cm (½in) across, with 4 or 6 spiked scales ripening in the autumn of their second year to red brown and opening to release seeds. Foliage (p10) does not have white marks on underside and has a rough texture since the leaf tips are usually not pressed against the twigs as seen in cone photograph. When crushed the leaves have a pungent catty smell.

Hinoki Cypress

Chamaecyparis obtusa (Seib. & Zucc.) Endl. Native of Japan where its timber is of great value. Cultivated for ornament in Europe and N. America. Height to about 36m (120ft) in its native environment, but slow growing in cultivation and often smaller. Male flowers (near right) shed pollen in April, when the bluish females (also near right) are produced on shoot tips. Cones (far right) are about 0·8cm (⅓in) across, with 8 scales bearing small points. Foliage (p10) has distinctively blunt ended leaves, with a thin line of blue around edges underneath. There are many cultivated varieties of differing shapes and colours.

Sawara Cypress

Chamaecyparis pisifera (Seib. & Zucc.) Endl.
Native of Japan, cultivated as an ornamental in
N. America and Europe. Height up to 45m
(150ft), usually less. Male flowers (near right)
shed pollen in April, females (also near right)
being produced at the same time. Cones (far right)
are about 1·2cm (½in) with 10 pointed scales.
Foliage (p10) has leaves with fine points and
bluish patches at their bases underneath. Again,
there are many garden varieties cultivated for
their colours and shapes.

White Cypress

Chamaecyparis thyoides (L.) Britt., Sterns &
Pogg.
Native to eastern N. America, where it grows in
swamps near the coast. Cultivated for ornament
in eastern United States and in Europe. Grows to
25m (80ft) in the wild but usually about 6–15m
(20–50ft) in cultivation. Male flowers (near right)
shed pollen in March, when females (also near
right) are produced. Cones (far right) are about
0·6cm (¼in) across with 6 scales. Leaves (p10)
have pointed tips.

Golden Chestnut

Chrysolepis chrysophylla (Hook.) Hjelmqvist,
family Fagaceae.
An evergreen, native to California and Oregon,
where it may grow to as much as 30m (100ft).
When cultivated in Europe it is usually lower and
sometimes bushy. Male and female flowers are
produced on the same catkins, about 2·5–3·7cm
(1–1½in) long, males for most of their length
with a few females clustered at the base. These
open in July (far left). Fruit (near left) is formed
in clusters similar to those of Sweet Chestnut
(*Castanea sativa*) about 2·5–4cm (1–1½in)
across, ripening in the second autumn to release
1 or 2 golden brown nuts, which contain sweet,
edible kernels. Leaves (p24) last for 2 or 3 years,
when they colour yellow and fall from the tree.

Yellow Wood

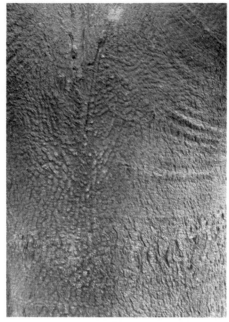

Cladrastis lutea (Michx.) K. Koch, family
Leguminosae.
Deciduous tree, native to south-eastern United
States, grown for ornament in eastern States and
Europe. The wood is bright yellow when first cut
and yields a yellow dye. Height to about 12m
(40ft) but may be taller in forest conditions.
Blossom is white and fragrant and opens in June
in bunches 20–35cm (8–14in) long, though not
always produced in Europe. Each flower is about
2·5cm (1in) long on a hairy stalk. Seed pods are
7·5–10cm (3–4in) long, 1·2cm (½in) wide
containing 4–6 seeds and ripening in September.
Leaves (p53) are the best feature in Europe,
turning bright yellow in autumn (near right).
Bark is shown far right.

Chinese Yellow Wood

Cladrastis sinensis Hemsl.
Deciduous tree, native of China, cultivated in
gardens and botanical collections. Height to 15m
(50ft) or more in the wild. Fragrant flowers (near
right) open in July in bunches as much as 30cm
(12in) long. Seed pods (far right) are about
5–7·5cm (2–3in) long when ripe, falling in late
September. Leaves (see near right) have 11–13
leaflets, arranged alternately on a central stalk.

Cornus alternifolia L. f. **Alternate-leaf
Dogwood**, family Cornaceae.
Deciduous, native to eastern N. America.
Height to 6m (20ft). Flowers in flat heads 5cm
(2in) open in June. Fruit round, black 0·6cm
(¼in). Leaves (p35) are alternate.

**Table
Dogwood**

Cornus controversa Hensl.
Deciduous, native to Japan. Height to 9–15m
(30–50ft). Flowers (near left) open in late June in
heads 5–10cm (2–4in) across. Fruit is round,
black 0·6cm (¼in) wide. Leaves (p35) are
alternate. (Drawing above left.)
Cornus florida L. **Flowering Dogwood**
(drawing above right)
Deciduous, native to eastern N. America.
Height to 3–6m (10–20ft) or more. Flower
clusters surrounded by large bracts (far left)
which unfold in May. Fruit in tight clusters, oval
red berries 1·2cm (½in) long, ripen in October.
Leaves (p35) may colour red, yellow and orange
in autumn.

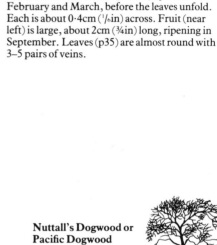

Cornelian Cherry

Cornus mas L.
Native to central and south-east Europe, planted in gardens of all sizes for its winter blossom and attractive fruits. Wood, though in short pieces, has been of value for small domestic items, and the berries may be made into a syrup or jam. Height to as much as 14m (45ft) but often low and shrub-like. Flowers (far left) open in February and March, before the leaves unfold. Each is about 0·4cm (¹⁄₆in) across. Fruit (near left) is large, about 2cm (¾in) long, ripening in September. Leaves (p35) are almost round with 3–5 pairs of veins.

Nuttall's Dogwood or Pacific Dogwood

Cornus nuttallii Audubon
Native of western N. America, where it may reach a height of 12–18m (40–60ft). Flowers are in a tight head, about 2cm (¾in) across surrounded by 4–8 large bracts (far left), which make this tree a stunning sight in flower. The flower buds are visible all winter, finally opening in May. Fruit is a tight cluster of red berries. Leaves (p35) colour red, orange and yellow in autumn (near left).

Corylus family Corylaceae, **Hazel**.
Deciduous trees or shrubs with alternate, toothed leaves. Male and female flowers are separate, but on same tree: males in bunches of hanging catkins, females a tassel of tiny styles. Fruit is a nut surrounded by a leafy bract.

Hazel or Cobnut

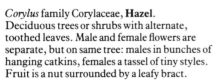

Corylus avellana L.
Native to west Asia, north Africa and Europe, including Britain. Often grown for its edible nuts, and as hedging. Coppicing produces thin flexible rods useful for woven fencing and diviners' rods. In the wild it forms bushy thickets 4–6m (13–20ft) high and sometimes forms a small tree. Male catkins expand to 3·7–6cm (1½–2½in) and shed their pollen in February and March; females are tiny red tassels (both near right). Fruit (far right) ripen in October and make good eating. Leaves (p39) are coarse and hairy.

Turkish Hazel

Corylus colurna L.
Native to south-east Europe and west Asia,
cultivated for ornament in large gardens and
botanical collections. Height to 21–24m
(70–80ft). Male catkins expand to 5–7·5cm
(2–3in), shedding pollen in February; females
are tiny red tassels (both shown near right). Nuts
(far right) are 1·2cm (½in) wide surrounded by
4cm (1½in) wide bract, easily distinguished from
other hazel fruits. Leaves (p39) are larger than
Cobnut (*C. avellana*) and are often almost lobed.

American Smoketree

Cotinus obovatus Raf., synonym *C. americanus*
Nutt., family Anacardiceae
Native to south-eastern United States,
apparently becoming rare due to exploitation for
an orange-red dye extracted from its wood.
Cultivated as an ornamental in eastern States and
Europe. Height to 9m (30ft) in the wild but often
bushy in cultivation. Male and female flowers
open in June on separate plants. Male flowers are
shown far left. Female flowerheads look similar
but have fewer flowers, leaving a mass of empty
threadlike stalks which give a cloudy appearance
to the tree, hence the name Smoketree. Fruit is
likewise sparse, about 0·3cm (⅛in) long. Leaves
(p32) are bronze when they first unfold and
colour beautiful clear reds in autumn (near left).

**Himalayan
Tree-cotoneaster**

Cotoneaster frigidus Wall., family Rosaceae.
A small deciduous tree or shrub, native to
Himalaya, grown for ornament in gardens and
parks. Height to 4·5–6m (15–20ft). Flowers
(near right) open in June and are about 0·8cm
(⅓in) across in flat clusters which can be as much
as 5cm (2in) wide. Perhaps the most striking
feature are the fruits (far right) which clothe all
branches. They ripen in September and remain
on the tree through winter. Leaves (p32) are
downy when young but become hairless through
the summer.

Crataegus family Rosaceae, **Hawthorn**.
A large group of deciduous shrubs and trees, usually bearing sharp spines. Leaves are toothed, may also be lobed and usually have two leafy bracts, or stipules, where their stalks meet the twig. Flowers contain both sexes and are usually produced in clusters. Fruit is fleshy, containing hard nutlets, like a tiny apple.

Azarole or Mediterranean Medlar

Crataegus azarolus L.
Native of south Europe, north Africa and west Asia, grown for its apple-flavoured fruits which are used in jams and liqueurs. Height to about 9m (30ft). Flowers (far left) open in June, each about 1·2cm (½in) across in bunches about 5–7·5cm (2–3in) wide. Fruit (near left) is 2–2·5cm (¾–1in) in diameter, ripening in September, usually orange-yellow, but varies and may be red or white. Leaves are deeply cut and downy underneath.

Cockspur Thorn

Crataegus crus-galli L.
Native to central and eastern N. America, often grown for ornament or hedging in eastern States and also in northern Europe. It bears long thorns, usually 3·7–7·5cm (1½–3in) long but old ones may be 10–15cm (4–6in) long and branched. Height to 7·5m (25ft). Flowers (far left) are about 1·2cm (½in) across, produced in June in clusters 5–7·5cm (2–3in) across. Fruit (near left) is about 1·2cm (½in) across, ripens in October and persists on the tree through winter. Leaves (p37) colour scarlet in autumn.

Black Hawthorn

Crataegus douglasii Lindl.
Native to eastern and central N. America, cultivated for ornament in gardens and botanical collections in Europe. Height to 9m (30ft). Flowers (far left) open in May, 1·2cm (½in) wide in clusters about 5cm (2in) wide. Fruit (near left) is about 0·8cm (⅓in) across, ripens to glossy black and falls from the tree in August and September. Leaves are shown on p38. Thorns are thick, about 2–2·5cm (¾–1in) long, but may often be absent.

Oriental Thorn

Crataegus laciniata Ucria
Native of China, planted in Europe as an
ornamental. Height to 4·5–6m (15–20ft).
Flowers (far left) open in June, each about 2cm
(¾in) across, developing to fruit (near left) of
about 2cm (¾in) diameter, which ripen in
October. Leaves (p47) are deeply cut, and downy
on both sides but particularly underneath.
Oriental Thorn bears few spines.

Midland Hawthorn, May or English Hawthorn

Crataegus laevigata (Poir.) DC, synonym
C. oxyacantha L. emend Jacq.
Native of Europe, including Britain, smaller
than Common Hawthorn (*C. monogyna*),
reaching 4·5–6cm (15–20ft), with fewer thorns.
Flowers (far left) open in May, about 1·2cm
(½in) across with two, sometimes three styles.
Fruits (near left) are oval, about 0·6–2cm
(¼–¾in) long, containing two or sometimes
three stones. Leaves (p47) are less lobed than on
C. monogyna.

Crataegus laevigata cv. 'Paul's Scarlet'
Originated in England around 1858 from a tree of
the pink double flowered variety (below).
Commonly grown in parks and gardens of all
sizes. Flowers (far left) open in late May or June,
double and strongly coloured. Fruit is rarely
formed. Leaves are similar to those of the wild
type.

Crataegus laevigata cv. 'Punicea Flore Pleno'
A cultivated variety of Midland Hawthorn
(*C. laevigata*) thought to have originated
somewhere on the continent of Europe. Grown
for ornament in parks and gardens but is less
common than 'Paul's Scarlet' (above). Flowers
(near left) open in late May or June and are
double and pink.

Hybrid Cockspur Thorn

Crataegus × lavallei Herincq ex Lav.
A hybrid thought to have originated in France,
now planted as an ornamental in gardens and
collections. Height to 4·5–6m (15–20ft). Flowers
(far left) open in June, each about 2·5cm (1in)
across in bunches about 7·5cm (3in) wide. Fruit
(near left) persists on the trees through winter.
Each is about 2cm (¾in) wide, often speckled
brown. Leaves (p37) are darker glossy green than
on most hawthorns. Thorns are few, about
2·5cm (1in) long.

Downy Hawthorn

Crataegus mollis (Torr. & Gr.) Scheele
Native to central United States, planted as an
ornamental in Europe. Height to 9–12m
(30–40ft). Flowers open in June, white with red
disk in the centre, about 2·5cm (1in) across.
Fruit ripens in September; red, downy and
spherical, 2–2·5cm (¾–1in) across. Leaves (p38)
are downy, particularly on the undersides.
Thorns are about 5cm (2in) long.

Common Hawthorn

Crataegus monogyna Jacq.
Native to Europe, including Britain and has
ancient associations with May-day festivities and
superstitions. Height to 10·5m (35ft). Fragrant
flowers (far left) open in mid-May (around May
1st on the Old Style calendar). Fruit (near left)
ripen in September, each containing only one
stone. This is one of the main differences
between this and the Midland Hawthorn
(*C. laevigata*). Leaves (p47) are 5- to 7-lobed.
Bark (p217) is dark brown and cracked into thin
rectangular plates.

C. monogyna cv. 'Biflora' **Glastonbury Thorn**
Legend has it that this variety arose at
Glastonbury from the staff of Joseph of
Arimathea. He drove it into the ground and it
burst into flower although it was then Christmas
Day. It produces flowers and leaves through mild
winters.

Crataegus oxycantha L. see *Crataegus laevigata*
p107

Scarlet Hawthorn

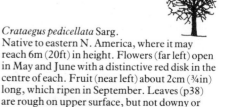

Crataegus pedicellata Sarg.
Native to eastern N. America, where it may
reach 6m (20ft) in height. Flowers (far left) open
in May and June with a distinctive red disk in the
centre of each. Fruit (near left) about 2cm (¾in)
long, which ripen in September. Leaves (p38)
are rough on upper surface, but not downy or
hairy. They usually have about 5 shallow lobes
on each side and are coarsely toothed. Thorns are
shiny, brown and 5cm (2in) long.

Broad-leaved Cockspur Thorn or Frosted Thorn

Crataegus prunifolia (Lam.) Pers.
Origins of this thorn are uncertain, but it is certainly similar to the Cockspur Thorn (*C. crusgalli*). Height to 6m (20ft). Flowers (far left) open in June 1·8cm (¾in) across. Fruit (near left) is about 1·2cm (½in) across, ripening in September, soon falling from the tree. Leaves (p37) turn red in the autumn. Thorns are hard 3·7–7·5cm (1½–3in) long and sharply pointed.

Japanese Cedar

Cryptomeria japonica (L. f.) D. Don, family Taxodiaceae
An evergreen conifer, native to China and Japan. It is an important forestry tree in Japan, where it yields valuable timber. Cultivated as an ornamental in Europe and N. America. Grows to 30–55m (100–180ft) in Japan, usually smaller in cultivation. Male and female flowers (near right) are separate, but on the same tree. Male catkins are present throughout winter, then turn yellow, then shed pollen in late February or early March. Females are the tiny green rosettes at tips of shoots. They develop into green cones (far right) about 1·5cm (⅗in) across by autumn. These dry out, turn brown (also far right) and release their seed the following autumn. Foliage is shown on p12. Bark is reddish-brown and peels away in thin vertical strips.

Chinese Fir

Cunninghamia lanceolata (Lamb.) Hook., family Taxodiaceae
An evergreen conifer, native to China, where it plays a major role in forestry. Named after James Cunningham, who discovered it in 1701 and was the first European plant-hunter to visit China. Grown in large gardens and botanical collections. Height to 45m (150ft) in home environment, but usually about 30m (100ft) in cultivation. Male and female flowers (far left) are separate on the same tree. Males are in large bunches at tips of shoots, and shed pollen in April. Females are also at shoot tips, about 1·2cm (½in) across. Cones (near left) are up to 4·5cm (1¾in) across. Foliage (p13) consists of hard, pointed needles. Bark is brown and scaly.

109

Leyland Cypress

×*Cupressocyparis leylandii* (Dallim. &
Jacks.) Dallim., family Cupressaceae
A hybrid between Nootka Cypress
(*Chamaecyparis nootkatensis*) and Monterey
Cypress (*Cupressus macrocarpa*). Mainly planted
as ornamentals in gardens, or as hedging. Height
to about 30m (100ft) so far. Male and female
flowers (near right) are on the same tree. Males
appear in the autumn and open to shed pollen the
following March. Females, small and green,
develop into shiny cones (far right) about 1–2cm
(½–¾in) across. A large number of clones now
exist. The two most important are:
×*C. leylandii* cv. 'Haggerston Grey' (clone 2) has
blue grey foliage, and the branchlets are set at all
angles round the brown woody twigs. Flowers
and fruit are shown right and foliage on p10.
×*C. leylandii* cv. 'Leighton Green' (clone 11) has
stouter green shoots, and branchlets from woody
twigs in one plane. Silhouette above is of this
clone.

Cupressus family Cupressaceae, **Cypress**
Evergreen coniferous trees, with tiny scale-like
leaves pressed against the branches and twigs.
Male and female flowers are separate on the same
plants. Wood is resinous and fragrant.

Rough-barked Arizona Cypress

Cupressus arizonica Greene
Native to south-west United States and north
Mexico. Planted as an ornamental in large
gardens and botanical collections. Height to 23m
(75ft) in native environment. Flowers (far left)
are on separate branches; males shed pollen in
February, and the tiny rose-like females develop
into cones (near left) about 1·8cm (¾in) with 6–8
scales bearing stout bosses. Foliage is shown on
p11. Bark of young trees is brown and stringy,
breaking into thin plates, and turns grey with
age.

Smooth Arizona Cypress

Cupressus glabra Sudw.
Native to Arizona, to the west of *C. arizonica*
with which it has often been confused. Height to
14–18m (45–60ft). Male flowers (far left) shed
pollen in February: females develop into cones
(near left) about 1·5cm (⅝in). Foliage (p11) is
blue-grey with depressions on leaf backs. Bark is
smooth and reddish brown, breaking into scales
which are shed.

Monterey Cypress

Cupressus macrocarpa Gord.
Native of California, cultivated in western N.
America in gardens and as hedging and
shelterbelts. Also planted in Europe, S. America
and Australia. Height to 18m (60ft) in the wild
but may be twice as tall in cultivation (silhouettes
of both shown). Flowers (far left) open in March,
the males turning yellow and shedding pollen.
Females develop into cones (near left) which are
about 2·5–3·7cm (1–1½in) across, made up of
4–6 scales. Foliage is shown p11. Bark is red
brown, ridged and broken into scales.

Italian Cypress

Cupressus sempervirens L.
Native to Mediterranean Europe, cultivated in
much of Europe and in N. America. It yields a
strong, long-lasting wood, used in the Middle
Ages to build chests, its pleasant odour making
them particularly suitable for storing clothing.
Height to 25–45m (80–150ft) and may be either
narrow with upright branches as shown above or
wider with horizontal branches. Flowers (far
left) open in March, the yellow males shedding
pollen. Female flowers develop into cones (near
left) which are about 1·8–3cm (¾–1¼in) with
8–14 spiked scales. Foliage is shown p11. Bark is
reddish brown, thin and shallowly ridged.

Quince

Cydonia oblonga Mill., family Rosaceae
Deciduous tree, probably native to Central Asia,
though long cultivated in Mediterranean Europe
for its fruit, now naturalised in many parts.
Height to 4·5–6m (15–20ft). Flowers (near right)
open in May each about 5cm (2in) across. Fruit
(far right) is pear-shaped, about 7·5–10cm
(3–4in) long, usually covered with a thick, white
felt. Despite its wonderful mouth-watering
fragrance, the unprepared quince fruit is most
unpalatable, being hard and acid. The main use,
in Britain, is for flavouring cooked apple and
pear dishes and for making jams and jellies. A
candy, 'Contignac', is made in France from
quinces and sugar. Leaves (p32) are covered with
felty down when young.

Dove Tree or Handkerchief Tree

Davidia involucrata Baill., family Davidiaceae.
Deciduous, native to China where it was
discovered by the French Jesuit, the Abbé David
in 1869. Height to 12–19m (40–65ft). Flowers
open in May in a tiny round head about 2cm
(¾in) across, almost hidden by the large, up to
20cm (8in), showy white bracts (far left). Male
and female parts are produced in separate
flowerheads. Fruit (near left) is solitary, about
3·7cm (1½in) long, ripening to reddish brown in
October and containing 3–5 seeds. Leaves (p41)
are bright, light green, the lower surface downy
and the upper with fine white hairs. They are
fragrant when they first unfold.
D. involucrata var. *vilmoriniana* (Dode) Wanger
has similar flowers and fruit but the leaves lack
down on the undersides.

Date Plum

Diospyros lotus L., family Ebenaceae.
A deciduous tree, native to China, cultivated for
its fruit in the Far East and Italy and for
ornament in gardens and collections in the north
of Europe. Height to 12m (40ft) but may be twice
as tall in warm climates. Flowers open in July:
males (near right) are in clusters in leaf axils,
females look similar but single and on a separate
tree. Each flower is about 0·6cm (¼in) across.
Fruit (far right) is 1·2–2cm (½–¾in) wide,
ripening yellow to purple. Leaves (p27) are dark
shiny green.

Common Persimmon

Diospyros virginiana L.
Deciduous tree, native to eastern and central
United States. In some parts, particularly the
southern States, the astringent fruit is gathered
in abundance from wild trees. Height to 12–20m
(40–65ft), occasionally much taller. Flowers
open in July. Female flowers (near right) are
solitary, about 2cm (¾in) long; males are
clustered and slightly smaller. Fruit is similar to
that of Date Plum (*D. lotus*), about 2·5–5cm
(1–2in) across, coloured pale orange and often
with a reddish flush on one side. Leaves are
shown on p27. Bark (far right) is very dark,
thick, and deeply cut into small rectangular
blocks.

Dipteronia sinensis Oliver, family Aceraceae. Deciduous tree, native to central China. Height to 9m (30ft) though may sometimes be bushy. Flowers (far left) contain both sexes. They open in June in clusters 15–30cm (6–12in) long. Fruits (near left) have wings 2–2·5cm (¾–1in) long and are completely distinctive. Leaves (p57) usually have 7–11 leaflets, with small tufts of hair in the vein axils beneath.

Winter's Bark

Drimys winteri J. R. & G. Forst., family Winteraceae.
An evergreen tree, or sometimes shrub, native to South and Central America. This form is sometimes known in gardens as var. *latifolia*. It was first discovered by Captain William Winter, on a voyage with Sir Francis Drake. He brought back pieces of its bark which he found to be useful in spicing meat and preventing scurvy. Fragrant flowers (near right) open in June, about 3·7cm (1½in) across. Fruit (far right) ripen in October when they fall from the tree. Several black fleshy fruit, containing 15 or so seeds, cluster together at the ends of long stalks, 5–7·5cm (2–3in) long. These are also clustered. The photograph (far right) shows only one stalk bearing two fruits. Leaves (p24) vary from long and narrow to oval. Bark (p217) is aromatic and smooth grey-brown or orange-brown.

Oleaster

Elaeagnus angustifolia L., family Elaeagnaceae. Deciduous tree, or sometimes shrub, native to west Asia and naturalised in south Europe. Cultivated in parks and gardens, particularly in central Europe. In the Far East a sweet sherbet is made from its fruit. Height to 12m (40ft). Flowers (far left) open in June, and are about 0·6cm (¼in) wide with an unusual heavy fragrance. Fruits are oval, about 1·2cm (½in) long silvery yellow and sweet. Leaves (p24) are distinct for their silver scales on undersides. Bark is shown near left.

Chilean Fire Bush

Embothrium coccineum J. R. & G. Forst, family
Proteaceae.
Evergreen tree, or shrub, native to Chile,
cultivated in gardens for ornament. Height to
12m (40ft). The distinctive scarlet flowers (near
right) open in June, each about 3·7–5cm
(1½–2in) long. The woody fruits (far right) are
5–7·5cm (2–3in) long, splitting to release winged
seeds. Leaves (p24) are rather variable in size and
shape, usually long, up to 15cm (6in), but often
much shorter and rounder.

Eucalyptus family Myrtaceae, **Gum Tree**
A large group of evergreen trees, almost entirely
native to Australasia. Leaves come in two types:
juvenile and adult, the former usually stemless
and rounded, the latter long and stalked.
Flowers look like tassels of stamens, opening a
year after the buds are formed.

Cider Gum

Eucalyptus gunnii Hook f.
Native to Tasmania, cultivated for ornament in
European gardens, young foliage often being
used in flower arranging. Height to about 30m
(100ft). Flowers (far left) open in July and
August, usually in bunches of 3. Fruits (near left)
are about 0·6cm (¼in) long (leaves in this
photograph are covered with spots caused by
scale insects). Leaves are shown p24: juvenile
leaves are almost round, clasping the stem in
pairs; adult leaves are alternate, long and thin on
a yellow stalk about 2·5cm (1in) long. Bark
(p217) is smooth, peeling off to expose almost
white wood which ages to dark brownish grey.

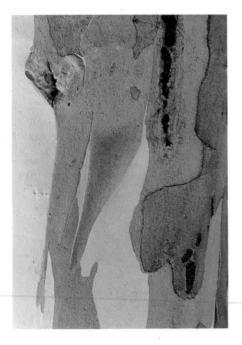

Snow Gum

Eucalyptus niphophila Maiden & Blakely
Native to mountains of New South Wales and
Victoria at high altitudes to 2000m (6,500ft).
Cultivated in gardens in Europe and quite
resistant to frost. Height to 6m (20ft) in the wild
but may grow larger in cultivation. Flowers (far
left) open in August in bunches of 9–11. Fruit
(also far left) is about 0·6cm (¼in) long. Leaves
(p24) are adult from very early, about one year,
unfolding orange brown, soon becoming grey-
green with stalks red on one side, yellow
underneath. They may be either short and
rounded but typically long, thin and curved.
Bark (near left) is grey, peeling in large plates, to
expose clear white new bark.

Eucalyptus perriniana Rodway
Native to Tasmania, Victoria and New South
Wales where it grows at altitudes of 300–600m
(1,000–2,000ft). Grown in Europe and often
coppiced to encourage juvenile foliage for flower
arranging and decoration. Height to 6m (20ft) in
the wild. Flowers (far left) open in August in
bunches of 3. Fruit (also far left) are about 0·5cm
(¹/₅in). Foliage (p24) consists of distinctive
juvenile leaves which are actually pairs joined
together to form a circular leaf surrounding the
stem. These eventually break off and spin around
the stem in the wind. Adult leaves are long, thin
and may be curved. Bark (near left) is dark and
distinctively ringed by old leaf scars.

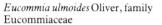

Eucommia ulmoides Oliver, family
Eucommiaceae
A deciduous tree, native to China, where it was
found by western botanists in cultivation rather
than in the wild. Also cultivated in European
gardens and botanical collections. A type of
rubber is produced and may be detected as thin
strands by carefully breaking a leaf. Height to
9–20m (30–65ft). Male and female flowers are
produced on separate plants and open in
February before the leaves unfold. Males (near
right) are clusters of anthers: females are single
green pistils and very inconspicuous. Fruit (far
right) is rather like an elm fruit, each about
3·7cm (1½in) long containing one seed. Leaves
are shown p33.

Eucryphia × nymansensis Bausch, family
Eucryphiaceae
An evergreen hybrid between *E. glutinosa* and
E. cordifolia, 2 species from Chile, first grown at
Nymans in Sussex early this century. Often
shrubby but as a small tree may reach 12–15m
(40–50ft) tall. Flowers (far left) open in August,
each about 6cm (2½in) across. They cover the
plant, giving a wonderful display of blossom.
Fruits (near left) are rather small, about 0·6cm
(¼in) long and do produce some fertile seed.
Leaves (p50) are mostly with 3 leaflets but many
are single: they reflect the leaves of parent trees.

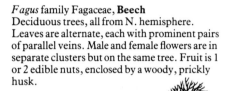

Korean Euodia

Euodia daniellii (Benn.) Hemsl., family Rutaceae
Deciduous tree, native to Korea and north China
cultivated for ornament in large gardens, parks
and collections in Europe. Height to 15m (50ft).
Flowers (near right) are strong-smelling and
open in August and September and are usually of
separate sexes: the flowerheads may be as much
as 10–15cm (4–6in) across, when fully open.
Fruits are reddish-black capsules with a hooked
point. Leaves (p53) colour clear yellow in
October (far right).

Fagus family Fagaceae, **Beech**
Deciduous trees, all from N. hemisphere.
Leaves are alternate, each with prominent pairs
of parallel veins. Male and female flowers are in
separate clusters but on the same tree. Fruit is 1
or 2 edible nuts, enclosed by a woody, prickly
husk.

Oriental Beech

Fagus orientalis Lipsky
Native to Asia Minor, the Caucasus and Balkans,
growing in lower more sheltered places than the
Common Beech, (*F. sylvatica*). Height to 30m
(100ft) in the wild. Flowers (far left) open in
May, drooping male clusters on stalks 2·5–5cm
(1–2in) long, the female produced at the tip of the
shoot. Fruit (near left) have husks about 2·5cm
(1in) long on stems 5–7·5cm (2–3in) long and
which split and fall in October to release the
triangular nuts. Leaves (p33) are longer than
Common Beech, with 7–12 pairs of veins. Bark is
smooth, dark grey and furrowed.

Common Beech or European Beech

Fagus sylvatica L.
Native to Europe, including south England,
much cultivated throughout Europe for timber,
ornament and shade. Also planted widely in N.
America. The edible nuts are a source of oil,
which was extracted on a large scale in Germany
during the World Wars, and may be made into a
kind of margarine. Height to 30m (100ft) with a
large thick trunk sometimes 2–2·5m (6–8ft)
across. Flowers (far left) open in May, numerous
drooping clusters of males and one or two female
clusters at the tip of the shoot. Fruit (near left) is
ripe in September or October, releasing
triangular nuts, about 1·5cm (⅝in) long. Leaves
(p33) have 5–9 pairs of veins. Bark (p117 top
right) is smooth and grey.

Fern-leaved Beech

Fagus sylcatica cv. 'Asplenifolia'
Often called 'Heterophylla' the leaves (p47 and far left) are deeply cut, though may occasionally revert to simple entire leaves. Flowers (far left) are similar to Common Beech (*F. sylcatica*). Bark is as *F. sylcatica* (near left).

Dawyck Beech

F. sylcatica cv. 'Dawyck' was first grown in Dawyck, Peeblesshire, and has an unusual columnar shape. Leaves and flowers are similar to the type *F. sylcatica*.

Weeping Beech

F. sylcatica forma *pendula* (Loud.) Schelle
Usually smaller than Common Beech (*F. sylcatica*) and has masses of drooping, pendulous branches. Flowers and leaves are similar to those of the type.

Purple Beech

F. sylcatica forma *purpurea* (Ait.) Schneid
Much planted in gardens and parks, Purple Beech has dark purple leaves (p33). Flowers (far left) and fruit (near left) also have a pinkish brown tint.

Fig

Ficus carica L., family Moraceae
Deciduous tree, native to west Asia and eastern Mediterranean, cultivated through south Europe and in California for its sweet fruits which are eaten raw, tinned, dried or sugared. They have a mild laxative effect. Height to 9m (30ft), but often low and bushy. Male and female flowers are produced on separate trees and are unusual in that they are borne inside a fleshy receptacle (near right) which develops into the fruit. They are pollinated by fig wasps, which crawl through a tiny hole at the tip. Fruit (far right) is fleshy and may be green, purple or brown. Varieties cultivated for fruit may often produce several crops in one year, but in cool climates flowers form in May and ripen in October. Leaves (p44) may have 3 or 5 lobes.

Fraxinus family Oleaceae, **Ash**
Deciduous trees. Flowers usually have no petals, and may be one sex only, or both together. One sexed flowers may sometimes be on separate trees, sometimes together. Leaves have 2 rows of leaflets either side of a central stem. Fruit have single wings.

White Ash

Fraxinus americana L.
Native of eastern N. America, where it yields a valuable timber useful in house interiors, furniture etc. Also grown for ornament and shade in eastern states and west and north Europe. Height to 35m (120ft) in the wild. Male and female flowers are borne on separate trees, opening in May. Male flowers shown near right; females are also petalless, in looser clusters. Fruit is about 2·5–6·2cm (1–2½in) long, about 0·6cm (¼in) wide with slightly pointed tips in clusters about 15cm (6in) long. Leaves (p53) have 7–9 leaflets and turn clear yellow in the autumn. Bark (far right) is thick and grey, and older trees have diamond-shaped ridges.

Narrow-leaved Ash

Fraxinus angustifolia Vahl
Native to west Mediterranean and north Africa, cultivated in collections and large gardens. Height to 18–25m (60–80ft). Flowers open in May; females are shown near right; males are in tighter clusters at the same time of year. Fruit is 2·5–3cm (1–1¼in) long, ripening in September. Leaves (p55) have 7–13 narrow hairless leaflets. Bark (far right) is dark grey, more deeply ridged and knobbly than Common Ash (*F. excelsior*). Easily distinguished from narrow leaved forms of Common Ash by its brown rather than black winter buds.

Patagonian Cypress

Fitzroya cupressoides (Mol.)
I. M. Johnston, family Cupressaceae
An evergreen, coniferous tree, native to Chile and Argentina where it yields a valuable timber. Named after Robert Fitzroy who commanded the famous 5-year surveying voyage of the *Beagle* which carried the young Charles Darwin as its naturalist. Cultivated in botanical collections and large gardens. Height to 50m (160ft) and slender in the wild, but in cultivation (see silhouette above) it may be very low and shrubby. Female flowers (far left) open in April and are about 0·5cm (⅕in) across. Males are yellow about 0·2cm (¹⁄₁₂in) long. Cones (near left) are about 0·8cm (⅓in) across and ripen from green to brown, splitting to release seed, but remaining on the tree through winter. Foliage (p11) has blunt leaves in rings of 3, each with 2 white bands on either side. Bark is deep reddish brown, peeling off to expose smooth grey trunk.

Common Ash or European Ash

Fraxinus excelsior L.
Native to Europe, including Britain, Common Ash is an important timber tree, its light coloured wood being strong and hard-wearing, and useful for furniture, house interiors and many wooden implements. Height to 30–42m (100–140ft). Flowers open in April with male and female in separate clusters on the same tree, on different trees or in the same flower. Male clusters (near right) are purple turning yellow when pollen is shed. Female clusters are pale green and looser in appearance. Fruit (far right) has wings about 4cm (1½in) long with slightly notched tip and a tiny spike. They turn brown in October and remain on the tree for some time after leaves have fallen. Leaves (p55) usually have 9–11 leaflets and turn clear yellow in autumn. Winter buds (see near right) are black.

Single-leaved Ash

F. excelsior forma *diversifolia* (Ait.) Lingelsh
Has simple leaves i.e. one leaflet only (p33), though may have 3 leaflets, but otherwise similar to Common Ash.

Weeping Ash

F. excelsior cv. 'Pendula'
Has drooping branches, forming a dome-shaped tree. Leaves and flowers similar to Common Ash.

Oregon Ash

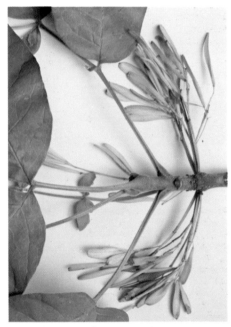

Fraxinus latifolia Benth.
Native to western N. America, where a valuable timber is produced. Height to 23m (75ft). Male and female flowers (both near right) open in April on separate trees. Fruit (far right) are about 2·5–5cm (1–2in) long in dense clusters. Leaves (p53) have 5–9 rather broad leaflets, the side ones with no stalks. Bark is dark grey, or tinged red with broad scaly ridges.

Manna Ash or Flowering Ash

Fraxinus ornus L.
Native to south Europe and Asia Minor, cultivated as an ornamental in other parts of Europe. The stems exude a sweet sap, manna, which is used medicinally as a mild laxative. Height to 15–20m (50–65ft). Flowers (near right) unlike most ashes, bear showy petals. They open in May in dense clusters about 7·5–10cm (3–4in) long. Fruit (far right) is narrow, about 2·5cm (1in) long. Leaves (p53) have 5–9 toothed leaflets, and are rather variable in size and form.

**Red Ash or
Green Ash**

Fraxinus pennsylvanica Marsh.
Native to east and central N. America, also
grown for timber in central and southern
Europe. Height to 12–18m (40–60ft). Male and
female flowers (near right) are produced on
separate trees, in April, just as the leaves are
beginning to emerge. Fruit is about 2·5–6·2cm
(1–2½in) long and may be pointed at the tip.
Leaves (p53) have 7–9 leaflets and may be similar
to those of Oregon Ash (*F. latifolia*) but side
leaves have short stems. Bark (far right) has scaly
ridges and may be red tinged.

**Velvet Ash or
Arizona Ash**

Fraxinus velutina Torr.
Native to south-west United States and Mexico.
The wood is not strong but was used in Arizona
to make wagons. Height to 7·5–12m (25–40ft).
Male and female flowers (near right) are
produced on separate trees in April. Fruits (far
right) are about 1·2–1·8cm (½–¾in) long, the
wing having a notch at the tip and only about half
the length of whole fruit. Leaves (p53) have only
5 leaflets, sometimes 7 or 3, covered with soft
down. Bark is dark grey with broad ridges
breaking into scales. Young shoots are velvety.

Maidenhair Tree

Ginkgo biloba L.,
family Ginkgoaceae
The only representative of a type of plant which
was widespread in prehistoric times. Native to
China but cultivated in gardens, streets and
parks in all temperate countries. Deciduous tree
to 30m (100ft). Flowers are produced on separate
trees: males (far left) about 2·5–3·7cm (1–1½in)
long shedding pollen in March; females tiny on a
stalk about 5cm (2in) developing into the fruit
(near left) which contains an edible nut. As the
flesh decays it becomes foul-smelling and slimy
and can be a hazard to traffic in busy town streets.
Leaves (p43) may be 2-lobed as shown, but often
fan-shaped with only shallow lobing. They
colour yellow in autumn before falling. Bark is
brown and corky, becoming ridged with wide
cracks on mature trees (p217) and often fluted.

Honey Locust

Gleditsia triacanthos L., family Leguminosae
A deciduous tree bearing stout branched thorns, native to central N. America, planted as an ornamental in Europe, particularly in the south. Height to 42m (140ft) in the wild. Male and female flowers open in June in separate clusters on the same tree. Male catkins (near right) expand to about 5cm (2in), each flower about 0·5cm (⅕in) wide with equal petals. Female clusters have few flowers. Fruit pod (far right) is 25–45cm (10–18in) long. They dry out around October and fall during winter. Leaves (p56) have 7–16 pairs of leaflets and turn yellow in autumn. The bark is dark brown, ridged and scaled, but the stem is most easily recognised by the masses of thick branched spines which grow from it (p217).

Gymnocladus dioica (L.) K. Koch, family Leguminosae **Kentucky Coffee Tree**
Native to eastern and central United States, where the seeds were supposed to have been roasted and ground to make a coffee-like beverage. Height to 33m (110ft). Male and female flowers open in June on separate trees: males are in bunches about 7·5–10cm (3–4in) long, females in bunches 3 times that size, each flower about 1·8–2·5cm (¾–1in) long. Leaves (p59) are branched, or bipinnate.

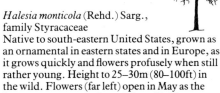

Mountain Snowdrop Tree or Silver Bell

Halesia monticola (Rehd.) Sarg., family Styracaceae
Native to south-eastern United States, grown as an ornamental in eastern states and in Europe, as it grows quickly and flowers profusely when still rather young. Height to 25–30m (80–100ft) in the wild. Flowers (far left) open in May as the leaves emerge, each about 2·5cm (1in) long. Fruit (near left) are about 3·7–5cm (1½–2in) long. Leaves (p26) are downy when they first appear.

Ilex family Aquifoliaceae, **Holly**
Deciduous and evergreen trees and shrubs. Male and female flowers on separate trees; fruit is one or more seeds, with a fleshy covering, and is poisonous.

Highclere Holly

Ilex × altaclarensis (Loud.) Dallim.
A group of evergreen hybrids between Common Holly (*I. aquifolium*) and another called Canary Holly (*I. perado*). Many cultivars have been produced, and most differ from Common Holly in having larger, less prickly leaves, and larger flowers and fruit. Height to 15m (50ft).
I. × altaclarensis cv. 'Camelliifolia'
A female clone, flowers (near right) open in May and develop into fruit (far right) about 1·2cm (½in) across, which are ripe by November. Young shoots, leaf stems and petal bases are tinged purple. Leaves (p36) may be up to 12·5cm (5in) long and may sometimes have a few short spines.

Ilex × altaclarensis cv. 'Golden King'
Despite its name this is a female clone. Flowers
are similar to other Highclere Hollies and open in
May. Fruit (near right) about 1cm (²/₅in) across,
ripening in November. Leaves (p36) are the
main feature, having an almost smooth edge and
yellow margins. Some may be completely yellow
(near right).

Ilex × altaclarensis cv. 'Hendersonii'
A female clone with flowers opening in May and
sparse large fruits (far right) about 1·2cm (½in)
ripening in December. Leaves (p36) are broad,
dull green with few spines. Young shoots are
usually green.

Ilex × altaclarensis cv. 'Hodginsii'
A male clone, so does not produce berries.
Flowers (near right) are tinged purple, about
1·2cm (½in) across and open in May. Leaves
(p36) are similar to 'Hendersonii' but are shiny
rather than dull. Young shoots are tinged with
purple. This cultivar is very resistant to
atmospheric pollution so is commonly planted
in industrial areas.

Ilex × altaclarensis cv. 'Wilsonii'
A female with flowers opening in May and
berries (far right) about 1cm (²/₅in) across
ripening in November. The leaves (p36) are
shiny green and have more spines, about 4–10 on
each side, than other Highclere Hollies. Leaf
edges and spines are clear yellow.

**Common Holly or
English Holly**

Ilex aquifolium L.
Evergreen tree, native to west Asia and Europe,
including Britain, much planted throughout
Europe and parts of N. America for shelter and
ornament. The wood is hard and fine-grained, so
used in detailed work such as turnery,
marquetry, engraving and making printing
blocks. The bright red berries are well known in
Europe as traditional Christmas decorations.
Height to 25m (80ft). Flowers (near right, males
on upper twig, females below) are about 08cm
(⅓in) across, ripening to 4-seeded berry (far
right) also 0·8cm (⅓in) in November. Leaves
(p36) are distinctive: glossy, wavy and sharply
spiney, though may be almost spineless on old
trees. Bark (p217) is smooth grey with some dark
marks. People often carve names and initials on
old holly trunks. Naturally variable and many
cultivated varieties have also been produced,
some of which are shown below.

122

Ilex aquifolium cv. 'Argentea Marginata'
A female, with flowers similar to Common Holly,
berries about 0·8cm (⅓in) ripening in
November. Leaves (p36) are green with whitish
cream edges.

Ilex aquifolium cv. 'Aurea Marginata'
Similar to 'Argentea Marginata' but with narrow
yellow, rather than cream leaf edges. This
difference is clearer on leaf photograph (p36).
Berries (far right) are about 0·8cm (⅓in) ripening
in November.

Ilex aquifolium bacciflava (West.) Rehd.
Leaves and flowers (near right) are similar to
Common Holly but the fruit is bright yellow (far
right).

Hedgehog Holly

Ilex aquifolium cv. 'Ferox'
This is a male clone so does not bear berries, but
this is more than made up for by its unusual
leaves (near right with flowers and p36) with
upper surfaces covered with prickles. Leaves are
smaller than Common Holly, about 3·7cm
(1½in).

Ilex aquifolium cv. 'Recurva'
Also male, flowers shown far right. Leaves (p36)
are small, about 3·7–5cm (1½–2in) and curved
backwards.

Himalayan Holly

Ilex dipyrena Wall.
Evergreen tree, native to Himalaya and further east. Grown as an ornamental in large gardens and botanical collections. Height to 12m (40ft). Flowers (males shown right) are in tight clusters in leaf axils. Fruit (far right) is about 1·2cm (½in) long, widely spaced along the twigs. Leaves (p36) are dull green, usually with no or very few spines on mature trees, but may have several on each side.

American Holly

Ilex opaca Ait.
Evergreen tree, native to central and eastern United States, where many cultivated varieties and hybrids have been produced. Wood has similar uses to the European Common Holly and berry-bearing branches are also used in N. America for Christmas decoration. Height to 12–15m (40–50ft) in the wild. Flowers open in June, males and females (near right) on separate trees. Berries (far right) are about 0·6cm (¼in) across, ripen in November and persist on the tree through winter. Leaves (p36) dull with sharp spines, though leaves in upper parts of old trees may have entire margins.

Perny's Holly

Ilex pernyi Franch.
Evergreen tree, native to central and west China, and named after the French missionary, Paul Perny, who discovered it. Now cultivated as an ornamental in gardens and collections. Height to 6–9m (20–30ft). Flowers (near right) are yellowish and open in June, each about 0·3–0·6cm (⅛–¼in). Fruit (far right) is about 0·6cm (¼in) wide with no stalk. It ripens in November. Leaves (p36) are small, about 1·2–5cm (½–2in) long and of distinctive shape.

Juglans ailantifolia Carr. **Japanese Walnut**
Native to Japan. Height to 15m (50ft). Male catkins up to 30cm (12in), fruit about 5cm (2in) long. Leaves (p57) have 11–17 pointed leaflets, downy underneath. Bark (p218) is light grey with dark vertical cracks.

Juglans cinerea L. **Butternut or White Walnut**
Native to eastern N. America. Height to 15–18m (50–60ft). Male catkins about 5–10cm (2–4in) long; fruit about 3·7–6·2cm (1½–2½in) long. Leaves (p58) have 7–19 leaflets, hairy at first on upper surface.

Black Walnut

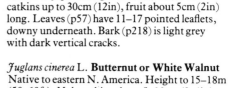

Juglans nigra L.
Native to eastern and central United States, grown in eastern States and in Europe as an ornamental. Height to 25–30m (80–100ft), sometimes more. Male and female flowers (far left) open in late May or early June, male catkins about 5–10cm (2–4in) long. Fruit (near left) ripens in October, and is usually round but may be tapered, about 3·7–5cm (1½–2in) across. Leaves (p58) have 11–23 leaflets with the end one often absent. Bark (p218) is dark brown, broken into a network of narrow ridges.

English Walnut or Persian Walnut

Juglans regia L.
Native distribution is uncertain, since it has long been cultivated throughout Europe, including Britain, and parts of Asia. The timber is highly prized for veneers and furniture and the fruit is harvested for pickling or for eating raw. Height to 30m (100ft). Flowers (far left) open in June, male catkins about 5–10cm (2–4in) long; fruit (near left) is smooth and about 3·7–5cm (1½–2in) across. Leaves (p54) usually have 5–7 leaflets, sometimes more. Young shoots have no down. Bark is smooth and grey with wide, deep cracks.

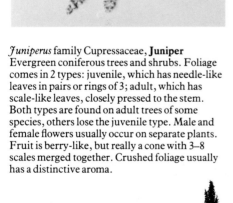

Juniperus family Cupressaceae, **Juniper**
Evergreen coniferous trees and shrubs. Foliage comes in 2 types: juvenile, which has needle-like leaves in pairs or rings of 3; adult, which has scale-like leaves, closely pressed to the stem. Both types are found on adult trees of some species, others lose the juvenile type. Male and female flowers usually occur on separate plants. Fruit is berry-like, but really a cone with 3–8 scales merged together. Crushed foliage usually has a distinctive aroma.

Chinese Juniper

Juniperus chinensis L.
Native to Japan, China and Mongolia. Height to 18m (60ft), often shrubby. Male flowers (near right) shed pollen in March, females usually on separate trees develop into cones (far right) which are about 0·6cm (¼in) across. Both adult and juvenile foliage (p12) are found on adult trees, juvenile needles usually in 3s. There are many cultivated varieties for growing in gardens.

Common Juniper

Juniperus communis L.
Native to northern Europe, N. America and
south-west Asia. The fruit are best known as a
flavouring for gin, and in various dishes, but
have also been used as a source of oil, as a diuretic
in medicine, and in Norway to make a beer.
Commonly a sprawling shrub, but may form a
tree about 2–4m (6–12ft) tall. Flowers (near
right) open in March, fruit (far right) are about
0·6cm (¼in) across and ripen to black in their
second or third year. Foliage (p12) is of
needle-type only, in whorls of 3 with a broad white
band on upper surface and grey undersurface.
Many garden varieties have been raised.

Syrian Juniper

Juniperus drupacea Labill.
Native to mountains of Syria, Greece and Asia
Minor. Height to 9–15m (30–60ft). Male flowers
(near right) are in small clusters, yellow when
fully open in March. Fruit are large, about 2·5cm
(1in) across, dark brown or blue-black. Foliage
(p12) is easily distinguished since needles are
1·2–2·5cm (½–1in) long and sharp with 2 bands
of white on upper surface. No adult, scale-type
leaves are produced.

Mexican Juniper

Juniperus flaccida Schlecht.
Native to Mexico and Texas, cultivated in
gardens and collections in Europe, particularly
the south. Height to 9m (30ft) with long
drooping branches. Male flowers (far right) open
in March; fruits are reddish-brown, about 1·2cm
(½in) wide. Foliage (p12) shows both types of
leaves.

One-seed Juniper or Cherrystone Juniper

Juniperus monosperma Sarg.
Native to south-west United States and
occasionally grown for ornament. Height to
9–15m (30–50ft). Flowers (females near right)
open in March. Fruit (far right) ripens to grey
blue, about 0·6cm (¼in) containing only one
seed. Foliage (p12) shows both adult and juvenile
types, the prickly juvenile eventually being lost
by old trees.

Drooping Juniper or Himalayan Juniper

Juniperus recurva D. Don
An unusual juniper native to China, Himalaya and Burma, grown in gardens and collections. Height to 9–12m (30–40ft). Male and female flowers (both near right) open in March on the same tree. Fruit (far right) are oval, ripening to dark purple in their second year. Foliage (p12) is all of the juvenile needle type but closely pressed to the stem and dull blue green, changing to brown before falling. They give the tree a rather straggly almost unhealthy appearance.

Temple Juniper or Needle Juniper

Juniperus rigida Sieb. & Zucc
Native to Japan, occasionally grown in western gardens where it often forms a shrub. Height to 6m (20ft) but may be twice as tall. Male and female flowers (both near right) open in March on separate trees, males in round yellow clusters about 0·3cm (⅛in) across, females half the size, green. Fruit (far right) ripen through brown to dark blue-black in second year. Foliage (p12) is always needle-like, in spreading rings of 3. Each has a band of white on upper surface.

Pencil Cedar or Eastern Redcedar

Juniperus virginiana L.
Native to eastern and central N. America, often cultivated in these areas as an ornamental, and also in west and central Europe. The wood has been used to line chests and cupboards for storing clothes as it has a pleasant smell and repels moths. One common name refers to its use in making lead pencils. Height to about 15m (50ft), occasionally twice this size, and the tallest of junipers grown in gardens. Male and female flowers (near right) open in March, sometimes on the same tree, but usually separate. Males are round, yellow; females smaller and green. Fruit is smaller than other junipers 0·3–0·6cm (⅛–¼in) long, blue. Foliage (p12) has both types; the needle-like leaves are usually in pairs and the scale-like leaves are pointed. There are several cultivated varieties: cv. 'Glauca', shown with berries far right has blue-green foliage.

Prickly Castor-oil Tree

Kalopanax pictus (Thunb.) Nakai, family Araliaceae

Native to Japan, east Russia, Korea and China, a tree which resembles a maple, but has alternate leaves and stout yellow prickles on its branches and suckers. Height to 25–28m (80–90ft) in the wild, usually much smaller in cultivation. Small white flowers open in August and September in round clusters, grouped into a large head sometimes as much as 60cm (2ft) across. Fruit (far left) is tiny, about 0·5cm (¹/₅in) ripening black and falling in December. Leaves are up to 18–25cm (7–10in) wide with 5 or 7 lobes, generally cut about ⅓ into the leaf, dark green above, and downy below when young (see photograph left). Bark (near left) is dark grey and ridged, often knobbly with spines.

K. pictus var. *maximowiczii* (Van Houtte) Li comes from Japan and has often been confused in gardens and collections with the type species. It has more deeply lobed leaves (p44).

Pride of India or Goldenrain Tree

Koelreuteria paniculata Laxm., family Sapindaceae

A deciduous tree, native to China, Korea and Japan, cultivated for ornament in large gardens and collections. Height to 9–18m (30–60ft). Flowers (near right) open in August in a cluster which may reach 30cm (1ft) long, each flower about 1·2cm (½in). Fruit (far right) is even more spectacular, each red pod about 3·7–5cm (1½–2in) long containing 3 black seeds. Leaves (p57) have 9–15 leaflets and turn yellow in the autumn, a fine complement to the red fruits.

Adam's Laburnum

+*Laburnocytisus adamii* (Poiteau) Schneid., family Leguminosae

A fascinating tree, originally produced by grafting Dwarf Purple Broom (*Cytisus purpureus*), onto the Common Laburnum (*Laburnum anagyroides*) forming a hybrid, or chimaera, at the graft junction. Flowers of a hybrid, yellow-purple type are produced along with flowers of both parent trees (left). The purple broom flowers occur on sprouts of broom type foliage. Height to about 7·5m (25ft), grown for its curiosity value in collections and gardens, but a rather unattractive straggly tree when not in flower. Leaves are shown p50.

Laburnum family Leguminosae
Small group of deciduous trees. Leaves have 3 leaflets and pea-type flowers are in large bunches. Fruit is a pod containing poisonous seeds, which have been known to prove fatal. The wood can be used as a substitute for ebony in furniture making.

Scotch Laburnum

Laburnum alpinum (Mill.) Bercht. & Presl
A small tree, originally from the Alps, Yugoslavia and Czechoslovakia, long cultivated in Europe, including Britain. Height to about 6m (20ft). Flowers (near right) open in June and are in larger, denser flowerheads than Common Laburnum (*L. anagyroides*). Each flower is about 1·8cm (¾in) long with hairless stalks. Seed pods are about 5–7·5cm (2–3in) long. Leaves (p50) are less downy than Common Laburnum.

Common Laburnum or Golden Chain

Laburnum anagyroides Med.
Native to central and southern Europe, widely cultivated for ornament throughout Europe, and naturalised in some places. Height to 6–9m (20–30ft). Flowers (above right) open in May, each about 2·5cm (1in). Seed pods (near right) are 5–7·5cm (2–3in) and similar to those of Scotch Laburnum (*L. alpinum*) but with a thickened edge. Leaves (p50) are rather downy on undersides.

Voss's Laburnum

Laburnum × watereri (Wettst.) Dipp. cv. 'Vossii'
A hybrid between Common and Scotch Laburnum, (*L. anagyroides* and *L. alpinum*). Blossom (far right) has large flowers 2·5cm (1in) in long dense heads and open in June. Foliage (p50) is thicker than Common Laburnum. Fruit is sparsely produced, only a few in each cluster.

Larix family Pinaceae, **Larch**
Deciduous conifers, with needle-like leaves in bunches. Male and female flowers separate on same tree. Fruit a woody cone, remaining on tree after seeds have been shed.

Common Larch or European Larch

Larix decidua Mill.
Native to mountains of central and southern Europe, cultivated in plantations and shelterbelts or as an ornamental in Europe and N. America. Height to 30–42m (100–140ft). Male and female flowers (far left) open in late March, early April; males turning yellow when pollen is shed; females about 1cm (²⁄₅in) long curve round to sit pointing vertical and may be pale or nearly white. Cones (near left), ripen from green to brown in autumn: they may be long, about 4·5cm (1¾in) or short and oval, 1·5–3cm (³⁄₅–1¹⁄₅in) long, each scale slightly wavy. Foliage (p23) turns golden yellow in November before falling. Bark (p218) is grey or pinkish grey with vertical cracks and scaly ridges.

129

Dunkeld Larch

Larix × eurolepis A. Henry
A hybrid between European Larch (*L. decidua*) and Japanese Larch (*L. kaempferi*) first raised in Dunkeld, Scotland, at the end of the last century and now used as a forestry tree in plantations and shelterbelts. Characters may be variable, but always intermediate to the 2 parents. Height to about 30m (100ft). Flowers (far left) open in March; females about 1cm (^{2}/sin) vary in colour from purple to cream tinged with red. Cones (near left) are long, about 3–4cm (1^1/s–1½in), like European Larch (*L. decidua*) and usually have scales turning outwards, though less dramatically than on Japanese Larch (*L. kaempferi*). Foliage (p23) consists of needles, dark green above with 2 grey bands beneath. Bark is dark blackish brown split into scales.

Dahurian Larch

Larix gmelinii (Rupr.) Kuzeneva
Native to Siberia, cultivated in botanical collections. Height to 30m (100ft) in the wild. Flowers (far left) open in early March; males greenish yellow becoming yellow when pollen is shed; females red and green, about 0·5–1cm (^{1}/s–^{2}/sin), ripening through the summer to a purple cone, which finally turns brown (near left) in October or November, opening to release seed. Cones are about 2·5cm (1in) long with glossy rounded scales turned slightly outwards. Foliage (p23) has needles flat on upper surface and slightly keeled underneath. Bark is dark reddish brown, broken into long scales.

Japanese Larch

Larix kaempferi (Lamb.) Carr.
Native to Japan, widely used as a forestry tree in western Britain. Height to 25–30m (80–100ft). Flowers (far left) open in March; males yellow when shedding pollen, females about 1cm (^{2}/sin) red and greenish cream each scale showing both colours. Cones (near left) are distinctive, usually rather round, about 2·5cm (1in) across. The back-turned bracts give the appearance of a small rose. Foliage (p23) has leaves with dark green upper surface and 2 bands of grey on underside. Bark is dark reddish brown, cracked or broken into scales.

Tamarack, Hackmatack or American Larch

Larix laricina (Du Roi) K. Koch
Native to Alaska and Canada south to
Pennsylvania, where its timber has been used for
telegraph poles and railway sleepers. Cultivated
in north-east N. America and occasionally in
Europe as an ornamental tree. Height to 18–25m
(60–80ft). Flowers (far left) open in March
smaller than other larches; females dark red
usually less than 1cm (²/₅in), males yellow. Cones
(near left) are also small, about 1·5cm (³/₅in) long
with smooth scales. Foliage (p23) turns golden in
September and October. Bark is reddish brown
and scaly.

Western Larch or West American Larch

Larix occidentalis Nutt.
Native to western N. America from British
Columbia to northern Montana. Cultivated in
eastern states of N. America and in Europe. An
important forestry tree in British Columbia,
producing a timber useful for construction, mine
timbers and railway sleepers. It has an attractive
figure when used for flooring and interior finish.
Height to 30–60m (100–200ft). Flowers (far left)
open in March, males yellow and females red and
green, about 1·2cm (½in) long. Cones (near left)
are about 2·5–3·7cm (1–1½in) long, with long
thin bracts sticking out from scales before they
open (top cone). After seed has been shed the
scales turn backwards on themselves and the
bracts fall away (2 lower cones). Foliage (p23) is
made up of 3-sided pointed needles. They colour
golden in September and October. Bark is dark
grey-brown and scaly, reddish brown on old
trees.

Tibetan Larch

Larix potaninii Batal.
Native to western China and Tibet, cultivated in
botanical collections. Height to 18–21m
(60–70ft). Flowers (far left) open in March,
males emerging green (as in photograph) and
turning yellow when pollen is shed; females are
about 1·5cm (³/₅in) long, pink and green. Cones
(near left) are about 5cm (2in) long with shiny
brown scales and long bracts pointing about
0·5cm (¹/₅in) out above them. Foliage (p23) is on
rather stout shoots and needles are almost 4-
sided with 2 bands of white on lower side. They
have a strong distinctive smell when crushed.
Bark is dark pinkish grey with scaly cracks.

131

Bay or Laurel

Laurus nobilis L., family Lauraceae
Evergreen tree or shrub, native to the
Mediterranean. Long cultivated, its aromatic
leaves being used as a herb in cooking all sorts of
dishes. The ancient Romans made the leaves into
wreaths to crown heroes and poets. Also makes a
decorative tree for gardens and patios,
commonly grown in tubs and placed at entrances
to hotels, restaurants and houses. Height to
12–18m (40–60ft), though often low and bushy
and trimmed like a hedge. Flowers are on
separate trees, opening in June. Males and
females are both about 0·5cm (¹/₅in) long,
females shown near right, males with clusters of
pollen shedding anthers. Fruit (far right) is about
1·2cm (½in) long and ripens to black. Leaves
(p32) are dark green, almost leathery, and have a
strong aroma when broken.

Libocedrus chilensis (D. Don) Endl.
see *Austrocedrus chilensis* (p88).

Libocedrus decurrens Torr.
see *Calocedrus decurrens* (p92).

Tree Privet or Glossy Privet

Ligustrum lucidum Ait. f., family Oleaceae
An evergreen tree, or shrub, native to China and
making a fine ornamental or shade tree in Europe
especially in cities. Height to about 15m (50ft) as
a tree, less than half that as a shrub. Flowers (far
left) open in late August and September, when
few other trees are flowering. Fruit ripens to
black oval berries about 1·2cm (½in) long.
Leaves (p32) are also noteworthy, being dark
green and very glossy on upper surface. Bark
(near left) is dark grey and smooth with light
streaks.

Liquidambar orientalis Mill., family
Hamamelidaceae **Oriental Sweet Gum**
Deciduous tree, native to Asia Minor. Height to
30m (100ft) in the wild. Leaves (p44) are hairless
and more rounded at lobe tips, and with deeper
rounded teeth on main lobes than on
L. styraciflua.

Sweet Gum

Liquidambar styraciflua L.
Deciduous tree, native to eastern United States
and Central America. The timber is sometimes
known as 'satin walnut'. Height to 45m (150ft) in
the wild. Flowers (near right) open in May:
males in round heads on a spike 5–7·5cm (2–3in)
long; females solitary or in pairs about 1·2cm
(½in) across. Fruits (far right) are about
2·5–3·7cm (1–1½in) across. Leaves (p44) are 5,
sometimes 7 lobed, with fine toothed edges. The
vein axils on the underside bear rust coloured
tufts. Autumn colours are purple, deep red and
orange (p188).

Liriodendron chinense (Hemsl.) Sarg., family Magnoliaceae **Chinese Tulip Tree**
Deciduous tree, native to China. Similar to *L. tulipifera*, but generally smaller, with leaves (p43) narrower in the middle. Pale orange flowers open in July about 6cm (2¼in) across.

Tulip Tree or Whitewood

Liriodendron tulipifera L.
Deciduous tree, native to eastern N. America, cultivated as an ornamental in eastern states and west and north Europe. The timber, called 'white wood' is used in N. America for house interiors, and a heart stimulant has been extracted from the bark. Height to 45–58m (150–190ft) in the wild. Flowers (far left) open in June and July, each petal about 3·7cm (1½in) long. Fruit (near left) is about 5cm (2in) long, ripening from green to brown in September. Leaves (p43) have 4 lobes and turn orange and yellow in autumn (near left and p188).

Tanbark Oak

Lithocarpus densiflorus (Hook. & Arn.) Rehd., family Fagaceae
Evergreen tree, native to California and Oregon, where its bark is used in tanning leather. Height to 21m (70ft), sometimes twice as much. Flowering is irregular, occurring in April or May and again in September. Male flowers (near right) are in catkins 7·5–10cm (3–4in) long. A few females are usually produced below the male catkins and develop into acorns about 1·5–2·5cm (³/₅–1in) in 2 years (far right). One year old acorns are shown with flowers near right. Leaves (p26) have 12–14 pairs of parallel veins and are covered with thick pale orange wool when young, becoming smooth and glossy with age. Young shoots are also covered with this down. Bark is thick, broken into scaly ridges.

Osage Orange

Maclura pomifera (Raf.) Schneid., family Moraceae
Deciduous tree, native to south and central United States, Arkansas and Oklahoma south to Texas. The bark has been used in tanning leather, but also yields a yellow dye, and the Osage Indians used the wood to make weapons. Cultivated as hedging around the Mississippi, and as an ornamental in eastern states and sometimes in Europe. Height to 12m (40ft). Male and female flowers are on separate trees. They open in June, males (far left) about 1·5–2·5cm (³/₅–1in) across, females with shorter stalk but about the same size and green. Fruit (near left) is large, about 7·5–12·5cm (3–5in) across and very heavy, ripening yellow and falling in November. When broken it exudes a white milky sap. Leaves are shown on p35.

Magnolia family Magnoliaceae
Deciduous and evergreen trees and shrubs, with large showy flowers containing both male and female parts. Leaves are simple, untoothed and alternate. Most have strongly aromatic barks. Named in honour of Pierre Magnol, a professor of botany and medicine at Montpelier in late 17th century.

Cucumber Tree

Magnolia acuminata L.
Deciduous forest tree, native to eastern N. America. Cultivated in eastern states and in Europe as an ornamental. Height to 18–27m (60–90ft). Flowers open in May (near right, not fully open) with erect petals about 5–7·5cm (2–3in) long. Fruits (far right) are usually about 7·5cm (3in) long, and when young and green look something like a cucumber, giving this tree its common name. Leaves are shown p28.

Campbell's Magnolia

Magnolia campbellii Hook. f. & Thoms.
Deciduous tree, native to Himalaya, much cultivated for its wonderful flowers. Height to about 18m (60ft) though may be twice as much in the wild; often with several trunks. Flowers (near right) open in February and March, may be 25cm (10in), varying from deep to pale pink or white. Fruits are about 20cm (8in) long. Leaves shown p28.

Yellow Cucumber Tree

Magnolia cordata Michx.
Small deciduous tree or shrub, native to south-east United States. Height to about 6m (20ft). Flowers (far right) are also smaller, petals about 3·7cm (1½in) long. Fruit is about 2·5–3·7cm (1–1½in) long, red and often curved. Leaves (p32) are rounder than most magnolias and slightly heart-shaped at the base.

Yulan

Magnolia denudata Desrouss.
Deciduous tree, native to China, long cultivated there as an ornamental, especially near temples. Height to 9–14cm (30–45ft). Hairy winter buds open in March to produce clear white flowers (near right) which usually have 9 petals about 6cm (3in) long. Fruit is tapered, about 11cm (5in) long, leaves about 8–15cm (3–6in) long narrowing sharply to a point at the tip.

Fraser Magnolia or Ear-leaved Umbrella Tree

Magnolia fraseri Walt.
Deciduous tree, native to south-east United States. Height to 9–12m (30–40ft). Strong-smelling flowers (far right) open in May and June, petals about 7·5–10cm (3–4in) long. Fruit is red, about 10–12·5cm (4–5in) releasing scarlet seeds. Leaves (p28) are a distinctive shape.

**Evergreen Magnolia,
Southern Magnolia or
Bull Bay**

Magnolia grandiflora L.
Evergreen, native to southern United States.
Height to 18–30m (60–100ft) in the wild.
Fragrant flowers (near right), open in July
through to September in northern Europe, but
usually earlier in N. America. They are about
20–25cm (8–10in) across when fully open. Fruit
is orange-green, cylindrical 5cm (2in) long.
Leaves (p27) are glossy green above, with thick
orange down on underside.

**Japanese Big-leaved
Magnolia**

Magnolia hypoleuca Sieb. & Zucc.,
synonym *M. obovata* Thunb.
Deciduous tree, native to Japan. Height to
15–25m (50–80ft) or more. Strong-smelling
flowers (far right) open in June, 20cm (8in)
across. Fruit is red, 12·5–20cm (5–8in) long.
Leaves (p28) are rather wider than most
magnolias and tend to be clustered at tips of
shoots.

**Northern Japanese
Magnolia**

Magnolia kobus DC.
Deciduous tree, native to Japan. Height 9–12m
(30–40ft). Flowers (near right) are about 10cm
(4in) across and have a downy covering when in
bud. They open in April. Fruits are pink, about
5cm (2in) long, splitting all over to release bright
red seeds which dangle by threads before
dropping. Leaves are shown p27.

Magnolia × loebneri Kache cv. 'Leonard Messel'
A cultivated hybrid believed to be between *M.
kobus* and a pink form of the shrubby *M. stellata*.
Flowers (far right) are produced in great
profusion in April, 12 narrow petals about 5cm
(2in) long, pale pink on outside. Leaves are
shown p32.

Willow-leaved Magnolia

Magnolia salicifolia
(Sieb. & Zucc.) Maxim.
Deciduous tree, native to Japan. Height to
6–12m (20–40ft). Flowers (near right) open in
March, about 7·5–10cm (3–4in) across. The
flower bud is hairy. Fruits are 5–7·5cm (2–3in)
long, pink, with scarlet seeds. Leaves are shown
p24. Bark has a sweet lemony scent when
bruised.

Magnolia × soulangiana
Soulange-Bodin
A hybrid between Yulan (*M. denudata*) and a
shrubby magnolia (*M. liliflora*). Popular in all
sizes of garden in Europe. May eventually form a
small tree, to about 7·5m (25ft) tall. Flowers (far
right) open late April, each petal about 7·5–10cm
(3–4in) long. Many cultivars have been
produced and all have white petals stained
purple-pink, deepest at the base on outer side. A
leaf is shown on p27.

135

Umbrella Tree

Magnolia tripetala L.
Deciduous tree, native to eastern N. America.
Cultivated as an ornamental in northern states
and in Europe. Height to 9–12m (30–40ft).
Flowers (near right) have a strong scent and open
in May and June, outer petals about 10–12·5cm
(4–5in) long. Fruit (far right) is about 10cm (4in)
long. Seeds are scarlet. Leaves (p28) are large
and distinguished by their tapering bases. They
grow in umbrella-like clusters, giving the tree its
common name.

Magnolia × veitchii Bean
A deciduous hybrid between *M. campbellii* and
the Yulan (*M. denudata*), first raised early this
century by Peter Veitch of the Royal Nurseries,
Exeter. It has so far attained a height of around
28m (85ft). Flowers open in April, about 15cm
(6in) long and are pale pink, although white
flowered clones have also been raised. Leaves
(p28) are purplish when young becoming dark
green in the summer.

Sweet Bay

Magnolia virginiana L.
Native to eastern United States, evergreen in the
southern part of its range, deciduous in the
north. In Britain it may retain some leaves in the
winter or be deciduous. Height to 9m (30ft).
Fragrant flowers (near right) are produced from
June to September, about 5–7·5cm (2–3in) wide.
Fruits are red about 5cm (2in) long, with scarlet
seeds. Leaves (p35) are smaller than most
magnolias.

Wilson's Magnolia

Magnolia wilsonii
(Fin. & Gagnep.) Rehd.
Deciduous tree, or shrub, native to China.
Height to 7·5m (25ft). Flowers (far right) are
fragrant, about 7·5–10cm (3–4in) across. They
open in May and June from the underside of
branches and so point downwards. Fruit is pink,
about 5–7·5cm (2–3in) long, ripening to release
shiny red seeds in September. Leaf (p27) has a
velvety underside.

Malus family Rosaceae, **Apple** or **Crab**
Deciduous trees, with simple toothed leaves.
Flowers are in clusters, varying from white to
deep rose pink. Fruit is fleshy and may be round
or oval. Many cultivated forms grown for either
blossom or fruit.

Siberian Crab

Malus baccata (L.) Borkh.
Native to a large area from east Siberia to
Manchuria and north China. Height to 6–15m
(20–50ft). Flowers (far left) open in April, each
about 3·7cm (1½in) across. They are easily
distinguished by rather narrow widely spaced
petals. Fruits (near left) are about 1–2cm
($^2/_5$–$^4/_5$in) across, may be yellow, and persist on
the tree during winter. Leaves (p37) are rather
slender.

Sweet Crab Apple or Garland Tree

Malus coronaria (L.) Mill.
Small tree, native to eastern N. America, often grown in gardens as it makes a charming ornamental. Height to 6–9m (20–30ft). Flowers (far left) open in May and June, with a beautiful sweet fragrance, each about 2·5–5cm (1–2in) across in clusters of 4–6. Fruits (near left) are about 2·5–3·7cm (1–1½in) across ripening in October, but not palatable, being rather acid. Leaves (p37) may be almost 3-lobed and turn yellow in the autumn.
M. coronaria cv. 'Charlottae' is a cultivated variety with double, pink tinted flowers and leaves colouring well in autumn.

Hawthorn-leaved Crab Apple

Malus florentina (Zucc.) Schneid.
Small tree or bush, native to north Italy, bearing some resemblance to a common hawthorn (*Crataegus monogyna*). Flowers (far left) are about 1·8cm (¾in) across, 5–7 in a cluster and open in June. Fruit (near left) are oval, about 1·2cm (½in) long, ripening from yellow to red in October. Leaves (p47) are dark green above, and covered with white down underneath.

Japanese Crab

Malus floribunda Sieb. ex Van Houtte
A Japanese tree, probably a hybrid rather than wild, now widely planted in Europe in gardens, parks and streets, as it flowers profusely every year. Height to about 6–9m (20–30ft). Flowers (far left) open in late April and early May, each about 2·5–3cm (1–1¼in) wide in clusters of 4–7. Fruits (near left) are about 2cm (¾in) in diameter, ripening yellow in October. Leaves are usually more toothed than is shown on p37, and may occasionally be lobed.

Oregon Crab

Malus fusca (Raf.) Schneid.
Native to western N. America, sometimes cultivated in eastern states and in Europe. The wood has been used in western America for making tools, tool handles and suchlike, as it is hard and heavy. Height to about 6–12m (20–40ft). Flowers (far left) are about 1·8cm (¾in) across and open in clusters of 6–12 in May. Fruits (near left) are oval, 1·2–2cm (½–¾in) and may be red or yellow. They have a pleasant sharp flavour. Leaves (p37) colour bright red and orange in the autumn.

Hupeh Crab

Malus hupehensis (Pampan.) Rehd.
Native from Himalaya to central and western China, where a tisane called red tea is made from the leaves. Cultivated in European gardens for its spring blossom. Height to as much as 12m (40ft) which is tall for a crab. Fragrant flowers (far left) open in April, each about 2·5–3·7cm (1–1½in) wide in clusters of 3–7. Fruits (near left) are about 0·8cm (⅓in) across, ripening to red from yellow and orange in September. Leaves are oval, and pointed, about 5–10cm (2–4in), usually rounded at the base, dark green above, and downy beneath. They may be purple tinged when young. Bark is dark grey-brown and breaks into flakes when older.

Prairie Crab Apple

Malus ioensis (Wood) Britt.
Native to central United States, similar to Sweet Crab Apple (*M. coronaria*). Height to 9m (30ft). Flowers (far left) are 3·7–5cm (1½–2in) across, 4–6 in a cluster and open in June. Fruits are yellow, green and round, about 3·7cm (1½in) across: similar to *M. coronaria* fruit but with duller surface. Leaves (p37) and branchlets are more downy.
M. ioensis cv. 'Plena', **Bechtel Crab**, has large double flowers about 5–6·2cm (2–2½in) and is much planted in American gardens.

Magdeburg Crab

Malus 'Magdeburgensis'
A hybrid between Chinese Crab (*M. spectabilis*) and the French Paradise Apple (*M. pumila*). Flowers (near left) open in late April and May, about 2·5cm (1in) across. Leaves are shown on p37.

Purple Crab

Malus × purpurea (Barbier) Rehd.
A cultivated hybrid, first raised in France, taking its bright red colours from one of the parents which itself does not grow well in cultivation nor flowers reliably. Height to 7·5m (25ft). Flowers (far left) are about 4cm (1⅜in) across, in clusters of 6–11, opening in April. Fruits (near left) are about 2cm (⁴/₅in) ripening from red to purple. Leaves (p37) are purple-red through summer, fading to purple tinted green at fruiting time (see photographs left). There are many other purple hybrids, one being *Malus* 'Profusion' which is considered by many to be a better tree in Europe than Purple Crab. Flowers are abundant and dark crimson, but turn pale pink quickly. Leaves are larger, about 7·5cm (3in) long.

Chinese Crab

Malus spectabilis (Ait.) Borkh.
A decorative tree from China where it was found in cultivation, but not in the wild. Height to 9m (30ft). Flowers (far left) are usually profuse, opening in late April and May; each is about 5cm (2in) across when fully open, 6–8 in a cluster. Fruit is round, yellow, about 2·5cm (1in) across. Leaves are oval or almost round, about 5–7·5cm (2–3in) long, round at base, and pointed at the tip. Bark (near left) is dark brown with fine ridges, often spiralled, and breaking into scales.

Crab Apple or Wild Crab

Malus sylvestris (L.) Mill.
Native of Europe, including Britain, found in hedgerows and thickets. Rarely cultivated but undoubtedly a parent of orchard apples. Height to 9m (30ft). Flowers (far left) are about 2·5–3·7cm (1–1½in) wide opening in late May. Fruits (near left) are about 2·5cm (1in) across and ripen in September or October when they may be flushed orange red. They are rather sour and bitter but make delicious conserves, especially mixed with other fruits. Leaves (p37) usually have a partly red stalk, and some branches may bear thorns. Bark is brown and broken into square flakes.

Medlar

Mespilus germanica L., family Rosaceae
A deciduous tree or shrub, native to south-east
Europe and west Asia, cultivated throughout
Europe for its fruits which are made into a
conserve, but are edible raw only when left to
turn half rotten. It has become naturalised in
parts of Britain and north Europe. Height to
about 6m (20ft). Flowers (near right) are similar
to a hawthorn (*Crataegus*) flower but are solitary
and larger, about 2·5–3·7cm (1–1½in) across.
They open in late May and early June. Fruits (far
right) are also distinctive, about 2·5cm (1in)
across, with a large 'open' end. Leaves (p26) are
downy, and old trees may bear hard thorns,
about 1·2–2·5cm (½–1in) long.

Dawn Redwood

Metasequoia glyptostroboides
Hu & Cheng, family Taxodiaceae
A deciduous conifer, native to China, of great
interest to botanists as it is the only living
member of a genus, which before 1944 was only
described from fossils. It was discovered by
Chinese scientists in 1941 and seeds were sent a
few years later to the Arnold Arboretum from
where it was distributed through N. America
and Europe. Grows to about 35m (115ft) in the
wild. Male flowers have not yet been seen in
Britain, females (far left) are about 0·6cm (⅓in)
long, produced when leaves first emerge. Cones
(near left) are about 1·8–2·5cm (¾–1in) long,
ripening in their first year to dark brown. Leaves
(p13) are similar to *Taxodium distichum* but
branchlets and leaves are in opposite pairs. They
turn beautiful reddish brown in autumn before
falling. Bark is dark grey, cracked and peeling.

White Mulberry

Morus alba L., family Moraceae
Deciduous tree, native to China but long
cultivated in other eastern countries and south
Europe as the food plant of the silkworm. Height
to about 9m (30ft). Flowers (near right) are in
separate catkins, males in longer spikes than
females, which are about 1·2cm (½in) long.
Fruits (far right) are about 1·2–2·5cm (½–1in)
long, usually white or pink, sometimes dark
purple. Leaves (p39) are shinier and less downy
than the common mulberry.

Common Mulberry or Black Mulberry

Morus nigra L.

A deciduous tree, probably native to the Far East, but has been cultivated in Europe and Asia for so long that its origins are obscure. The fruit has an unusual flavour, and some people love to eat it raw, but often used in jam and wine making. Often a crooked tree, to about 9m (30ft), occasionally low and domed. Male and female flowers are in separate catkins, females (near right) are about 1·2cm (½in) long, males about twice that length. Fruit (far right) grow to as much as 2·5cm (1in) long. Leaves (p39) may be unevenly lobed or simple but always heart-shaped at the base. They are covered with short rough hairs above and downy below.

Nothofagus family Fagaceae, **Southern Beech**
Evergreen and deciduous trees which represent the beech family in the southern hemisphere. Male and female flowers are in separate clusters, males 1–3 together, females usually in 3s. Fruits are like miniature beech nuts.

Antarctic Beech or Nirre

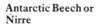

Nothofagus antarctica (Forst. f.) Oerst.
Deciduous tree, native to southern Chile, where it may reach 15m (50ft) in height, but often low and straggly on exposed mountain sites. Flowers (far left) open in April and May; males in profusion about 0·4cm (¹/₆ in) long, the females just visible in the photograph as a tiny nut shape with a red tassel. Fruit (near left) with 3 nutlets, about 0·6cm (¼in) long. Leaves are shown p29. Bark is dark brown with deep cracks forming thick flaking plates.

Dombey's Southern Beech or Coigüe

Nothofagus dombeyi (Mirbel) Blume
Evergreen tree, native to Chile and Argentina. Height to 25m (80ft), or more in the wild. Flowers open in late May, males (far left) have red anthers and are about 0·4cm (¹/₆in) long. Females are tiny, similar to those of Antarctic Beech. Fruit (near left) is about 0·6cm (¼in) long, splitting to release seed in October. Leaves (p29) are glossy green and covered with minute dark spots (see fruit photograph). Bark is dark greyish brown with broad shallow cracks, and eventually peels in strips to expose orange underneath.

Roblé Beech

Nothofagus obliqua (Mirbel) Blume
Deciduous tree, native to Chile and western
Argentina, where it once formed extensive
natural forests and is still an important timber
tree. Its wood being similar to that of oak, the
Spanish gave it their name for oak, Roblé.
Height to 30m (100ft) in the wild. Flowers (far
left) open in May; males are single with as many
as 30–40 stamens; females are tiny green and nut-
shaped. Fruits (near left) are about 1cm (^{2}/sin)
long, opening in September to release the
nutlets. Leaves (p29) usually have 8 or 9 pairs of
veins. Bark (p218) on mature trees is brown and
broken into small rectangular curved flakes.

Raoul or Rauli

Nothofagus procera (Poepp. & Endl.) Oerst.
Deciduous tree, native to the Andes in Chile, and
in Argentina near the Chilean border, where it is
one of the most important timber trees. Its use in
forestry is being extended to Britain where it
apparently has great potential. Its wood is
superior to the Roblé Beech (*N. obliqua*) and it
has a fast growth rate. Height to 25m (80ft) and
more. Flowers (far left) open in May; males
about 0·6cm (¼in) long, females tiny green and
nut-shaped in leaf axils towards the ends of
shoots. Fruits (near left) are about 1cm
(^{2}/sin)
long, breaking open in September to release
seeds. Leaves (p29) have more pairs of veins than
N. obliqua, usually 14–18 pairs. Bark is smooth,
greyish-brown with vertical wide dark cracks.

Tupelo, Black Gum or Pepperidge

Nyssa sylvatica Marsh., family Nyssaceae
A deciduous tree, native to eastern N. America
where it grows in swamps or damp ground.
Cultivated as an ornamental in eastern states and
in Europe. Height to 30m (100ft) in the wild,
with a tapering trunk. Male and female flowers
(near right) are produced in June on separate
trees: both in round heads about 1·2cm (½in)
across, but females have only a few flowers to the
cluster. Fruits (far right) are about 1·2cm (½in)
long, and ripen to dark bluish-black in October.
Leaves (p35) are usually long and tapered at both
ends. They colour brilliant orange and red in the
autumn (p77). In the United States it is one of the
earliest trees to display autumn foliage.

Ostrya family Carpinaceae, **Hop Hornbeam**
A small group of deciduous trees, similar in
many ways to the hornbeams (*Carpinus*), but
distinguished mostly by the fruits: each nutlet is
completely enclosed by a bladder-like, thin
papery husk.

European Hop Hornbeam

Ostrya carpinifolia Scop.
Native to southern Europe, Asia Minor and the
Caucasus. Grows to 15–18m (50–60ft) tall, the
crown becoming rounded with age. Flowers (far
left) open in April, male catkins about 3·7–7·5cm
(1½–3in) long, the females rather small and
green, opening among the emerging leaves. Fruit
clusters (near left) are about 3·7–5cm (1½–2in)
long, turning light brown in September and
October. They look very much like hops, hence
the English name. Leaves (p33) have 12–15 pairs
of veins and are rather hairy on the upper
surface, less so underneath.

Eastern Hop Hornbeam or Ironwood

Ostrya virginiana (Mill.) K. Koch
Native to eastern N. America, where it yields a
very hard timber used for making mallets and
fence posts amongst other things. Sometimes
cultivated for ornament in European gardens and
collections. Height 9–18m (30–60ft). Flowers
(far left) open in April, male catkins about 5cm
(2in) long, females often red among the emerging
leaves. Fruit clusters (near left) are about
3·7–5cm (1½–2in) long on hairy and longer
stalks than *O. carpinifolia*. They turn light brown
in autumn. Leaves (p33) are hairy on upper
surface and more downy beneath with hairy
stalks.

Sorrel Tree or Sour Wood

Oxydendrum arboreum (L.) DC., family
Ericaceae
Deciduous tree, native to eastern N. America.
Cultivated in parks and gardens, in eastern
states, and in western Europe. The leaves are
rather acid and have been used medicinally as a
tonic and diuretic. Height to about 18m (60ft) in
the wild, but often half this height or even
shrubby in cultivation. Flowers (near right) open
in August and September, each about 0·6cm
(¼in) long in clusters which may be as much as
25cm (10in) long. The fruits are hard, woody
bell-shaped capsules about 1·2cm (½in) long.
Leaves (p27) are alternate, tapered and
sometimes hairy on the mid vein and stalk. They
colour bright red in the autumn (far right).

Persian Ironwood or Iron Tree

Parrotia persica (DC.) C. A. Mey., family Hamamelidaceae
Deciduous tree or shrub, native to the area to the south and south-west of the Caspian Sea, from north Persia to the Caucasus. Both in the wild and in gardens it can be very shrubby, forming dense thickets, but may be found as a tree to about 12m (40ft) tall. Flowers (far left) open in February and March before the leaves emerge; the clusters are about 1·2cm (½in) across, with bright red anthers. Fruit is like a small brown nut about 1·2cm (½in) in a cluster of 3–5. Leaves (p32) colour brilliant reds, orange and yellow (near left). Bark (p218) is smooth and grey, breaking off in flakes, to expose light green patches.

Foxglove-tree

Paulownia tomentosa (Thunb.) Steud., family Scrophulariaceae
Deciduous tree, native to China, cultivated in Japan, roadsides in south Europe, and in gardens throughout Europe, but does not do well in colder parts as the flowerbuds are produced in autumn and lie waiting through the winter. Height to 12m (40ft). Flowers (near right) open in May, each about 5cm (2in) long, in large upright clusters. Fruit (far right) is up to about 5cm (2in) long, drying up, and splitting to release lots of winged seeds. Leaves (p42) are variable, smaller ones unlobed, and larger ones with 3 or 5 shallow lobes. They have silky hairs on top surface and grey down on lower surface.

Amur Cork-tree

Phellodendron amurense Rupr., family Rutaceae
Deciduous tree, native to China, including the Amur region. Height to about 15m (50ft). Flowers open in July, male and female on separate trees, similar to *P. japonicum* flowers, about 0·6cm (¼in) long, in erect clusters about 7·5cm (3in) tall. Fruits (far left) are about 1·2cm (½in) across. Leaves (p55) have 5–11 leaflets, which are hairless except around the edge and at the base of the main vein.

Phellodendron japonicum Maxim.
Deciduous tree, native to Japan and growing to about 9m (30ft). Flowers open in July, male clusters (near left) about 10cm (4in) long. Females, on separate tree, are in a more slender cluster. Fruits are black, about 1·2cm (½in) across. Leaves have broader leaflets which are very downy on the underside.

Picea family Pinaceae, **Spruce**
Evergreen coniferous trees, with needle-like leaves arranged singly and spirally around the shoot. Bare shoots bear tiny peg-like projections where the leaves were once attached. Male and female flowers are on the same tree. Fruit are hanging woody cones.

Norway Spruce

Picea abies (L.) Karsten
Native to mountains from Scandinavia to north-west Russia and in central Europe, grown throughout northern and central Europe and in eastern United States. The timber, known as white wood, or deal, has many uses, including roofing, house interiors and paper pulp. Turpentine is extracted from the stem and the bark is still used for tanning in Germany, but Norway Spruce is perhaps best known in Britain as the Christmas tree. Height to about 36m (120ft) but may be larger. Flowers (near right) open in May, males are about 1cm (²/₅in) long, clustered at shoot tips. They turn yellow when shedding pollen. Females are erect, pink turning green at the end of May, turning downwards as the cone ripens. Cone (far right) ripens from green to shiny brown in the autumn, 12·5–15cm (5–6in) long. Foliage (p17) has hard pointed needles and dark brown round buds. Bark is reddish brown flaking into thin scales, but on very old trees is darker and broken into plates.

Dragon Spruce

Picea asperata Mast.
Native to western China, cultivated in collections and large gardens. Height to about 30m (100ft) in the wild, but rather less has been attained in cultivation. Flowers (near right) open in April, each about 2cm (5in) long, males pink turning yellow when shedding pollen, females dark crimson. Cones (far right) are about 7·5–12·5cm (3–5in) long, with round scales. Foliage (p17) is rather blue, needles more dense on upper part of the shoot, with lower needles bending round to point upwards. Bark is dark brown, flaking into lighter brown papery scales.

Sargent Spruce

Picea brachytyla (Franch.) Pritz.
Native to central and western China, cultivated in botanical collections and large gardens. Height up to about 25m (80ft), though often much less. Flowers (near right) open in late May, males about 1·5cm (³/₅in) long, turning yellow, females slightly larger at shoot tip. Cones (far right) are about 6·2–7·5cm (2½–5in) long. Foliage (p17) is distinctive since needles are flattened, rather than 4-sided as in most spruces, and are arranged only on sides and upper parts of the twigs. They are bright glossy green above and white beneath. Bark is smooth, grey and covered with white spots of resin.

Brewer's Weeping Spruce

Picea breweriana S. Wats.
Native to a small part of California and Oregon at altitudes up to 2,000m (7,000ft). Its decorative curtains of hanging branchlets make this a graceful ornamental for gardens. Height to 36m (120ft) in the wild, but usually much less. Flowers (near right) open in May; males rather round, about 1·5cm (³⁄₅in) long, females erect about 2·5cm (1in) long, usually dark pink (but shown pinkish green) developing into a purple cone, about 7·5cm (3in) long, with round scales, ripening to brown in autumn (far right). Foliage (p17) is made up of needles pointing forwards all round the twigs. Bark is dark pinkish grey, with round peeling plates.

Blue Engelmann Spruce

Picea engelmannii (Parry) Englem.
forma *glauca* Beissn.
The blue form of the Engelmann Spruce, native to the mountains of western N. America. Height to about 30m (100ft). Flowers open in May, males are dark purple (not shown) and females (near right) are reddish purple, about 3cm (1¹⁄₅in) long. Cones (far right) are about 5–7·5cm (2–3in) long and differ from the White Spruce (*P. glauca*) in having slightly toothed scales. Foliage (p17) is also distinctive, as the needles point forwards and are soft to the touch with spiney tips, and have a smell of camphor when crushed. Bark is orange, and flakes into papery scales.

White Spruce

Picea glauca (Moench) Voss
Native across the northern regions of N. America, often planted in Canada, New England and northern Europe as an ornamental. Height to about 21m (70ft). Flowers (near right) open in April, males about 2·5cm (1in) long when shedding pollen, females about the same, developing into a cone (far right) about 3·7–5cm (1½–2in) long with rounded scales. Foliage (p17) is made up of rather blue 4-sided needles which are denser on top of the shoot and point forwards. They are hard but do not have a spined tip, and when crushed produce a strong unpleasant smell. Bark is purplish-grey, and breaks into rounded flakes.

Hondo Spruce

Picea jezoensis (Seib. & Zucc.) Carr.
var. *hondoensis* (Mayr) Rehd.
Native to Japan, grown in collections and large
gardens. A variety of a species which is widely
distributed through north-east Asia. Height to
28m (90ft) in the wild. Flowers (near right) open
in May, males are about 2·5cm (1in) long when
shedding pollen, females a bit larger (shown
right on leading shoot). Cones (far right) are
about 5cm (2in) long with toothed, inward-
curved scales. Needles (p17) are spine tipped,
with 2 white bands underneath and point
upwards and forwards, attached on top and sides
of shoots. Bark is smooth brown, or paler and
greyish, cracked and plated.

Koyama's Spruce

Picea koyamai Shirasawa
Native to central Japan at altitudes between
1,500–1,800m (5,000–6,000ft) and also Korea.
Height to about 18m (60ft). Flowers (near right)
open in May, males about 2·5cm (1in) long,
females dark purple and slightly longer. Cones
(far right) are about 10cm (4in) long with scales
rounded and slightly wavy. When dry, they
expand to half their length. Needles (p17) are
very sharp at the tip, 4-sided and rather blue.
They radiate all round the twig but lower ones
curve and point upwards, upper ones point
forward. Bark may be dark brown or light
purplish grey, with grey flakes breaking away.

Likiang Spruce

Picea likiangensis (Franch.) Pritz.
Native to a large area of western China and Tibet,
first discovered in the Lichiang mountains in
Yunnan province. Grown as an ornamental in
botanical collections and gardens. Height to 45m
(150ft) in the wild. Flowers (near right) open all
over the tree in April. Cones (far right) are
usually about 5cm (2in) long, with round but
wavy scales. Foliage (p17) may be rather variable
in colour, from green to blue-green; needles are
4-sided and upper ones point forwards. Bark is
light grey and rough, with some long dark
cracks.

147

Black Spruce

Picea mariana (Mill.) Britt., Sterns and Pogg.
Native across northern regions of N. America
south to Wisconsin and Virginia. Sometimes
cultivated but short-lived. Its timber has been
used locally in Canada, but is of no great value,
and spruce-beer is made from its leaves. Height
to about 9m (30ft) but may be found three times
as high. It takes a columnar form in Canada but
rather pyramidal when cultivated (both
silhouettes are shown). Flowers (near right) open
in May in great profusion, male and female both
about 2cm (⁴/₅in) long. Cones (far right) are
2·5–5cm (1–2in) long with rounded or slightly
toothed scales, and may persist on the tree for
many years. Foliage (p17) consists of needles
pointed at the tip, but not sharply. They are 4-
sided, with a blue-grey band on each face. Bark is
pinkish or purplish-grey and flaky.

Siberian Spruce

Picea obovata Ledeb.
A spruce similar to Norway Spruce (*P. abies*)
from north Europe right across north Russia.
Height may reach 30m (100ft) in the wild but is
often less in cultivation. Flowers (near right) and
fruit (far right) are similar to *P. abies*, opening in
May, but cones are usually smaller, about 7·5cm
(3in) long. Foliage (p18) is distinguished by a
single needle pointing out below the buds at a
different angle to all the others.

Serbian Spruce

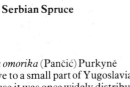

Picea omorika (Pančić) Purkyně
Native to a small part of Yugoslavia, of interest
because it was once widely distributed through
Europe before the Ice Age. Now cultivated in
parks and gardens in Britain, and occasionally in
north Europe for timber. Height may reach 30m
(100ft). Flowers (near right) open in May, males
about 1·2cm (½in) long, expanding to shed
pollen, females slightly larger. Cones (far right)
are about 2·5–5cm (1–2in) long with broad,
rounded scales. Foliage (p18) is distinctive as the
needles are flattened rather than 4-sided, with 2
white bands underneath. Bark is reddish-brown
breaking into plates and papery flakes.

Oriental Spruce or Caucasian Spruce

Picea orientalis (L.) Link
Native to the Caucasus and Asia Minor, grown
for ornament in Europe and eastern states of
N. America and sometimes for timber in
Belgium, Italy and Austria. Height to about 30m
(100ft). Flowers (near right) open in late April,
males about 1·2cm (½in) long, females twice as
long and slender greenish purple or violet. Cones
(far right) are about 5–9cm (2–3½in) long,
ripening to shiny brown. Foliage (p18) is easily
recognised as the needles are much shorter than
on any other spruce, about 0·5–1cm (¹/₅–²/₅in).
Bark is pinkish brown, breaking into small
rounded flakes.

Tiger-tail Spruce

Picea polita (Sieb. & Zucc.) Carr.
Native to Japan, cultivated in Europe and
eastern N. America for ornament. Height to over
30m (100ft), but may be rather smaller in
cultivation. Flowers (near right) open in May,
males about 2cm (⁴/₅in) long, females larger,
about 2·5cm (1in). Cones (far right) are usually
about 10cm (4in) long and ripen to dark brown,
the scales rounded with a pale edge. Needles
(p18) are 4-sided, hard and sharply pointed.
Bark is pinkish-brown with large rough plates.

Colorado Spruce

Picea pungens Engelm.
Native to the Rocky Mountains in western
N. America, particularly at the south end of the
range. Grown for ornament and sometimes for
timber in northern and central Europe. Height to
about 30m (100ft) but may reach 45m (150ft) in
favourable conditions. Flowers (near right) open
in May, males about 2cm (⁴/₅in) long, females
twice that. Cones (far right) are a distinctive pale
colour, with wavy toothed scales. They are about
7·5–10cm (3–4in) long. Needles (p18) are 4-sided
with whitish-blue buds on each face. They are
spine tipped when young, becoming blunter
with age. Bark is purplish-grey, breaking into
coarse plates.

Blue Spruce

Picea pungens Engelm. forma *glauca* (Reg.)
Beissn.
The blue-leaved form of Colorado Spruce
(*P. pungens*), perhaps more commonly grown in
European parks, gardens and collections than
the type. Flowers and cones (near and far right)
are similar to Colorado Spruce. Foliage (p18)
differs from Blue Engelmann Spruce (*P.
engelmanni glauca*) in having harder spiney
needles and leaf buds having scales curved
outwards. Many named cultivars of this form are
available for planting.

Red Spruce

Picea rubens Sarg.
A native of eastern N. America, where it was
once used, along with its ally the Black Spruce
(*P. mariana*), to make a spruce-beer. Its timber
has been put to use for flooring and suchlike in
north-eastern states of America, and also made
into paperpulp. Height to about 25m (80ft) or
more. Flowers (near right) open in May, male
and female both about 2–3cm (⁴/s–1¹/sin) long.
Cones (far right) are up to 5cm (2in) long with
rounded scales, very similar in size and shape to
P. mariana but these fall from the tree as soon as
they open, whereas *P. mariana* cones persist for
many years. Needles (p18) are 4-sided with light
bands on each face and a more yellow-green than
those of *P. mariana*. Bark is dark purplish-
brown, breaking into small curved plates.

Sitka Spruce

Picea sitchensis (Bongard) Carr.
An important timber tree, native to the coast of
western N. America, now widely planted in
western, northern and central Europe as a
plantation tree, as its timber is quickly produced
and of high quality. It thrives in areas of high
rainfall, making it suitable for north-western
Europe. Height to 50m (160ft) or more. Flowers
(near right) open in May, males about 2·5–3·7cm
(1–1½in) long, females a bit longer, usually red
or pinkish green. Cones (far right) are distinctive
with wavy edged scales, and feel soft when
squeezed. They are about 5–10cm (2–4in) long,
ripening from green to brown. Needles (p18) are
4-sided, and spined at the tip making foliage
prickly. Upper needles lie flat pointing down the
shoot. Bark (p218) is dark purplish grey or
brown and breaks into coarse irregular plates
which fall away.

Morinda Spruce or West Himalayan Spruce

Picea smithiana (Wall.) Boiss.
Native to west Himalaya, named after Sir James Smith who was the first president of the Linnean Society. Height to about 36m (120ft) but sometimes twice as much, with a weeping appearance, as *P. breweriana*, but less marked than in that species. Flowers (near right) open in early May, males about 2cm (⁴/₅in) long; females longer. Cones (far right) may be 10–18cm (4–7in) long, ripening to shiny brown from light green. Scales become toothed as the cone dries. Needles (p18) are longer than other spruces, pointing outwards on all sides of the shoot. Bark is purplish-grey, and breaks into shallow, rounded plates.

Sikkim Spruce or East Himalayan Spruce

Picea spinulosa (Griff.) Henry
Native to eastern Himalaya, where it grows to more than 60m (200ft). In cultivation however it has not attained this height. Flowers (near right) open in May, males about 2·5cm (1in) long, females slightly longer. Cones (far right) are about 6–9cm (2¼–3½in) long, green with purple edges, ripening to brown. Needles (p18) are 2-sided, point forwards and have sharp points. Bark is light grey and breaks into round plates and shallow cracks.

Picea wilsonii Mast.
Native to China, cultivated elsewhere only in botanical collections and large gardens. Height to about 21m (70ft). Flowers (near right) open in May, males about 2cm (⁴/₅in) long, females larger. Cones (far right) are about 3·7–7·5cm (1½–3in) long with rounded scales and may persist on the tree for several years. Needles (p18) are 4-sided, green on all faces, and are sharply pointed. Bark is pinkish-grey, breaking into thin flakes.

Picrasma

Picrasma quassioides (D. Don) Bennett, family Simaroubaceae
Deciduous tree, native to Japan, Korea, China and Himalaya. Very decorative but little cultivated in other areas. Height up to about 12m (40ft). Flowers (far left) open in June, each about 0·5cm (¹/₅in) across in a loose cluster. Fruits (near left) are about 1cm (²/₅in) long, and ripen red in September or October. Leaves (p55) colour orange and scarlet in the autumn. They have 9–13 pairs of leaflets.

Pinus family Pinaceae, **Pine**
Evergreen coniferous trees and shrubs. Leaves are needle-like, long and slender in clusters of 2–5, rarely single or up to 8 together which when pressed together form a thin cylindrical shape. Male and female flowers are separate on the same tree, males clustered at base of new shoots, females at the tips. Fruit is a woody cone which usually takes 2 years to ripen.

Whitebark Pine

Pinus albicaulis Engelm.
A small tree, native to western N. America, at altitudes between 1,500–3,000m (5,000–10,000ft) forming a tree of about 15m (50ft) or a low shrub about 3m (10ft) in exposed sites. The edible sweet seeds were collected for food by American Indians. Flowers open in June, males red and clustered, females (near right) red, about 1·2cm (½in) long. Cones (far right) are about 3·7–7·5cm (1½–3in) with thick scales bearing sharp spines and ripening from purple to brown. They fall from the tree, eventually breaking up to release unwinged, edible seeds, about 1·2cm (½in) long. Needles (p21) are in bundles of 5, sometimes 6, or rarely 8, with pale lines on all surfaces, 5–6cm (2–2¼in) long. Leaf-buds are dark reddish-brown, with scales closely pressed. Bark of mature trees is rather white in appearance.

Bristle-cone Pine

Pinus aristata Engelm.
Native to mountains of Colorado, Arizona and New Mexico at altitudes above 2,500m (8,000ft). Height to about 15m (50ft), though may be smaller in exposed sites. Flowers open in June, males dark red, females (near right) red purple, about 0·6cm (¼in) long. Cones (far right) are about 7·5cm (3in) long and have distinctive long bristles on each scale. They also show white patches of resin which may be found all over the leaves and stem. Needles (p21) are in bundles of 5, rather short and stout, with paler inner surfaces. They all bunch together pointing forwards on the shoots to give the appearance of a bottle brush or a foxtail.

David's Pine

Pinus armandii Franch.
Named after the French missionary Père Armand David, a great naturalist, who discovered this pine in its native China. Also found in Burma and Formosa. Cultivated in botanical collections. Height to about 22·5m (75ft). Flowers (near right) open in June, males yellow and often sparse, female is reddish purple developing to cone (far right) about 7·5–15cm (3–6in) long, with thick scales and ripening from green to light brown. Foliage (p22) is made up of long needles in bunches of 5 which are often strongly bent or crinkled near the base. They are bright green on the outside with a pale band on inside. Twigs are often bare for much of their length and covered with drops of resin.

Knobcone Pine

Pinus attenuata Lemm.
Native to western N. America from Oregon through California. Height is usually around 9m (30ft) but may grow to 30m (100ft) in the wild. Flowers open in May, males orange brown in large clusters at the base of new shoots, females (near right, shown on a leading shoot) about 1·5cm (³/sin) long, usually borne in whorls. Cones (far right) are about 10–12·5cm (4–5in) long, scales more developed into knobs on outer sides, and bearing small sharp spines. They persist for a long time on the tree, sometimes for 30 or 40 years, only releasing seed after fire or the death of the tree. (The white patches in the photograph are dried resin.) Needles (p21) are in clusters of 3 and buds are cylindrical and resinous. Bark (p218) is dark grey with fine flakes, often covered with dried resin.

Mexican White Pine

Pinus ayacahuite Ehrenb.
Native to Guatemala and Mexico, where it grows in mountain valleys at altitudes 2,500–3,000m (8,000–10,000ft). Height to about 30m (100ft) or more in the wild. Flowers (near right) open in June, males yellow in clusters at base of new growth, females red, about 1cm (²/sin) long. Cones (far right) grow to about 15–30cm (6–12in), turning pale brown and opening as they ripen, scale tips usually resinous and the lowest scales curve back. Seeds have wings at least 2·5cm (1in) long with a seed about 0·6cm (¼in). Needles (p22) are slender in clusters of 5.
P. ayacahuite var. *veitchii* Shaw
A variety from Mexico which has often been confused with the species in gardens and collections. It has larger seeds, about 1·2cm (½in) long with shorter, broader wings. Cones may reach 38cm (15in) in length.

Jack Pine

Pinus banksiana Lamb.
Native to Canada and north-eastern United States, cultivated for timber on poor sandy soils in central Europe. Height to about 21m (70ft) though may be shrubby in cultivation. Flowers (near right) open in May, males yellow or reddish yellow, clustered at base of new growth, females red and prickly, about 0·5cm (1/5in) long. Cones (far right) are about 3·7cm (1½in) long, very tapered and usually curved. They ripen from green to light brown and although some cones open on the tree, most remain closed until triggered by the heat of a fire. Seeds therefore become viable after a forest fire so Jack Pine is often one of the first trees to colonise burnt areas. Needles (p19) are short, 2–4cm (¾–1½in), flattish and grouped in pairs.

Lacebark Pine

Pinus bungeana Zucc.
Native to east and central China, cultivated in botanical collections and some gardens. Height may reach around 30m (100ft), the trunk usually divided into several stems low down, sometimes bushy. Flowers (near right) open in late May, males yellow and clustered at base of new growth, females yellowish green, about 1cm (2/5in) long, developing to round cones about 5–7·5cm (2–3in) long, each scale having a short spine. Seeds are hard, about 0·8cm (⅓in) long with a short wing. Needles (p21) are shiny and hard, grouped in 3s. The bark (p218) is perhaps the most noteworthy feature, being more like a plane than a pine. On old trees it becomes almost white but this is rarely seen in cultivation.

Arolla Pine or Swiss Stone Pine

Pinus cembra L.
Native of the Alps and Carpathians, growing at altitudes up to 3,000m (10,000ft), cultivated in collections and gardens for ornament in Europe and north-eastern United States, and occasionally for timber in Scandinavia. Height to about 25m (80ft) or more. Flowers (near right) open in late May, males clustered at base of new growth, females at the tips, about 1cm (2/5in) long. Cones (far right) are round or egg-shaped, about 5–7·5cm (2–3in) long, ripening from dark purple to light brown and falling from the tree in their third year. The scales do not open, the seeds being released as the cones rot on the ground or are broken up by birds or animals in search of food. Needles (p22) are in clusters of 5, which only partially open and are green on outer surface and bluish grey on the inner surface. Twigs are clothed by an orange down.

Pinyon,
Mexican Nut Pine or
Mexican Stone Pine

Pinus cembroides Zucc.
Native to Arizona, California and Mexico where
the seeds are harvested and sold as nuts. Height
to about 12m (40ft) in the wild. Flowers open in
late May, males yellow in dense clusters, females
(near right) red, about 1cm ($^2/_5$in) long. Cones
(far right) are round, about 5cm (2in) across
becoming flat and flower-like as the scales ripen
and open to release the large, about 1·2cm (½in)
long, wingless seed. Needles (p21) are usually in
3s, but sometimes pairs, each needle curved
inwards. Three other pinyons occur in south-
west United States. These are considered
varieties of this Mexican species, differing in the
leaf thickness and the number of leaves in a
cluster.

Shore Pine or
Beach Pine

Pinus contorta Loud.
Native to the coast of western N. America, from
Alaska to California, an important forestry tree
in Britain especially on peaty soils in the west.
Also planted in central and northern Europe.
Height to about 25m (80ft). Flowers (near right)
open in May, males abundant, yellow, about 2cm
($^4/_5$in) long, females red, about 0·6cm (¼in) long.
Cones (far right) are usually curved, about 5cm
(2in) long, and each scale bears a sharp spine,
which gradually wears off. Scales open to release
winged seeds. Needles (p19) are often twisted
and are grouped in pairs. Twigs are also twisted.
The bark is usually reddish brown, and deeply
cracked into square plates, or long narrow plates
on old trees.

Lodgepole Pine

Pinus contorta var. *latifolia* S. Wats.
Native to the Rocky Mountains from Alaska to
Colorado, this is the inland form of Shore Pine
(*P. contorta*), and intermediate types may be
found at the boundary of their ranges. Planted as
a forestry tree in Britain, particularly on high
ground. Height may reach 25m (80ft), making a
more slender tree than *P. contorta*. Flowers (near
right) open in late May. Cones (far right) are
usually more reddish brown than *P. contorta*,
also shorter and more rounded. Although some
cones open each year, many remain closed and
persist on the tree. Needles (p19) are in pairs and
are longer, broader and paler than *P. contorta*
leaves. A thin, smoother bark also distinguishes
it.

Big-cone Pine

Pinus coulteri D. Don
Native to California, where the Indians used to
harvest the seeds for food, and to north-western
Mexico. Cultivated in botanical collections and
gardens. Height may reach about 30m (100ft).
Flowers (near right) open in early June, males
dark purple then yellow and females red, about
1·5cm (³/₈in) long. Cones (far right) are the
heaviest of all pines. They may grow to about
30cm (12in) long and weigh about 2·27kg (5lb)
when fresh, but generally found much smaller.
The scales are hard and bear a sharp incurved
claw-like spine. Seeds are also large, about 1·2cm
(½in) with a wing twice as long. Most cones
remain closed and persist on the tree, but some
open to release seeds in autumn. Needles (p21)
are long and narrow in clusters of 3 together.

Limber Pine

Pinus flexilis James
Native of the Rocky Mountains from Canada
south to California and New Mexico. Height to
about 18m (60ft). Flowers (near right) open in
early June, males yellow or reddish yellow,
females often clustered, red, about 0·6cm (¼in)
long. Cones (far right) are up to 15cm (6in), or
more in America, similar in appearance to cones
of *P. albicaulis*, but longer and opening to release
seeds when ripe. They are solitary or 2 or 3
together. Needles (p22) are in clusters of 5, and
each is the same colour on each face. The edges
are usually smooth, rather than finely toothed as
in most 5-needle pines, though may be toothed
near the tip.

Aleppo Pine

Pinus halepensis Mill.
A native of south Europe from Spain around the
Mediterranean to Asia Minor. It is particularly
common on drier soils on mountains and by the
coast. Its wood has little value, but the resin
yields oil of turpentine and is also used in making
the Greek wine, retsina. Height to about 15m
(50ft) though may be taller. Flowers open in
May, females (near right) about 1cm (²/₅in) long.
Cones (far right) are about 7·5cm (3in) long,
usually borne in pairs or threes and persist on the
branches for several years. Needles (p19) are in
pairs, growth buds are free of resin and have
scales curving back.

Bosnian Pine

Pinus heldreichii Christ var. *leucodermis* (Ant.) Markgraf ex Fitschen, synonym *Pinus leucodermis* Ant.
Native to northern Italy, Yugoslavia and the Balkans and is more common than *P. heldreichii* itself. Height to about 28m (90ft) but usually much smaller. Flowers (near right) open in late May, males abundant, yellow, females dark red-purple about 0·8cm (⅓in) long developing into a dark purple cone (far right) about 2cm (⁴/₅in) long which expands and ripens in its second year to pale brown (also far right), about 5–7·5cm (2–3in) long. The specimen in the cone photograph has some of its needles cut away to show the young cones more clearly. Needles (p19) are dark green, spine tipped and arranged in pairs.

Holford's Pine

Pinus × holfordiana A. B. Jacks
A hybrid raised at Westonbirt, England, from seed of a Mexican White Pine (*P. ayacahuite*) which had been pollinated by a Himalayan Pine (*P. wallichiana*) standing nearby. It may be found in British collections and large gardens. Height has reached about 28m (90ft) so far. Flowers (near right) open in June, males yellow and clustered around the base of new shoots, females dark red and narrow, about 2cm (⁴/₅in) long. Cones (far right) ripen in the second year from green to woody orange brown, about 20–30cm (8–12in) long. Cone scales open to release winged seeds. Needles are in clusters of 5 (p22) and are shining green on outer surface, pale grey-blue on inner surface. Compare with *P. ayacahuite* and *P. wallichiana*.

Jeffrey Pine

Pinus jeffreyi Balf.
Native to southern Oregon, to lower California, at altitudes to 1,000m (3,500ft) in the north and 3,000m (10,000ft) in the south. Cultivated as an ornamental in European gardens and in eastern states of N. America. Height to 60m (200ft) in the wild but usually half this. Flowers (near right) open in early June, males reddish, then yellow, females dark purple, about 0·8cm (⅓in) long. Cones (far right) are up to about 20cm (8in) long when ripe. Each scale bears a narrow sharp spine and opens to release winged seeds. Needles (p21) are in bundles of 3, and are rather long and slender, producing a strong lemon smell when crushed. Bark is smooth, with a few deep cracks and is very dark brown.

Western White Pine or Mountain White Pine

Pinus monticola D. Don
Native to western N. America, where it produces a light timber used in house interiors. Cultivated in eastern N. America and Europe, but is susceptible, like other 5-needled pines from America, to a fungal disease, white pine blister-rust, which has been responsible for killing the oldest ornamental specimens. Height to about 50m (160ft) but often much less. Flowers (near right) open in early June, males pale yellow in clusters, females red, about 0·5cm (¼in) long. Cones (far right) are 12·5–25cm (5–10in) long, usually slightly curved and covered with resin. (In Britain they usually reach 15cm (6in).) Needles (p22) are rough to the touch and are in groups of 5. Inner surfaces are paler than outer. Young shoots are downy which easily distinguishes this from Weymouth Pine (*P. strobus*).

Bishop Pine

Pinus muricata D. Don
Native to the coast of California, occasionally felled for timber. Cultivated in Europe as an ornamental and found to be particularly useful as a shelter-tree in seaside areas as it withstands salt spray. Height to around 15m (50ft) but may grow to nearly twice as much. Flowers (near right) open in late May, the male in long spikes rather than short clusters, females red, about 0·6cm (¼in) long, in whorls of 3–5. Cones (far right) are about 7·5cm (3in) long, and each scale bears a sharp spine. They persist on the tree for at least 25 years, releasing seed only after a fire has forced the scales to open. Needles (p19) are hard, deep glossy green and arranged in pairs.

Austrian Pine

Pinus nigra Arnold
Native to Austria, Italy, Yugoslavia and Greece. Planted in Britain for shelter and for ornament. Height may reach over 30m (100ft) in the wild, with a shorter trunk and more branches, covered with thick foliage, than Corsican Pine (*P. nigra* var. *maritima*). Flowers (near right) open in late May, males golden yellow, females red, about 0·5cm (¼in) long. Cones (far right) are 5–7·5cm (2–3in) long and the scales open to release winged seeds. Needles (p19) are stiffer and usually shorter and straighter than on *P. n. caramanica* and *P. n. maritima*. They are arranged in pairs in dense clusters separated by bare lengths of twig.

Crimean Pine

Pinus nigra var. *caramanica* (Loud.) Rehd.
Native to Asia Minor, the Caucasus, Crimea, the
Balkans and Carpathians. Height to around 30m
(100ft). Flowers (near right) open in late May,
and are similar to those of the Austrian Pine
(*P. nigra*). Cones (far right) are similar to *P. nigra*
and *P. n. maritima* but may be larger. They open
to release seeds when ripe, but are often difficult
to find as birds and squirrels soon break them up.
Only the unripe conelets are shown in the
photograph. Needles (p19) are longer than
P. nigra and straighter than *P. n. maritima*. They
are arranged in pairs. Young shoots are orange.

Corsican Pine

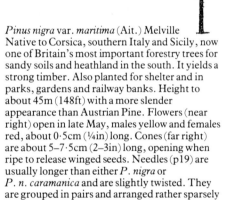

Pinus nigra var. *maritima* (Ait.) Melville
Native to Corsica, southern Italy and Sicily, now
one of Britain's most important forestry trees for
sandy soils and heathland in the south. It yields a
strong timber. Also planted for shelter and in
parks, gardens and railway banks. Height to
about 45m (148ft) with a more slender
appearance than Austrian Pine. Flowers (near
right) open in late May, males yellow and females
red, about 0·5cm (¼in) long. Cones (far right)
are about 5–7·5cm (2–3in) long, opening when
ripe to release winged seeds. Needles (p19) are
usually longer than either *P. nigra* or
P. n. caramanica and are slightly twisted. They
are grouped in pairs and arranged rather sparsely
on the branches, not in distinct whorls as in
P. nigra. Bark is shown on p218.

Japanese White Pine

Pinus parviflora Sieb. & Zucc.
Native of Japan, grown as an ornament in
gardens. The most common form is thought to
be a Japanese cultivated variety and forms a
rather low tree to about 10m (33ft). The wild
type can grow to about 25m (80ft) or more and is
less drooping in appearance. Flowers (near right)
open in early June, the males in spikes along base
of new shoots, pale purple or white turning to
yellow when shedding pollen. Females are deep
pink about 1·2cm (½in) long and often produced
in abundance. Cones (far right) are about 5cm
(2in) long, opening to release seeds and
persisting on the tree for some years. Needles
(p22) are slightly twisted with pale inner
surfaces. They are clustered in groups of 5.

Macedonian Pine

Pinus peuce Griseb.
Native of the Balkans, planted in collections and large gardens. Height to about 36m (120ft) in the wild. Flowers (near right) open in early June, males pale yellow in a cluster, females dark red, about 1·2cm (½in) long. Cones (far right) are about 12·5cm (5in) long with drops of resin. The scales open wide to release winged seeds. Needles (p22) have dark green outer surfaces and pale inner ones. They are in clusters of 5 which point strongly forwards on young shoots.

Maritime Pine or Cluster Pine

Pinus pinaster Ait.
Native to the western Mediterranean and north Africa, now naturalised in Portugal and France, and cultivated in California and Britain. It is sometimes felled for timber, but its greatest value lies in its resin which yields a high quality oil of turpentine. The trunk is tapped by making a diagonal slit through which the resin slowly flows or is sprayed with dilute sulphuric acid which causes the resin to exude. Height to about 36m (120ft). Flowers (near right) open in late May, males golden, females dark red, about 1·8cm (¾in) long. Cones (far right) may reach about 15cm (6in) long and persist on the tree for many years in whorls or clusters. Needles (p20) are in pairs and are longer than on any other 2-needled pine. Bark (p219) is reddish brown, or dark deeply cracked into plates.

Stone Pine or Italian Stone Pine

Pinus pinea L.
Native to south-west Europe around the Mediterranean to Greece and Asia Minor. The seeds are eaten raw, roasted like peanuts or added to stews and ragouts, a traditional Italian dish. Remains of husks have been found in Roman camps in Britain, indicating a long history of their use. Height may reach 30m (100ft) but in the open it forms a much lower umbrella-shaped tree. Flowers (near right) open in June, males golden and clustered, females pale yellowish green, about 1·2cm (½in) long. Cones (far right) are large, about 12·5cm (5in) long and heavy. They remain closed for 3 years. When harvesting the seeds the cones are left in direct sun which forces them open. Needles (p20) are dark green, thick, slightly twisted and pointed. They are in pairs and often rather sparse. Bark (p219) is reddish brown with deep dark cracks forming long plates.

Western Yellow Pine

Pinus ponderosa Laws.
Native to western N. America from British
Columbia south to Mexico, and variable in
length of needles and size of cones throughout its
range. Planted for timber in N. America and
central Europe, and for ornament in large
gardens and collections. Height may be more
than 60m (200ft) in the wild. Flowers (near right)
open in May, males red, about 3cm (1¼in) long,
females also red. Cones (far right, some needles
have been cut to show the cone clearly) are about
7·5–15cm (3–6in) long, ripening from purple to
dark brown and opening to release winged seeds.
Each scale bears a tiny bristle. Needles (p21) are
in clusters of 3 and may be 12·5–25cm (5–10in)
long. They are hard and curved and densely set
around twigs.

Monterey Pine

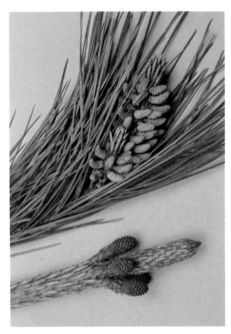

Pinus radiata D. Don
Native to a coastal part of Monterey, California.
Cultivated for ornament in most Pacific states, in
western and southern Europe, particularly for
shelter by the sea and for timber in Australia,
New Zealand and South Africa. Height to 35m
(115ft) but may be much taller; over 60m (200ft)
has been recorded in New Zealand. Flowers
(near right) open in early April, males bright
yellow in large clusters, females dark purple red,
about 1·8cm (¾in) long. Cones (far right) are
about 10cm (4in) long, with scales much more
developed on one side. They are borne in whorls
and may remain closed on the tree for 30 years or
more. Needles (p21) are in bunches of 3, rarely 2,
shiny, bright green.

Red Pine

Pinus resinosa Ait.
Native to south-eastern Canada, the Lake States
and north-eastern United States on dry rocky or
sandy soils and planted in northern parts of
N. America for timber and as an ornamental in
parks and gardens. Found in Europe in botanical
collections and large gardens. Height to 30m
(100ft) in the wild. Flowers open in late May,
males dark purple in clusters, females (near
right) reddish purple about 1cm (²/₅in) long.
Cones (far right) are about 5cm (2in) long. Scales
do not bear spines and open in autumn of their
second year to release winged seeds (some
needles have been cut off to show the cone more
clearly). Needles (p20) are long and slender and
grouped in pairs, densely packed on branches.
They snap easily when bent in two. Shoots are
orange and give off a strong lemon smell when
broken. Bark of upper trunk in crown is orange
red.

161

Northern Pitch Pine

Pinus rigida Mill.
Native to eastern N. America. Its wood has been used for fuel and occasionally for timber, and it is of little ornamental value, but found in collections and large gardens. Height to 25m (80ft). Flowers (near right) open in late May, males red in clusters, females also pinkish red, about 1cm ($^2/_5$in) long in whorls around shoots. Cones (far right) are about 3–6cm (1¼–2¼in) long and may persist in their clusters for some time. Each scale bears a sharp prickle. Needles (p21) are in groups of 3, dark green and twisted and shorter and thicker than other 3-needled pines. The trunk usually bears leafy growth sometimes on short twigs.

Weymouth Pine or White Pine

Pinus strobus L.
Native to eastern N. America. Planted for its light timber in central Europe and occasionally in the United States. Also planted in gardens and parks for ornament, but is susceptible in Britain to a fungal disease called blister-rust which has destroyed many old specimens. Height to 30m (100ft), or much more in the United States. Flowers (near right) open in early June, males yellowish green in a dense cluster, females pinkish green, about 1cm ($^2/_5$in) long. Cones (far right) are slender, about 12·5–15cm (5–6in) long, ripening from green to brown. Scales do not bear spines or prickles and open wide to release winged seeds. Needles (p22) are in bundles of 5 and are shorter than most other 5-needled pines, dark green on outsides and pale on inner surfaces. Young shoots may have tufts of short hair below the base of leaf bundles.

Scots Pine

Pinus sylvestris L.
Native to western and northern Europe and Russia, once more widespread through central Europe but now restricted by competition from other trees. A few native stands remain in Scotland, but not now elsewhere in Britain. Much planted in Europe and N. America for timber and ornament. Height to 36m (120ft). Flowers (near right) open in May, males round and yellow clustered or scattered along weaker shoots, females red, about 0·5cm ($^1/_5$in) long. Cones (far right) are about 2·5–6cm (1–2½in) long, ripening in their second year from green to brown or reddish brown. Scales do not bear prickles and open to release winged seeds. Needles (p20) are about 5cm (2in) long, blue-green, twisted and set in pairs. They may be 7cm (2¾in) on young vigorous trees. Scots Pine is recognised by orange flaky bark on the upper trunk (p219) and branches, and short needles.

Chinese Pine

Pinus tabuliformis Carr.
Native to China and Korea, cultivated in botanical collections. Height to 25m (80ft) in the wild. Flowers (near right) open in May, males pale yellow, oval, in a spike, females, dark purple 0·5cm (¹/₅in) long. Cones (far right) are about 5–6cm (2–2½in) long, ripening from a shiny green conelet to pale or dark brown, each scale bearing a very tiny prickle. They may persist on branches for many years. Needles (p20) are dark shiny green, usually set in pairs, but sometimes in threes.

Japanese Black Pine or Kuro-matsu

Pinus thunbergii Parl.
Native to Japan, cultivated in gardens and botanical collections. Height to about 30m (100ft) or more in the wild. Flowers (near right) open in early June, males red, turning to yellow, grouped in clusters, females purplish red, about 0·5cm (¹/₅in) long. Cones (far right) may be up to 6cm (2½in) long, each scale with a small spine. They are produced in large numbers, up to 100 on a shoot, even on young trees. Needles (p20) are thick, pointed and slightly twisted. They are grouped in pairs.

Mountain Pine

Pinus uncinata Mirb., synonym *P. mugo* var. *rostrata* (Ant.) Hoopes
Native to the Pyrenees east to the Alps. A good timber is produced in Spain and Mountain Pine is used in France for reafforestation on poor soils. Height to about 25m (80ft). Flowers (near right) open in early June, males dark pink or yellow in thick clusters, females dark reddish purple, about 0·5cm (¹/₅in) long. Cones (far right) are about 2·5–5cm (1–2in) long. Lower scales bear short downcurved spines. Needles (p20) are stiff, with grooves on inner surfaces. They are set in pairs.

Scrub Pine

Pinus virginiana Mill.
Native to eastern N. America, sometimes grown
in botanical collections. Height to about 15m
(50ft). Flowers (near right) open in May, males
red turning yellow, females reddish white, about
0·5cm (⅕in) long and spiky in appearance.
Cones (far right) may be long and narrow, about
5–6cm (2–2½in) long or short and oval, 3cm
(1¼in) long. Each scale has a distinct bristle.
Needles (p20) are set in pairs. They are short,
thick and twisted with a paler inner surface.
Young shoots have a pale greyish bloom.

Himalayan Pine or Bhutan Pine

Pinus wallichiana A. B. Jacks
Native to Himalaya, sometimes grown for timber
in Europe and for ornament in parks, gardens
and old churchyards in Britain. Height to 45m
(150ft) in the wild. Flowers (near right) open in
June, males reddish in loose groups at base of
new shoots, females pale pinkish green or
purple, about 2cm (¾in) long. Cones (far right)
are usually in bunches and may be 15–30cm
(6–10in) long when completely ripe and usually
covered with resin. Needles (p22) are long and
slender and are set in groups of 5, the whole
bunch crinkled and bent. They are soft and
droop from branches. Bark is orange-brown, and
may be cracked into plates.

Kohuhu

Pittosporum tenuifolium Gaertn., family
Pittosporaceae
An evergreen tree, native to New Zealand,
grown in gardens and for its foliage which is
commonly used by florists, especially in winter.
Height to 9m (30ft). Flowers (far left) are about
1·8cm (¾in) across, open in May and have a
strong sweet scent, most apparent in the evening.
Fruits (near left) are about 1·2cm (½in) across
and become dry and wrinkled as they ripen.
Leaves (p27) are pale green, glossy and have a
wavy edge. There are several cultivated varieties
with leaves purple, golden or variegated.

London Plane

Platanus acerifolia (Ait.) Willd.
synonyms *P. × hispanica* Muenchh.,
P. hybrida Brot., family Platanaceae
A deciduous tree, thought to be a hybrid between
Oriental Plane (*P. orientalis*) and Western Plane
(*P. occidentalis*). Grown in town and city streets,
parks and gardens in most of central and western
Europe. Its wood is fine grained and makes a
good veneer. Height to over 30m (100ft).
Flowers (near right) open in May, male and
female in separate round clusters, females larger
and reddish growing at the tip of the shoot and
males yellow, growing further back on old wood.
There are usually 2–4 fruit clusters on one stem
(far right). They are about 2·5cm (1in) across and
turn brown in the autumn, breaking up in late
winter, often blocking drains and gutters with
debris. Leaves (p46) can be extremely variable,
even on the same tree, with deeper lobes, more
teeth, and of different sizes. They colour yellow
and orange in autumn (p188). The bark (p219) is
distinctive, peeling off in flakes leaving lighter
smooth bark exposed and producing a mottled
effect.

Oriental Plane

Platanus orientalis L.
Deciduous tree, native to Greece, Bulgaria,
Yugoslavia and Albania. Long planted for shade
in southern Europe and the Middle East,
particularly in villages where it provides a shady
meeting place. Less common in Britain than the
London Plane (*P. acerifolia*), but distinguished
by being shorter and thicker. Flowers (near
right) open in May with separate male and female
clusters. Fruit clusters are also similar to London
Plane fruits but usually 3–6 balls on each stem.
Leaves (p46) are also distinctive, as they are more
deeply cut with narrow central lobes and more
teeth. Bark peels off in flakes, but is more rough
looking and knobbly.

Plum-fruited Yew or Chilean Yew

Podocarpus andinus Endl., family Podocarpaceae
Evergreen tree, native to Chile and Argentina.
Found in botanical collections. Height to about
15m (50ft) in the wild and, so far, much taller in
cultivation. Flowers (far left) open in June, male
and female on separate trees: males are yellow in
clusters about 2·5cm (1in) long, females tiny and
green. Fruits (near left) are about 1·8cm (¾in)
long and ripen to yellow. They have a sweet
edible flesh surrounding a stone containing a nut
which was eaten by Indians. Leaves (p13) on
older trees and side shoots are narrow and
pointed, dark dull green above, with 2 bluish
bands on undersides. They are set all round the
shoots.

Populus family Salicaceae, **Poplar**
Deciduous trees, with alternate broad leaves.
Male and female flowers are in catkins usually on
separate trees. Fruits are small capsules
containing seeds tufted by cottony down.

White Poplar or Abele

Populus alba L.
Native to western and central Europe and central
Asia. Cultivated in Europe and N. America for
ornament in streets, parks and gardens, and
found to be useful for shelter near the sea as it
withstands salt spray. Height to 30m (100ft), but
much less in Britain. Flowers open in April
before leaves unfold, males reddish crimson and
hairy about 7·5cm (3in) long; females (near right)
greenish-yellow about 5cm (2in) long. Fruit
catkins release white cottony seeds in June.
Leaves (p47) are lobed and covered entirely by
thick white down when first open, but becoming
dark glossy green on upper surface and pure white
underneath. Bark (far right) is smooth, white or
grey with diamond-shaped marks and becomes
black and rough at the base.

Balsam Poplar or Tacamahac

Populus balsamifera L.
Native to a large area across the north of
N. America, occasionally planted for ornament
in European collections and gardens. Height to
30m (100ft) in the wild, often half this in Britain.
Flowers open in March, male (near right) bright
red, about 7·5cm (3in) long, females greenish
10–12·5cm (4–5in) long. Fruit capsules have 2
valves and form a cluster 20–30cm (8–12in) long.
Leaves (p40) are round or slightly heart-shaped
at the base, round-toothed and pointed, dark
green above, paler beneath. Commonly forms
many suckers, and winter buds are covered by a
thick resin which has a balsam smell. Bark is
shown far right.

Hybrid Black Poplar

Populus × canadensis Moench, synonym
P. × euramericana Guinier
A group of hybrids from the European Black
Poplar (*P. nigra*) and Cottonwood (*P. deltoides*)
of N. America, planted throughout Europe as
the hybrids proved to be more vigorous and
easily propagated than either parent. Many
named clones are now available (see 2 of these
below).

Railway Poplar

Populus × canadensis 'Regenerata'
This is a female clone which arose in France in
1814; it became widely planted in France and
Britain particularly near railways as a screen.
Now little planted, as it is susceptible to a
bacterial disease. Height to about 30m (100ft).
Flowers (near right) open in March and April
and the fruit (far right) is ripe in June but is
usually sterile. Leaves are shown p40.

Populus × canadensis 'Robusta'
This is a vigorous, male clone, which arose in
France at the end of the 19th century. Widely
planted in Britain for shelter, screening,
ornament and timber. Height to around 35m
(116ft) so far. Flowers (near right) are bright red,
about 6cm (2½in) long and open in March.
Leaves (p40) are also a fine sight in spring, as
they unfold a bronzy colour, turning to blue-
green through the summer. (Catkin shown far
right is *P. canescens*).

Grey Poplar

Populus canescens (Ait.) Sm.
Native to south, central and western Europe,
probably including Britain. Commonly grown
for ornament and shelter, especially by the sea.
Height to 30m (100ft). Flowers open in March,
males (above right) red and silky grey, about
5–10cm (2–4in) long, females (near right)
greenish and silky about 2–5cm (¾–2in).
Fruiting catkins (far right) are about 10cm (4in)
long and release cottony seeds in June. Leaves
(p40) are at first covered with a white down
which falls away remaining only on undersides
and sometimes only faintly. Some consider this
to be a hybrid between White Poplar (*P. alba*)
and Aspen (*P. tremula*). Bark is dark greyish-
brown and ridged, but in the crown (p219) it is
white with black streaks and diamonds.

**Cottonwood or
Necklace Poplar**

Populus deltoides Marsh
Native to eastern N. America. Planted in central
Europe by roads and for timber, and in eastern
states of America for shelter and ornament.
Height to 30m (100ft) or more in the wild.
Flowers open in March, males (near right) red,
up to 5cm (2in) long, females greenish, up to
10cm (4in) long. Fruit capsules have 3 or 4 valves
and release cottony seeds in June. Leaves (p40)
have finely hairy edges and glands at join with
leaf stem. Buds and leaves have a strong balsam
fragrance.

Big-toothed Aspen

Populus grandidentata Michx.
Native to eastern N. America. Height to about
21m (70ft). Flowers open in March, males red
with grey silky hairs about 5cm (2in) long,
females (far right) greenish also about 5cm (2in)
long. Fruit catkins are about 12·5cm (5in) with 2-
valved capsules and ripen in May or June. Leaves
(p40) look similar to the American Aspen
(*P. tremuloides*) but are more deeply toothed.

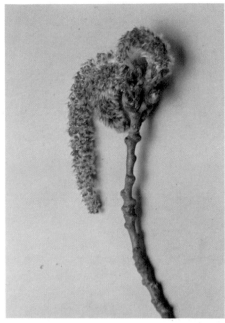

Chinese Necklace Poplar

Populus lasiocarpa Oliver
Native to central China, cultivated for interest in collections and large gardens. Height to about 18m (60ft). Flowers (near right) open in late April or May, males reddish up to about 10cm (4in) in length, females yellowish-green about 10cm (4in) long. Many trees have catkins with the lower, stalked end male and the top either female or bisexual. Fruiting catkins (far right) may reach about 20cm (8in) and release their cottony seeds in July. Leaves (p42) are remarkably large, 25cm (10in) or even more. They usually have thick red stems.

Black Poplar

Populus nigra L.
The true Black Poplar is native to Europe and western Asia, not often found, but its many cultivars and varieties are widespread. Many of these are superior timber trees though may not be so attractive. Two are described below.

Downy Black Poplar

Populus nigra L. var. *betulifolia* (Pursh) Torr.
Native to northern and central Europe. Planted by roads, and in parks and gardens. Height to about 30m (100ft). Flowers open in March, males (near right) red, about 5cm (2in) long, females greenish about the same length. Fruiting catkins are about 7·5cm (3in) long and shed white cottony seeds in June. Leaves (p40) have forward-pointing teeth and flattened stems. Young shoots, leaf stalks, main veins and flower stalks are downy but on the true Black Poplar they are hairless. Bark (far right) is dark brown, ridged and characteristically has thick bosses all over it.

Lombardy Poplar

Populus nigra cv. 'Italica'
A male clone, propagated by cuttings from a tree in Lombardy, N. Italy, early in the 18th century. Grown in Europe and N. America on roadsides, for shelter and for ornament. Height to about 30m (100ft) or more. Flowers (near right) open in March or April, up to about 5cm (2in) long. Leaves (p40) look similar to those of Black Poplar (*P. nigra*) with hairless stalks and shoots. Bark is greyish and usually fluted and cracked and often bears twiggy shoots (far right). The tree shape is perhaps its most distinctive feature.

Aspen or
European Aspen

Populus tremula L.
Native to Europe (including Britain), north
Africa and Asia. Commonly forms thickets in the
wild as it suckers easily. Height to about 15m
(50ft). Flowers open in February, male catkins
pinkish with grey silky hairs, about 5–10cm
(2–5in) long, females (near right) also grey and
silky. Fruiting catkins (far right) are about
10–12·5cm (5–6in) long and shed white woolly
seeds in May. Leaves (p40) are almost round
with wavy edges but on suckers may be wedge-
shaped. They have stems flattened which causes
them to quiver in the wind. They have pairs of
glands where the blade meets the stem and turn
clear yellow in autumn. Bark is smooth and
greyish with horizontal lines.

American Aspen or
Quaking Aspen

Populus tremuloides Michx.
Native to a large area of N. America, in Canada
south of the tundra, and western United States
from Mexico northwards. Occasionally
cultivated in Europe. Height to 30m (100ft) in
the wild but usually half that in cultivation.
Flowers open in February and March, male
catkins pinkish with long silvery hairs about 5cm
(2in) long and more slender than those of Aspen
(*P. tremula*); females (near right) also with silvery
hairs also about 5cm (2in) long. Fruiting catkins
are about 15cm (6in) long and release white
cottony seeds in May. Leaves (p40) are almost
circular and have fine teeth on their edges (not
wavy edges as *P. tremula*). They have flattened
stems causing them to quake in the wind. Bark is
paler and yellower than *P. tremula* and bark on
young trees has horizontal dark marks.

Western Balsam Poplar or
Black Cottonwood

Populus trichocarpa Hook.
Native to western N. America from Alaska south
to California. It yields a timber which has been
used as a veneer and for paper pulp. Commonly
planted in Britain by roads, for shelter and in
gardens. Height to as much as 60m (200ft) in the
wild but usually much smaller. Flowers open in
March, males (near right) stout and red, about
5cm (2in) long. Female catkins are greenish and
may be 15cm (6in) long when ripe. They bear 3-
valved downy capsules which release white
cottony seeds in June. Leaves (p40) are variable
in size usually about 5cm (2in) long or up to 25cm
(10in) on young vigorous shoots. The buds and
young leaves give off a strong balsam fragrance.
Bark (far right) is greenish grey and smooth
when young, becoming shallowly cracked on
mature trees.

Prunus family Rosaceae
A large group of trees and shrubs, usually bearing clusters of white or pink 5-petalled flowers and a single-celled fruit containing one seed. Much cultivated for either blossom or fruit.

Prunus 'Accolade'
An ornamental garden cherry, believed to be a hybrid between *P. sargentii* and *P. subhirtella*, making a small tree with spreading branches. Flowers (far left) open in March about 4cm (1½in) across with 12–15 petals. Leaves (p30) are deciduous, deeply toothed and colour red and yellow in autumn.

American Red Plum

Prunus americana Marsh.
A deciduous tree or bush, native to eastern United States. It has given rise to many named varieties and is cultivated in eastern states for its fruits. Height to 9m (30ft). Flowers (near left) open in April and are 1·2–2·5cm (½–1in) across. Fruit are round, about 2·5cm (1in) across, ripening from yellow to bright red, with yellow flesh. Leaves (p31) have tufts of down on midrib and vein axils beneath and downy stems.

**Gean,
Wild Cherry or
Mazzard**

Prunus avium L.
Deciduous tree, native to Europe, including Britain. Its fruits trend to be bitter but it is one of the parents of most European cultivated cherries. The wood is reddish-brown with a very straight grain, and used in cabinet making, and for anything requiring a straight bore such as pipes and musical instruments. To be found in hedges and woods, gardens and parks in most of Europe, also cultivated and naturalised in eastern N. America. Height to 18m (60ft) or more. Flowers (far left) open in mid April, each about 2·5cm (1in) across in clusters on previous year's growth. Fruits (near left) are about 2cm (¾in) across and may be light or blackish red, sweet or bitter. Leaves (p31) have stems red above and yellowish beneath with 2 or more glands or lumps near the base of the leaf blade and colour yellow and red in autumn. Bark (near left below) is reddish brown and clearly marked by lenticels in horizontal lines and broken by large cracks.

Prunus avium cv. 'Plena'
Double flowered cultivar planted in gardens and streets, often with pink Japanese cherries. Height to about 12m (40ft), the largest white double cherry. Flowers (far left) open in great profusion in early May. Each is about 4cm (1½in) across with 30–40 petals. Fruit is rarely set. Leaves and bark similar to those of *P. avium*.

Cherry Plum or Myrobalan

Prunus cerasifera Ehrh.
Deciduous tree, native to the Balkans, cultivated in central Europe for its fruits, found in Britain in hedgerows and by roads. Height to about 9m (30ft). Flowers (far left) are 2cm (¾in) and open in early March before Sloe (*P. spinosa*) with which it is often confused. Fruits are about 2·5cm (1in) across, ripening yellow to red in late summer. Leaves (p31) are deep glossy green above, paler beneath with a pinkish grooved stem.

Purple-leaved Plum or Pissard Plum

Prunus cerasifera cv. 'Pissardii', synonym *P. cerasifera* var. *atropurpurea* Dipp.
Often grown in streets, parks and gardens. Flowers (near left) open in early March, about 2cm (¾in) pale pink among red leaves, usually profuse but in country areas the buds are eaten by bullfinches so that flowers may be sparse. Fruit is about 2·5cm (1in) across, purple. Leaves (p31) darken through the summer.

Almond

Prunus dulcis (Mill.) D. A. Webb, synonyms *P. amygdalus* Batsch, *P. communis* (L.) Arcang., not Huds.
Deciduous tree, probably native to south-west Asia and the Balkans, cultivated for its blossom and nuts, and naturalised in most of Europe. Also cultivated in California, Australia and South Africa. Height to about 9m (30ft). Flowers (far left) open in March and April, up to 5cm (2in) across. Fruit is 3·7–6cm (1½–2½in) long with a green downy skin and little flesh which splits to release the oval pitted nut. Leaves are narrow, widest below the middle.

Prunus 'Hillieri'
Ornamental deciduous cherry. Height to about 10m (33ft). Flowers (near left) open in mid-April, about 3cm (1¼in) across on long stems (not yet developed in photograph). Leaves (p31) are double toothed and bronzy coloured when young. *Prunus* 'Spire' came from the same cross and has similar flowers but a narrow shape, about 3m (10ft) wide at the base and 8m (26ft) high.

Holly-leaved Cherry

Prunus ilicifolia (Hook. & Arn.) Walp.
An evergreen tree or shrub, native to California, cultivated as an ornamental in western and southern Europe. Height to 9m (30ft) in the wild. Flowers (far left) open in May in California but later in Britain. Each is about 0·8cm (⅓in) across in spikes about 4–8cm (1½–3in) long. Fruits (near left) ripen in November and December. They are about 1·2cm (½in) across with a pointed tip, and ripen from green to red to dark purple. Leaves (p36) are holly-like dark and glossy with prickle pointed teeth.

171

Cherry Laurel

Prunus laurocerasus L.
Evergreen shrub, native to eastern Europe near the Caspian Sea, cultivated throughout Europe from the 16th and 17th centuries onwards as an ornamental. Height to over 6m (20ft). Flowers (far left) open in April, each about 0·8cm (⅓in) across in spikes 7·5–12·5cm (3–5in) long. Fruits (near left) are about 1·2cm (½in) long, ripening to black from green and red in September. Leaves (p26) are glossy green and leathery with a few minute teeth on the edges. Many cultivated varieties are available with different growth habits, leaf sizes and colours.

Portugal Laurel

Prunus lusitanica L.
Evergreen shrub, native to Spain and Portugal, cultivated for ornament in gardens in most of Europe. Height to about 6m (20ft) but may be twice as tall. Flowers (far left) open in June in profusion each about 1·2cm (½in) across in spikes 15–25cm (6–10in) long. Fruits (near left) are cone-shaped, about 0·8cm (⅓in) long, ripening to dark purple in October. Leaves (p26) are smaller than Cherry Laurel (*P. laurocerasus*), and softer, glossy green above and shallowly toothed.

Manchurian Cherry

Prunus maackii Rupr.
Deciduous tree, native to Manchuria, Korea and neighbouring parts of Russia, cultivated for ornament in gardens. Height to 12m (40ft). Fragrant flowers (far left) open in early May each about 1·2cm (½in) across in spikes 5–7·5cm (2–3in) long. Leaves (p31) have tiny dots on undersides and downy stems. Bark (p219) is shiny brown or golden, and peels in thin strips.

St Lucie Cherry

Prunus mahaleb L.
Deciduous tree, native to central and southern Europe, cultivated in gardens for its blossom and naturalised in eastern N. America. Height to about 12m (40ft). Fragrant flowers (near left) open in late April or early May about 1·2cm (½in) across. Fruits are oval, about 0·6cm (¼in) long, ripening black. Leaves (p31) are rather small. The main vein is hairy on the underside and the stem usually bears 2 glands.

Bird Cherry

Prunus padus
Deciduous tree or shrub, native to Europe (including Britain) and Asia. Often planted in streets and gardens. Height to 15m (50ft). Flowers (far left) are fragrant about 1·2cm (½in) across and open in late May in spikes 7·5–15cm (3–6in) long. Fruits (near left) are about 0·6cm (¼in) across, black and bitter to taste, but may be used to flavour brandy and wines. They ripen in July and August. Leaves (p31) are finely toothed, may have tufts of down in vein axils and glands on stems. Bark is smooth, dark greyish-brown and has a strong unpleasant smell. Two cultivars which are popular for gardens and streets are:
P. padus cv. 'Plena'. Has larger double flowers which are open for a longer time.
P. padus cv. 'Watereri'. Flowerheads are in spikes, up to 20cm (8in) and the leaves have noticeable tufts of down in vein axils underneath.

Pin Cherry or Wild Red Cherry

Prunus pensylvanica L. f.
Deciduous, native to northern N. America from the Atlantic coast to the Rockies. Short-lived but provides useful shelter to other young trees. Height to about 12m (40ft). Flowers (far left) open in late April or May, 1·2cm (½in) across. Fruit is round, about 0·6cm (¼in) and ripens to red. Leaves (p25) are finely toothed with a hairless stalk.

Peach

Prunus persica (L.) Batsch
Deciduous tree, believed to be native to China, but cultivated for so long its origins are obscure. Grown in China, Europe and eastern N. America for its sweet fleshy fruit. Height to 6m (20ft). Flowers (near left) open in April, 2·5–3·7cm (1–1½in) across. Fruits are round and fleshy, about 5–7·5cm (2–3in) across with velvety skin, sweet yellow flesh and a ridged stone. Leaves (p25) are narrow widest at or above the middle.

Sargent Cherry

Prunus sargentii Rehd.
Deciduous tree, native to northern Japan and Sakhalin, cultivated by roads and in gardens in Europe and N. America. Height to 25m (80ft) in the wild. Flowers (far left) open in early or mid April about 3–4cm (1¼–1½in) across in closely set pairs. Fruits are round, black, about 0·8cm (⅓in) wide and rarely produced. Leaves (p31) have a long narrow tip, coarse teeth and glands at blade base. They colour dazzling orange and red in late September while other trees are still green (near left).

Black Cherry or Rum Cherry

Prunus serotina Ehrh.
Deciduous tree, native to N. America where its fruit has been used to flavour brandy and rum and its wood used by cabinet makers. Grown in central Europe for timber and other parts for ornament in larger gardens. Fruits have been used in cough mixture. Height to about 30m (100ft) in best conditions. Flowers (far left) open in late May or early June about 0·8cm (⅓in) across in spikes 10–15cm (4–6in) long. Fruits (near left) are 0·8cm (⅓in) and ripen in September. Leaves (p31) are dark green and glossy on upper surface, paler beneath with hairs on the main vein. They have pairs of tiny glands on the stem at the base of the leaf-blade. The bark has a strong, bitter fragrance.

Tibetan Cherry

Prunus serrula Franch.
A deciduous tree, native to western China, cultivated in gardens for its attractive bark. Height to about 15m (50ft), usually much smaller. Flowers (far left) are about 1·6cm (⅔in) across and open in April in clusters of 2 or 3. Fruits are red, oval, about 1·2cm (½in) long. Leaves (p25) are narrow and fine toothed. Bark (near left) is shining red-brown and peels in thin strips.

Japanese Cherry

Prunus serrulata Lindl.
Probably of Chinese origin, cultivated in Japan and now rather uncommon. Many cherries with decorative blossom have been produced in Japan and it has become usual to group them under this species, although the origins of most are obscure. In Japan they are known as Sato Zakura – domestic cherries. A few are shown below:

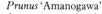

Prunus 'Amanogawa'
A very narrow deciduous tree to 8m (26ft), ideal for small gardens. Fragrant flowers (far left) open in early or mid-April, about 2·5cm (1in) across with about 9 petals. Leaves (p30) are bronzy when they first unfold, and turn yellow in the autumn.

Prunus 'Hokusai'
Deciduous tree to 7·5m (25ft). Flowers (near left) are about 5cm (2in) wide with about 12 petals and open in late April through May. Leaves (p30) are bronzy at first, becoming green, and colouring orange and red in the autumn.

Prunus 'Kanzan', synonym 'Sekiyama'
The names 'Kanzan' and 'Sekiyama' are derived
from the Chinese character representing a sacred
mountain; the first name is also sometimes spelt
'Kwanzan'. A popular cherry for gardens and
streets. Height to 12m (40ft). Flowers (far left)
open in late April or early May, each about 5·5cm
(2¼in) across with about 30 petals. Leaves (p30)
have long teeth and are dark reddish when they
first appear at flowering time and remain so for
some time. They colour golden or sometimes red
in the autumn. Bark is shown near left.

Prunus 'Mikurama – gaeshi'
Small deciduous tree, useful for small gardens
and hedges because of its upright shape. Flowers
(far left) have a light apple fragrance and open in
mid-April. Each is about 5cm (2in) across,
usually single with 5 petals and they cover the
otherwise gaunt looking branches. Leaves (p30)
have short teeth, are bronzy at first, soon green,
and turn dark red and yellow in the autumn.

Prunus 'Pink Perfection'
A hybrid between 2 other Japanese cherries.
Height to 7·5m (25ft). Flowers (near left) open in
mid or late April. They are similar to those of *P.*
'Kanzan' but are darker in bud and a purer less
purple pink, fading to a pale pink. Leaves (p30)
are a paler bronze when they unfold.

Prunus 'Shirofugen'
A deciduous tree, which may reach 7·5m (25ft).
Flowers (far left) open late in the season, in mid
or late May. They are about 5cm (2in) across with
around 30 petals, pink at first fading to white and
pink. Leaves (p30) are purple bronze at first with
red stems and turn deep copper-brown in the
autumn.

Prunus 'Shirotae'
A deciduous tree, to 9m (30ft). Flowers (near
left) are semi-double, about 5cm (2in) across
with a light fragrance. They open in early or mid-
April. Leaves (p30) are pale green at first and
have teeth with long hair-like tips, giving a
fringed appearance.

175

Great White Cherry

Prunus 'Tai-Haku'
An ancient Japanese cherry which had become extinct in Japan but has now been revived from a single specimen found in a garden in Sussex. Height to 12m (40ft). Flowers (far left) are single, up to 6cm (2½in) across and open in mid or late April. Leaves (p30) are bronzy when young, green in the summer, colouring yellow and orange in the autumn. They have a fringed edge.

Prunus 'Ukon'
A deciduous tree, popular for its unusual flowers (near left) which have a pale green or yellowish tinge. They are semi-double, about 5cm (2in) across and open in late April. Leaves (p30) are light bronzy green and colour red, and purplish brown in the autumn.

Sloe or Blackthorn

Prunus spinosa L.
A deciduous prickly shrub or small tree, native to Europe (including Britain) and N. Asia, cultivated and naturalised in eastern N. America. Its fruits are gathered from hedgerows and may be used to colour and flavour gin. The wood has been used for the teeth of hay rakes. Height to 4·5m (15ft) as a shrub but may be 6m (20ft) as a tree. Flowers (far left) open before the leaves in March or early April, about 1·2cm (½in) or more across. Fruits (near left) are about 1·2cm (½in) across and have a strongly astringent taste. Leaves (p31) are small with pointed teeth and hairs on the main vein beneath. Twigs bear hard sharp spines.

Spring Cherry or Rosebud Cherry

Prunus subhirtella Miq.
Deciduous tree, native to Japan, cultivated in gardens. Height to 9m (30ft). Flowers (far left) open in late March to mid-April, about 1·8cm (¾in) across. Fruits are black, round, 0·8cm (⅓in) across. Leaves (p31) are irregularly toothed with downy stem and main vein on underside.
P. subhirtella cv. 'Autumnalis', **Autumn Cherry**
This has semi-double pink flowers which open in November and December and sometimes again in the spring.

Choke Cherry

Prunus virginiana
A deciduous tree or shrub, native to eastern and central United States, occasionally planted and naturalised in central and western Europe. Height to 4·5m (15ft). Flowers (near left) are 0·8cm (⅓in) across in spikes 7·5–15cm (3–6in) long and open in late May. Fruit is round, red, 0·8cm (⅓in) across. Leaves (p31) have conspicuous tufts of down in vein axils beneath.

Yoshino Cherry

Prunus × yedoensis Matsum.
A deciduous tree, thought to be a hybrid between the Spring Cherry (*P. subhirtella*) and the Oshima Cherry (*P. speciosa*). Commonly planted in Japanese cities, in N. America, and sometimes in Europe. Height to 15m (50ft). Fragrant flowers (far left) open in late March or early April, about 2·5cm (1in), pale pink or white on red stems. Fruits (near left) are about 1cm (²/₅in) across and ripen black in August. They are bitter to the taste. Leaves (p30) are doubly toothed glossy on upper surface with hairy veins below.

Pseudotsuga family Pinaceae, **Douglas Fir**
Evergreen coniferous trees, with flat narrow leaves narrowed at the base and leaving a slightly raised scar when they fall off. Cones have 3-pronged bracts protruding from each scale.

Large-coned Douglas Fir

Pseudotsuga macrocarpa (Torr.) Mayr, synonym *P. douglasii* var. *macrocarpa* (Torr.) Engelm.
Native to California, occasionally planted in gardens and collections. Height to 9–28m (30–90ft). Flowers (near right) appear in April, males yellowish, about 1·2cm (½in) long, females reddish green about 5cm (2in) long. Cones are 9–12·5cm (3½–5in) long and may be even larger. They have short protruding bracts. Leaves (p16) are set around the shoot, and slightly curved glossy green above with 2 pale bands beneath. Bark (far right) is blue-grey with wide orangey brown cracks.

**Douglas Fir or
Green Douglas Fir**

Pseudotsuga menziesii (Mirbel) Franco, synonyms *P. douglasii* (Lindl.) Carr., *P. taxifolia* (Lamb.) Sudw.
Native to western N. America from Canada south to California. Cultivated throughout Europe for its high quality timber, known as Oregon or Columbian Pine. Also grown for ornament in eastern states of N. America and Europe. Height to 60–90m (200–300ft). Flowers (near right) open in late March and April, males yellow on underside of shoot and females yellowish green or pinkish green at tips of old growth, about 1·8cm (¾in) long. Cones (far right) ripen from green to brown in the autumn and are about 7·5cm (3in) long with bracts pointing straight. Leaves (p16) are densely set, needle-like with blunt tips and have a strong fruity fragrance. Bark on old trees is grey and rough with deep wide cracks.

Blue Douglas Fir

Pseudotsuga menziesii var. *glauca* (Mayr) Franco, synonym *P. douglasii* var. *glauca* Mayr
Native to the eastern Rocky Mountains from Montana south to Mexico. Occasionally grown for ornament in eastern states and in Europe. Height to 25m (80ft). Flowers open in late March, early April, males (near right) dull pinkish purple about 0·8cm (⅓in), females dark red, about 1·8cm (¾in) long. Cones (far right) are smaller than *P. menziesii* cones, about 5cm (2in) with bracts protruding and bent at right angles. Leaves (p16) are blue-grey above, with 2 blue-grey bands below, rounded tips and little fragrance when crushed. Bark is dark grey and scaly.

Hop Tree or Stinking Ash

Ptelea trifoliata L., family Rutaceae
Deciduous tree, native to southern Canada and eastern United States, planted in gardens and sometimes naturalised in central Europe. Height to 7·5m (25ft), often shrubby. Flowers (far left) may be almost white and open in June and July, each about 0·8cm (⅓in) in round clusters about 5–7·5cm (2–3in) across. Fruits (near left) are up to 2·5cm (1in) across, eventually ripening to a pale straw colour. Leaves (p50) have 3 leaflets, and like the bark and unripe fruits give off a strong aromatic smell when crushed.

Caucasian Wing-nut

Pterocarya fraxinifolia (Lam.) Spach, family Juglandaceae
Deciduous tree, native to the Caucasus and northern Iran, occasionally planted for timber or ornament in Europe. Height to 30m (100ft) with a short thick trunk. Flowers (near right) open in April, male catkins thick and green, 7·5–12·5cm (3–5in) long, females longer with more scattered flowers bearing red styles developing into fruiting catkins 30–50cm (12–20in) long with nuts surrounded by green wings about 1·8cm (¾in) across. Leaves (p54) may be over 60cm (2ft) long, but usually less with 7–27 stalkless leaflets, hairless on upper surface with tufts of hairs beneath. The common stalk is round and smooth.

Hybrid Wing-nut

Pterocarya × rehderiana Schneid.
A hybrid between the Caucasian Wing-nut
(*P. fraxinifolia*) and the Chinese Wing-nut
(*P. stenoptera*) first raised in the United States
towards the end of the 19th century. Deciduous
tree to about 25m (80ft). Flowers (near right)
open in late April or early May, male catkins
thick and dense, about 7·5cm (3in) long, females
slender with scattered flowers and may be twice
as long. Fruiting catkins may be as long as on
P. fraxinifolia but each nut has slightly smaller
rounder wings. Leaves (p54) have 5–25 leaflets
and the common stalk has narrow wings (the
Chinese parent has strongly winged leaf stems).

Pyrus family Rosaceae, **Pear**
Deciduous trees with simple toothed leaves, and
distinctively shaped fruits, with gritty flesh.

Almond-leaved Pear

Pyrus amygdaliformis Vill.
Native to southern Europe, particularly around
the Mediterranean, sometimes grown in other
parts of Europe for ornament. Height to about
12m (40ft) but may be shrubby. Flowers (far left)
open in April about 2·5cm (1in) across in clusters
of 8–12, sometimes massed together. Fruits
(near left) are spherical rather than pear-shaped,
slightly wider than long, about 2·5cm (1in)
across. They ripen yellowish brown in October.
Leaves are variable, usually narrow, about
3·7–6cm (1½–2½in) long, 1·2–1·8cm (½–¾in)
wide with pale hairs at first but becoming hairless
and shiny on upper surface and almost hairless
beneath.

Common Pear

Pyrus communis L.
Probably of hybrid origin, arising from
cultivated varieties mingling with wild species.
Found wild in most of Europe, including Britain
and many cultivated varieties are grown in
orchards and gardens. Height to about 12m
(40ft), occasionally more. Flowers (far left) open
in late April, early May about 2·5–3·7cm
(1–1½in) across in clusters. Fruits (near left) may
be almost round, up to about 10cm (4in) long,
ripening yellowish with sweet flesh. Leaves (p37)
are variable, but usually oval or almost round,
becoming hairless or starting hairless. Bark
(p219) is dark brown and broken into small thick
square plates.

Quercus family Fagaceae, **Oak**
Male and female flowers are separate on the same
tree, males in slender catkins, females single or a
few together developing into acorns, the most
important common feature. Many species are
deciduous but there are also a lot of evergreen
and semi-evergreen oaks.

Willow-leaved Pear

Pyrus salicifolia Pall.
Native of the Caucasus and Asia Minor to the
south and south-west of the Caspian Sea.
Cultivated for ornament in European gardens.
Height to around 6m (20ft). Flowers (far left)
open in April, each about 1·8cm (¾in) across.
Fruit is about 2·5cm (1in) long and is not
pleasant to eat. Leaves (p24) begin life covered in
silvery silky hairs, but eventually become dark
green on upper surface (compare flower and fruit
photographs). *P. salicifolia* 'Pendula' is often
cultivated and has more weeping branches than
the type.

Californian Live Oak or Encina

Quercus agrifolia Née
An evergreen, native to California, otherwise
only found in oak collections. Height to 25m
(80ft) although it is often shrubby with stems
prostrate or only a few feet high. Flowers (near
right) open in May with the appearance of the
young leaves. The sessile or nearly sessile acorns
are a long conical shape 3·7cm (1½in) long, often
deeply enclosed in the cup (far right). They ripen
in one year and fall in October. Leaves (p29) are
2·5–5cm (1–2in) long, dark and shiny above and
have tufts of down in the vein axils below.

White Oak

Quercus alba L.
Deciduous, native to central and eastern N.
America, where the strong heavy wood has been
used in shipbuilding, cabinet making, railway
sleepers, cooperage and extensively as fuel.
Height to 30m (100ft), sometimes more, at
altitudes to 1,400m (4,500ft) but at this altitude it
is a low bush. Flowers appear with the young
leaves (near right) at the end of May. The acorns
(far right) are 1·8cm (¾in) long, usually sessile
but not always, and fall in early October. The
leaves (p48) grow up to 12·5–22·5cm (5–9in)
long, the upper surface is dark glossy green, the
lower downy at first. When they open they are
tinted a violet colour and turn deep red in
autumn, often staying on the tree all winter.

Swamp White Oak

Quercus bicolor Willd.
Deciduous, native to south-eastern United
States. The wood is hard and heavy and has been
used in construction, cabinet-making, railway
sleepers and fencing. Height to 21m (70ft).
Acorns (near right) are 2·5cm (1in) long, a third
enclosed by cup. They mature in one year and
fall in October. Leaves (p49) are about
7·5–17·5cm (3–7in) long, dark green above, felty
below.

Mirbeck's Oak or Algerian Oak

Quercus canariensis Willd.,
synonym *Q. mirbeckii* Durieu
Deciduous, native to north Africa also found in
Spain. Height to 35m (120ft). Acorns (far right)
ripen in one year to 2·5cm (1in). Leaves (p49) are
9–15cm (3½–6in) long, the underside usually has
touches of flock on the midrib often concentrated
near the base. They remain on the tree until well
after Christmas.

Chestnut-leaved Oak

Quercus castaneifolia C. A. Mey.
Deciduous, native to the forests south and south-
west of the Caspian Sea. Although a striking tree
it is fairly rare in collections. Height to 30m
(100ft). The flowers (near right) appear with the
young leaves at the end of April or early May, the
female flowers are seen in the terminal axils of the
new shoots. The acorns (far right) which ripen in
the second year are about 2·5cm (1in) long and
fall in October. Leaves (p26) are 7·5–19cm
(3–7½in) long, dark glossy green above, dull
grey downy beneath.

Turkey Oak

Quercus cerris L.
Deciduous, native to southern and central
Europe from south-east France through the Alps
and Apennines to the Carpathian Mountains of
Rumania. Common in gardens and parks
elsewhere and naturalises quickly in woods and
hedges. Grows to a height of 40m (130ft). The
timber is inferior in quality compared to most
oaks, but it is useful as an ornamental tree as it is
elegant and quick-growing. The flowers (near
right) appear in May, the females are in the leaf
axils at the tip of the shoot. Acorns (far right)
have big woolly cups and fall in October; they
grow to 2·5cm (1in) or more long. Leaves (p49)
are 6–12·5cm (2½–5in) long, covered in down
both above and below and can be very diverse in
shape. Bark is shown on p219.

Canyon Live Oak or Maul Oak

Quercus chrysolepis Liebm.
Evergreen, native to the west coast of N. America from southern Oregon along the coastal ranges of California at altitudes to 2,800m (9,000ft). The strong hard wood has been used for making agricultural tools. Rare in collections. A small tree or shrub not normally reaching more than 18m (60ft) in height, but spreading to as much as 45m (150ft) in width. Flowers (near right) appear in late May, the females are in the young leaf axils. The acorns (far right) grow up to 3·7cm (1½in) long. The specimens shown are not fully ripe; the acorns will grow much longer and extend further from the cup. The leaves may have smooth margins as in the flower photograph or holly-like as in the acorn photograph (see also p24). They are 2·5–9cm (1–3½in) long.

Scarlet Oak

Quercus coccinea Muenchh.
Deciduous, native to north-eastern United States at altitudes to 1,500m (5,000ft). Widely planted in gardens and parks for its stunning autumn colour. Height to 25m (80ft). The flowers (near right) appear with the bright yellow young leaves, the females are in the axils of the new leaves. The acorns (far right) are about 2cm (¾in) long and ripen in October. Leaves (p48) are green through the summer then turn bright red (p188) about 6 weeks before they fall. They are 7·5–15cm (3–6in) long, lustrous green above and paler beneath.

Daimio Oak

Quercus dentata Thunb.
Deciduous, native to Japan, Korea and China and grown in a few collections. Height to 18m (60ft). Flowers open in May. Acorns (near right) are 1·2–1·8cm (½–¾in) long in cups bearing long narrow scales and drop in October. Leaves (p49) turn brown in autumn and often remain on the tree during winter. They are among the largest of all the oak leaves, sometimes over 30cm (1ft) long, both sides downy at first with the upper surface becoming smooth.

Hungarian Oak

Quercus frainetto Ten.
Deciduous, native to southern Italy, the Balkans and Rumania, grows well in cultivation. Height to 30m (100ft). Flowers open in May and the acorns (far right), 1·2–1·8cm (½–¾in) long, fall in October. Leaves (p49) grow to 20cm (8in) long; the upper surface soon becomes dark green the lower surface downy and greyish green.

Lucombe Oak

Quercus × hispanica Lam. 'Lucombeana'
A natural hybrid between *Q. cerris* and *Q. suber*
occurring in south Europe and found in many
gardens and collections. Semi-evergreen, in the
autumn the leaves turn partly brown, but they do
not fall until the new leaves grow in the following
June except in extremely hard winters. Height to
30m (100ft). Flowers (near right) open at the end
of May. The females are in the leaf axils at the tip
of the new growth. The fertile acorns (far right)
are produced in two years. Note the brown edged
semi-evergreen leaves in the flower photograph.
Leaves (p48) may be 5–12·5cm (2–5in) long, the
upper surface glossy green, the lower covered
with grey felt. The bark can be more or less corky
like the parent *Q. suber*, the Cork Oak.

Holm Oak or Holly Oak

Quercus ilex L.
Evergreen, native to the Mediterranean region,
common in parks and gardens and roadsides, it
makes a good solid healthy looking tree as wide as
it is tall with a dense dark appearance due to the
abundance of its foliage. It thrives with clipping.
The wood is hard and durable, used for joinery,
vine props and makes good charcoal. Height to as
much as 28m (90ft). Flowers (near right) appear
with the new leaves in June, female flowers are in
the new leaf axils. The acorns (far right) up to
1·8cm (¾in) long, fall in October; after good
summers there is usually a very heavy crop. The
leaves (p29) are variable in size, 3·7–7·5cm
(1½–3in) long, and may have spine-tipped teeth
or be untoothed. Young leaves have down on
both surfaces but this soon falls away from the
upper surface, leaving it dark glossy green. The
bark (p219) is nearly black and cracked into
small squares.

Shingle Oak

Quercus imbricaria Michx.
Deciduous, native to central and eastern United
States where it is found on rich hillsides and
fertile damp bottom land. Sometimes planted as
an ornamental tree in N. America, but it is rare in
collections in Europe. Pioneers used its timber
for clapboards and shingles, a type of roof tile,
hence the name Shingle Oak. A small tree to
about 15m (50ft) in the wild, but may reach 25m
(80ft) in cultivation. Flowers (near right) appear
in late May or early June, the females are in the
leaf axils of the new growth. The acorns (far
right) grow to 1·8cm (¾in) long and almost as
wide; the specimens shown are not yet fully
grown. The young leaves are a lovely yellow and
remain so until mid June; a mature leaf (p28) is
normally 10–17·5cm (4–7in) long and usually
unlobed but occasionally three-lobed near the
base.

Californian Black Oak

Quercus kelloggii Newberry
Deciduous, native to the valleys and coastal mountain ranges of California and Oregon to an altitude of 2,000m (6,500ft). Grown in botanical collections in Europe. The acorns were once the staple diet of the Californian Indians and the brittle wood used for fuel. Height to 25m (80ft) or more. The flowers (near right) can be seen in early May with the new leaves, the females are in the leaf axils. The acorns (far right) are 3·7cm (1½in) long, deeply enclosed in the cup, take two years to form and fall around October. Leaf (p48) 7·5–15cm (3–6in) long, dark shining green above, paler below.

Laurel Oak

Quercus laurifolia Michx.
Semi-evergreen, native to a wide belt along the southern coast of N. America, including Florida, otherwise rare, grown only in collections. Height to 30m (100ft). The flowers are seen at the end of May. Acorns (near right) have shallow hairless cups. Leaves (p24), normally 7·5–10cm (3–4in) long, occasionally lobed near the apex. Those shown with acorns are atypical as they are usually more narrowed at the base.

Lea's Hybrid Oak

Quercus × leana Nutt.
Deciduous, a natural hybrid between *Q. imbricaria* and *Q. velutina* found in south-eastern N. America with the parents, also in a few European collections. Height to 20m (65ft). Flowers not shown. Acorns (far right) fall in October. Leaves (p49) are variable in shape and pubescence.

Lebanon Oak

Quercus libani Olivier
Deciduous, native to Syria, Lebanon and Asia Minor. A fine tree, not as common as it might be in collections. Height to 21m (70ft). The flowers (near right) are seen with the bright yellow young leaves as early as the end of March, the females can be seen in the leaf axils. The acorns (far right) 2·5cm (1in) long fall in October. The distinctive leaves (p26) are 5–10cm (2–4in) long.

Ludwig's Oak

Quercus × ludoviciana Sarg.
Deciduous, a natural hybrid between *Q. phellos* and probably *Q. falcata* var. *pagodifolia* Elliott. found in Louisiana. Leaves are very variable up to 18cm (7in) long (p48).

Caucasian Oak

Quercus macranthera Fisch. & Mey.
Deciduous, native to the Caucasus and northern
Iran. Uncommon, found only in collections.
Height to 25m (80ft). Flowers in May. Acorns
(near right), up to 2·5cm (1in) long, fall in
October. Leaves (p49) are up to 15cm (6in) long.

Burr Oak or Mossy Cup Oak

Quercus macrocarpa Michx.
Deciduous, native to eastern N. America from
the deep south to the far north. The wood is
strong and durable. Height to 50m (160ft) in the
wild. Flowers in May. Acorns (far right) are very
variable in size but in the south may reach as
much as 5cm (2in) long. Leaves (p49) are
10–25cm (4–10in) long.

Black Jack Oak

Quercus marilandica Muenchh.
Deciduous, native to south-eastern and eastern
United States, a ragged tree of poor soils growing
to 10m (30ft) in height. The wood is hard and
good for fuel and charcoal. Flowers (near right)
at the end of May with females in the new leaf
axils. The acorns are small, 1·8cm (¾in) long.
Leaves (p49) are distinctive, 7·5–17·5cm (3–7in)
long.

Bamboo-leaved Oak

Quercus myrsinifolia Blume
Evergreen, native of south China and Japan,
rare, grown only in collections. Height to 15m
(50ft) in the wild but shrubby in cultivation. The
young leaves are a rich purplish red. Acorns (far
right) are small, up to 1·8cm (¾in) long in
unusual cups with concentric rings. Leaf p26.

Water Oak

Quercus nigra L.
Deciduous, native to south-eastern United
States. Height to 25m (80ft) in the wild. The
leaves may be broad at the apex like
Q. marilandica or long and narrow like
Q. phellos. They stay quite fresh
on the tree until January.

Pin Oak

Quercus palustris Muenchh.
Deciduous, native to north-eastern United
States. Successful in cultivation in Europe but
found mainly in some botanical collections. The
wood is hard and strong, used for construction
and clapboards. Height to about 25m (80ft), or
more. Flowers (near right) in early May with the
young bright yellow leaves, the females are in the
new leaf axils. Acorns (far right) mature after 2
years, about 1·2cm (½in) long and one third
covered by their cup. Those shown are in their
first year. Leaves (p48), deeply lobed, grow to
7·5–12·5cm (3–5in) long, with conspicuous tufts
of brown hairs on the vein axils underneath and
turn scarlet and deep red in autumn (p189).

Sessile Oak or Durmast Oak

Quercus petraea (Mattuschka) Lieblein
Deciduous, native to Europe and west Asia. This and *Q. robur* are the common British oaks. The wood has been widely used in joinery and shipbuilding. Height to 30m (100ft) but can grow taller. Very long lived. Flowers (near right) appear in May, the females are in the leaf axils on the end of the new shoot. Acorns (far right) are sessile which is the main difference between this oak and *Q. robur* where the acorns are on long stalks. The acorns grow to as much as 3cm (1¼in) long, with more scales on the cup than on *Q. robur*. Leaves (p48) have a stalk whereas *Q. robur* has sessile leaves, they are 7·5–12·5cm (3–5in) long.

Willow Oak

Quercus phellos L.
Native to south-eastern United States, usually deciduous but in the south of its range it is almost semi-evergreen. It grows in low wet lands generally near streams and swamps. Height to 20–30m (70–100ft). Flowers (near right) in May, the females in the new leaf axils. Acorns (far right) are not well formed in the photograph. When mature the cup will cover less than half of the acorn which will be roundish in shape about 1·2cm (½in) long. Leaves (p24) are long, up to 10cm (4in), and willow-like giving this oak its common name, they are yellow at first then bright green colouring golden yellow in the autumn (p189) to make a superb show.

Pontine Oak or Armenian Oak

Quercus pontica K. Koch
Deciduous, native to the Caucasus and north-east Anatolia. A shrub or small tree to a height of 8m (25ft). Remarkable for its large, 10–20cm (4–8in), leaves (p29) which resemble chestnut leaves. Acorns are 2·5–3·7cm (1–1½in) long and they ripen to a deep mahogany red. The leaves colour yellow in the autumn (p189).

Basket Oak or Chestnut Oak

Quercus prinus L.
Deciduous, native to eastern United States, often found on dry rocky soils and sometimes also called Rock Oak. The wood, which is hard and easily split, has been used for construction, cooperage, wheels, fences, fuel and basket making. Height to 30m (100ft). The flowers (near right) appear with young leaves in April, earlier than most oaks. The acorns (far right) are 2·5–3·7cm (1–1½in) in length and fall in October. Leaves (p49) resemble the leaves of the Sweet Chestnut (*Castanea sativa*) which gives this oak its alternative common name. They are 15–20cm (6–8in) long, evenly lobed, dark green above and silvery white and densely pubescent below. The bark is nearly black and deeply ridged.

Downy Oak

Quercus pubescens Willd.
Deciduous, native to southern Europe, west Asia
and the Caucasus. A rapid grower to a height of
20m (70ft). Flowers (near right) at the end of
May, the females are to be seen in the leaf axils on
the new growth. Acorns (far right) are 2·5cm
(1in) long and fall in October. Leaves (p48) are
downy when young but during the summer the
upper surface becomes smooth and hairless; they
are 5–9cm (2–3½in) long. Please note the leaf
shown on p48 is not typical; those shown with the
flower and acorn pictures are more normal. The
winter buds and new shoots are covered in down
which, with the downy leaves, gives this oak its
common name.

Pyrenean Oak

Quercus pyrenaica Willd.
Deciduous, native to south Europe and
Morocco, sometimes grown in collections.
Height to about 18m (60ft). Does not flower till
June, but then profusely, with the young, very
downy leaves (near right), the females are in the
new leaf axils. Acorns (far right) are found on a
downy erect stalk. (Those shown are dried
specimens.) Leaves (p48) are variable, often
fairly large, up to 20cm (8in) long and deeply cut,
covered with felt at first, later only felted on the
greyish underside.
Q. pyrenaica 'Pendula'. This form is more
common in gardens and collections than the
type.

English Oak or Pedunculate Oak

Quercus robur L.
Deciduous, native to Europe (including Britain),
east Russia, south-west Asia and north Africa.
This is the more common of the two native
British oaks and is extremely long lived, possibly
up to 800 years or more. Valuable for timber,
especially in the past when much of Britain was
covered in oak forests. Height to more than 30m
(100ft). Flowers (near right) in May, the female
flowers can be seen on the end of the new growth.
Acorns (far right) are on long stalks or peduncles,
hence the alternative common name which
separates it from *Q. petraea*, the Sessile Oak. The
acorns are 1·8–3cm (¾–1¼in) long and fall in
October. The leaves 10–12·5cm (4–5in) are
sessile (p48). There are many varieties of
interest, two of which are:
Q. robur cv. 'Filicifolia' **Cut-leaved Oak**. Leaf
p48.
Q. robur forma *purpurascens* (DC.) K. Koch
Purple English Oak. Leaf p48.

Sweet Gum
Liquidamber styraciflua (p132)

Scarlet Oak
Quercus coccinea (p182)

**Yellow Buckeye or
Sweet Buckeye**
Aesculus flava (p80)

**Tulip-tree,
Yellow Poplar or
Whitewood**
Liriodendron tulipifera (p133)

London Plane
Platanus acerifolia (p165)

Hers's Maple
Acer grosseri var. *hersii* (p70)

Norway Maple
Acer platanoides (p74)

**Pontine Oak or
Armenian Oak**
Quercus pontica (p186)

Willow Oak
Quercus phellos (p186)

Pin Oak
Quercus palustris (p185)

Shumard Oak
Quercus shumardii (p190)

Red Oak

Quercus rubra L., synonym *Q. borealis* Michx. f.
Deciduous, native to the eastern half of
N. America from central Florida and Texas to
northern Canada. This is the best growing oak
introduced from N. America to Europe; young
trees may grow at the rate of 2·5m (8ft) per year.
The wood, though hard, is not durable and has
been used mainly for fire-wood and the bark, rich
in tannin, is used in tanning leather. Height to
18–25m (60–80ft). Flowers (near right) appear in
May, the red females can be seen in the axils of
the new leaves. Acorns (far right) 1·8cm (¾in)
long, take two years to mature and fall in
October. Leaves (p48) are 10–22·5cm (4–9in)
long are a lovely bright yellow for the first three
weeks; the autumn colour is a deep red to brown.

Shumard Oak

Quercus schumardii Buckl.
Deciduous, native to south-eastern United
States. In the Mississippi valley it is used for
lumber and considered the most valuable oak.
Height to 30m (100ft) or more. Flowers (near
right) with the lovely yellow new leaves in May,
females can be seen in the leaf axils. Acorns (far
right) about 2·5cm (1in) long. The leaves (p48)
can be distinguished from *Q. rubra* and
Q. coccinea by the tufts of pale hairs on the
underside; they are 7·5–9cm (3–3½in) long, and
colour red in the autumn (p189).

Cork Oak

Quercus suber L.
Evergreen, native of the west Mediterranean
countries, found in collections and now grown
for its bark in California and other southern
states. The remarkable feature of this oak is the
thick cork bark (p220). In Spain and Portugal it
is stripped off every ten years to provide most of
the world's cork. Height to 20m (65ft), but in its
rocky native environment it is often smaller and
more stunted. Flowers (near right) are found at
the end of May or beginning of June, the females
are in the lead axils of the new growth. Acorns
(far right) form in one year and fall in October,
1·2–3cm (½–1¼in) long. The leaves (p29) are
dark glossy green above and clothed in grey felt
below, 2·5–6·2cm (1–2½in) long.

Macedonian Oak

Quercus trojana Webb, synonym *Q. macedonica* A.DC.
Evergreen, native to south-east Italy and the Balkans. A small tree growing in cultivation to as much as 20m (65ft). The flowers (near right) appear with the young fresh green leaves in May, the females are in the new leaf axils. Acorns (far right) 1·8–3cm (¾–1¼in) long fall in October. The leaf shown on p49 is not up to scratch; those shown with the acorns are much better, note the distinctive veining. Both leaf surfaces are smooth and hairless in the mature leaf, 3–7cm (1¼–2¾in) long.

Turner's Oak

Quercus × turneri Willd.
Deciduous or semi-evergreen, a hybrid between *Q. ilex* and *Q. robur* raised in the 18th century by Spencer Turner in Essex. Much planted in gardens and collections in Europe as it makes a well formed and decorative tree to a height of 16m (55ft). Flowers (near left) at the end of May or early June, the females are in the new leaf axils. Acorns (far right) are similar to *Q. ilex*, about 1·8cm (¾in) long on long stalks and fall in October. The leaves (p49) are 6–11cm (2½–4½in) long and stay on the tree until February at least and sometimes until after the new leaves are formed, note the flower photograph.

Black Oak or Quercitron Oak

Quercus velutina Lam.
Deciduous, native of eastern N. America. The bark is used as a source of quercitron, a yellow dye, and also for tannin. Height to about 23m (75ft) but may occasionally be much taller. Flowers (near right) are found with the young leaves in late May or early June, note the females in the leaf axils. Acorns (far right) fall in October, and are up to about 1·8cm (¾in) in length. The leaves are very variable; the specimen shown on p48 is not typical and should look more similar to *Q. coccinea* (p182) and (p48), though less deeply cut away. They are usually about 12·5cm (5in) long but may reach as much as 30cm (1ft) in length. The upper surface is dark shiny green, the lower surface is scattered with a thin scurf and has tufts of down in the vein axils.

191

Stag's Horn Sumac

Rhus typhina L., family Anacardiaceae
Deciduous tree or shrub, native to eastern
N. America, commonly grown in gardens in
central and northern Europe. Height to 7·5m
(25ft), but may reach 12m (40ft) in the wild.
Flowers (far left) open in late June and July, male
and female on separate trees. Females form a
dense downy head 10–20cm (4–8in) long, males
form larger looser clusters. Fruit (near left) is in a
cluster 10–20cm (4–8in) long, crimson and
velvety. Leaves (p58) are also covered with soft
velvety hairs. They colour bright orange in
autumn and this, combined with crimson fruits
on female bushes, make a stunning display for
any garden.

Varnish Tree

Rhus verniciflua Stokes
Deciduous tree, native to Himalaya and China,
cultivated in other parts of east Asia and
sometimes in Europe. A poisonous juice is
extracted from the stem to make the black
varnish used in making black lacquer in China
and Japan, and an oil from the fruits was used in
candle-making in China. Height to 18m (60ft) in
China. Flowers (far left) open in July in large
open clusters up to 25cm (10in) long. Fruits
(near left) are 0·6cm (¼in) across, ripening
yellowish brown. Leaves (p58) are 30–60cm
(1–2ft) long with 7–13 shortly stalked leaflets,
which are softly downy underneath.

False Acacia or Black Locust

Robinia pseudoacacia L.,
family Leguminosae
Deciduous tree, native to eastern and mid-
western United States, cultivated for ornament
in eastern states and throughout Europe, and
naturalised in south-western Europe. Common
in city streets and parks. Height to 25m (80ft),
often forming thickets by suckering. Flowers
(near right) have a sweet fragrance and open in
June in clusters 10–20cm (4–8in) long. Fruit
pods (far right) are 5–10cm (2–4in) long
containing kidney-shaped seeds. Leaves (p57)
are about 15–20cm (6–8in) long and usually have
13–15 rounded leaflets, each with a notched and
spined tip. Bark (p220) is dark brown and deeply
furrowed with a network of ridges. Twigs bear
short stout spines.
R. pseudoacacia cv. 'Frisia'. A cultivated variety
with golden-yellow leaves.

Clammy Locust

Robinia viscosa Vent.
Deciduous tree, native to Carolina and naturalised in many parts of eastern U.S.A. Cultivated for ornament in most temperate countries. Height to about 12m (40ft). Flowers (near right) have little perfume and open in June in clusters about 12·5cm (5in) long. Fruit are pods, 5–9cm (2–3½in), containing reddish brown seeds and covered with sticky hairs. Leaves (p57) are 17·5–30cm (7–12in) long with 13–21 leaflets on a sticky and hairy main stem. Young shoots are also stickily hairy and bear some thorns.

Salix family Salicaceae, **Willow**
Mostly deciduous trees and shrubs, with simple alternate usually narrow leaves, male and female flowers on separate trees. Fruits are tiny capsules enclosing seeds.

White Willow

Salix alba L.
Native to Europe (including Britain), northern Asia and northern Africa. Grows wild on riversides. Height to 25m (80ft). Catkins open in late April and May, males (far left) yellow about 3·7–5·5cm (1½–2¼in) long, females green about the same length ripening to form fruiting catkins (near left) which split to release white tufted seeds in June. Leaves (p25) are light green at first, becoming dark green with white silky hairs above and thick white down beneath, giving the tree a pale greyish white appearance.

Weeping Willow

Salix babylonica L.
Native to China, planted in gardens and parks by lakes and rivers in Europe and N. America. Superseded in Britain by the Golden Weeping Willow (*S.* × *chrysocoma*). Height to 10m (33ft). Catkins open in mid-May, males (far left) yellow, females green, up to 1·8cm (¾in) long. Leaves are narrow about 7·5–15cm (3–6in) long, hairless, dark green above and paler beneath. Young shoots are brown and hang down.

Goat Willow, Pussy Willow or Great Sallow

Salix caprea L.
Small tree or shrub, native to Europe (including Britain) and north-east Asia. Height to about 10m (33ft) but often shrubby. Catkins (near left) open on bare twigs in March and April, males grey and silky turning yellow, females green, both up to 3cm (1¼in). Female flowers develop into green capsules which release white tufted seeds in May. Leaves (p32) are broad for a willow on a red downy stem. Often rather wrinkled and with soft grey hairs underneath. Shoots have grey hairs at first and become shiny red brown.

Golden Weeping Willow

Salix × chrysocoma Dode,
synonym *S. alba* 'Tristis' Gaud.
A hybrid, commonly cultivated in parks and
gardens by water and on dry ground. Height to
20m (65ft). Catkins (far left) open in April,
usually male, about 7cm (2¾in) curving
upwards, sometimes with both male and female
flowers on the catkins. Leaves (p25) are narrow
and have silky hairs on both sides, paler than
S. babylonica. Branches and shoots are golden.

Grey Sallow

Salix cinerea L.
Small tree or shrub, native to Europe (including
Britain) and north-east Asia. Height may reach
10m (33ft) but usually shrubby. Catkins (near
left) open in March and April, similar to
S. caprea but more slender. Fruit capsules
release seed in May. Leaves (p25) are similar in
texture to *S. caprea* but narrower and less
wrinkled. Young shoots are covered with brown
down. Often forms hybrids with *S. caprea*.

Crack Willow or Brittle Willow

Salix fragilis L.
Native to Europe (including Britain) and west
Siberia south to Iran, growing on riverbanks.
Twigs snap off easily at their bases when
knocked, hence the common names. This allows
it to spread along a river as they root and form
new plants when washed ashore. Height to 25m
(80ft). Catkins open in April, males (far left)
yellow about 1·8–5cm (¾–2in) long. Female
catkins are green developing to fruiting catkins
(near left) about 10cm (4in) long which release
white fluffy seeds in May. Leaves (p25) are
narrow and coarsely toothed, slightly hairy at
first but turning glossy green and hairless when
mature.

Contorted Willow

Salix matsudana Koidz. cv. 'Tortuosa'
A cultivated variety of the Pekin Willow
(*S. matsudana*) which is a rare Chinese species.
Planted in streets and gardens. Height to 12m
(40ft). Catkins (far left) are female and open in
April, about 2·5cm (1in) long. They develop into
fruiting catkins which release white cottony
seeds in June. Twigs and leaves (p25) are
curiously twisted and curled.

Black Willow

Salix nigra Marsh.
Native to eastern N. America, where it yields a light timber used in making boxes. Height to 12m (40ft). Catkins open in April, males (far left) yellow about 2·5–5cm (1–2in) long, females green, about the same length, releasing seeds in May and June. Leaves (far left) are narrow often slightly curved, pale shining green when mature.

Bay Willow or Laurel-leaved Willow

Salix pentandra L.
Native to central and northern Europe (including Britain) and Asia Minor. Grows by rivers and is sometimes cultivated in gardens. Height to 20m (65ft). Catkins (near left) open in late April or May, males yellow, about 1·8–6cm (¾–2¼in) long, females green, more slender and shorter. Fruiting catkins (below left) may be 10cm (4in) long and release cottony seeds in June. Leaves (p25) are dark shiny green and broader than most willows.

Almond-leaved Willow or French Willow

Salix triandra L.
Small tree or shrub, native to Europe (including Britain). Height to 10m (33ft). Cultivated in Europe for basket making. Catkins open in March or April, males slender and yellow, females green. Seeds released in May and June. Leaves (p25) are narrow and shiny. Recognised by its flaky, peeling bark.

Osier

Salix viminalis L.
Shrub or small tree to about 10m (33ft), native to central and western Europe (including Britain). Often coppiced and used in making baskets and fences. Catkins open in April and May before the leaves unfold, males (near left) grey and silky with yellow anthers, about 1·8cm (¾in) long, females green, releasing seeds in June. Leaves (p24) are narrow with inrolled margins, dark green above and covered with silky hairs underneath.

Elder

Sambucus nigra L., family Caprifoliaceae
Deciduous shrub or small tree, native to Europe (including Britain), north Africa and western Asia. Grows wild in woods and scrub and waste places. Often thought of as a weed and the flowers and fruits are used in wine-making. May grow to 10m (33ft). Flowers (near right) open in June, each about 0·6cm (¼in) across in bunches 10–20cm (4–8in) across. Fruits (far right) ripen in August and September, each about 0·6cm (¼in) across. They are especially rich in vitamin C. Leaves (p53) usually have 5 or 7 toothed leaflets which have a distinctive, unpleasant smell.

Sassafras albidum (Nutt.) Nees,
family Lauraceae **Sassafras**
Native to eastern United States. Bark and roots
produce a fragrant oil and Choctaw Indians used
its leaves to make a soap. Height to 21cm (70ft).
Male and female flowers on separate trees, small
and yellowish in clusters. Fruit oval, bluish, about
0·8cm (⅓in) long. Leaves (p47) are 2 or 3-lobed or
entire, colour yellow and orange in autumn and
have a sweet, tangy smell.

Prince Albert's Yew

Saxegothaea conspicua Lindl.,
family Podocarpaceae
Evergreen coniferous tree, native to Chile and
Argentina. Sometimes bushy or forms a slender
drooping tree to about 18m (60ft) high, or less in
S. America. Flowers (far left) open in May, males
deep pinkish purple, about 0·2cm (¹/₁₀in) long;
females on same tree, pale blue-green and
developing into cones of the same colour (near
left) about 1·2cm (½in) long. Leaves (p13) are
flat, hard and curved with a sharp tip. They have
2 whitish bands on underside.

Umbrella Pine

Sciadopitys verticillata (Thunb.) Sieb. & Zucc.,
family Taxodiaceae
Evergreen coniferous tree, native to Japan,
cultivated in large gardens. Height to about 21m
(70ft) or less in cultivation but up to 36m (120ft)
in native habitat. Flowers (near right) open in April
and May, males yellow about 1·2cm (½in) long in
clusters at shoot tips, females dark. Cones (far
right) ripen over 2 years from green to brown,
about 5–7cm (2–2¾in) long. The scales open to
release seeds and are loosely attached – the cone
usually breaks up easily when handled. Leaves
(p18) are distinctively arranged in whorls along the
branches. They are narrow and shining green with
a deep groove both above and below. Bark is
reddish brown, peeling in long strips.

Coast Redwood

Sequoia sempervirens (D. Don)
Endl., family Taxodiaceae
Evergreen coniferous tree, native to the Pacific
coast from Oregon south through California.
Grown for timber in N. America and sometimes
in Europe in large gardens, parks and estates for
ornament. Thought to be the tallest tree in the
world, one having reached over 111m (367ft) in
California. Flowers (far left) open in February,
males yellow or brown about 0·6cm (¼in) long at
tips of shoots, females about the same size,
green. Cones (near left) ripen from a hard green
conelet to woody brown cone about 1·8cm (¾in)
long in one year. Foliage (p13) consists of scale-
like leaves pressed closely to the stem and flat
needle-like leaves in 2 rows on each side of the
shoots. Bark (p220) is bright orange-red, soft and
fibrous.

Wellingtonia or California Big Tree

Sequoiadendron giganteum (Lindl.) Buchholz, synonym *Sequoia gigantea* (Lindl.) Decne., family Taxodiaceae Evergreen conifer, native to western slopes of the Sierra Nevada, California. Cultivated for ornament in eastern states and in western and southern Europe. Some of the tallest trees in the word have been Wellingtonias, some recorded at 110m (365ft) and 4,000 years old. In Europe it may reach about 50m (165ft). Male and female flowers (near right) appear on same tree. Males appear in October, then turn yellow and shed pollen in March. Females are tiny green conelets about 1·2cm (½in) long with spine tipped scales. Cones mature in 2 years from green conelets (far right) about 7·5cm (3in) long to dark brown. They may remain on the tree for up to 20 years. Seeds are winged. Foliage (p12) consists of scale-like leaves and have an aniseed-like smell when crushed.

Sophora japonica (L.) **Pagoda Tree,** family Leguminosae. Native to China. Height to 25m (80ft). Clusters of white flowers in August.

Sorbus family Rosaceae, **Whitebeam** and **Rowan** Deciduous trees of 3 forms, 2 of which are commonly found: the Whitebeams with simple, sometimes lobed leaves; and the Rowans with pinnate leaves. Flowers are small, in clusters, and fruits are berry-like.

American Mountain Ash

Sorbus americana Marsh.
Native to eastern N. America, cultivated there and sometimes in Europe for attractive fruit and autumn colour. The fruit has a sharp flavour, is rich in vitamins and has been used in herbal remedies. Height to about 9m (30ft), often low and shrubby. Flowers (far left) open in May, about 0·3cm (⅛in) across in flat clusters 7·5–10cm (3–4in) across. Fruit (near left) are about 0·6cm (¼in). Leaves (p56) have 11–17 leaflets, on a dark red or green stem, and colour bright yellow in autumn.

Whitebeam

Sorbus aria (L.) Crantz.
Native to central and southern Europe (including Britain), growing on chalk and limestone. Planted in parks, gardens and streets, along with its many cultivated forms. Height to 25m (80ft). Flowers (far left) open in May, each about 1·2cm (½in) across in heads 5–7·5cm (2–3in) across. Fruits (near left) are up to about 1·2cm (½in) across and ripen red from green in September, quickly taken by birds. Leaves (p34) are irregularly toothed and covered with thick white down when they first emerge. The upper surface loses this down but the lower one remains white and felty. They colour yellow and brown in the autumn.

**Rowan,
Mountain Ash or
European Mountain Ash**

Sorbus aucuparia L.
Native to Europe (including Britain), N. Africa
and Asia Minor. Once planted by houses in the
Scottish Highlands as a protection against
witchcraft, and still popular in gardens, parks
and streets, and now widely planted in
N. America. The wood is hard and useful for
small items such as tool handles and spinning
wheels, and the berries, rich in vitamin C, make a
delicious jelly; and have also been used in herbal
remedies. Height to about 15m (50ft). Flowers
(far left) open in May in clusters about 10–15cm
(4–6in) across. Fruits (near left) ripen from green
in September, and are quickly eaten by birds.
Leaves (p56) have 9–15 leaflets, untoothed at
their bases, smaller than the American Mountain
Ash (*S. americana*). Leaf buds are long, slender,
dark purple and hairy. The bark (p220) is shiny
grey-brown, with dark dots, or lenticels.

Japanese Rowan

Sorbus commixta Hedl.
Native to Japan, Korea and Sakhalin, sometimes
grown in gardens and streets. Height to about
15m (50ft). Flowers (far left) open in May in
clusters about 7·5cm (3in) across. Fruits are
about 0·8cm (⅓in) across and ripen bright
orangey-red in August and September. The
leaves (p56) have 11–15 leaflets, dark green
above and whitish beneath. They colour deep
purple then red in October and November. A
good distinguishing feature is the pointed
shining red leaf bud, about 1cm (½in) long.

Service Tree

Sorbus domestica L.
Native to southern Europe, north Africa and
west Asia, often planted in central Europe for
ornament and for its fruit, which is very sour, but
edible when over-ripe or frosted, and used in
making a type of beer. Height to about 15m
(50ft). Flowers (far left) open in May, about
1·2cm (½in) across in rounded clusters up to
about 10cm (4in) across. Fruits (near left) are
about 2·5cm (1in) long, pear-shaped or rounded,
green tinged red to brownish when ripe. Leaves
(p56) have 11–21 leaflets, softly downy beneath
and may be rather yellowish above. Their buds
are oval, bright green and resinous. Bark is dark
brown and orange, broken into small cracks and
plates.

Chinese Scarlet Rowan

Sorbus 'Embley', synonym *S. discolor* Hort.
Of Chinese origin, now grown in parks, gardens
and streets. Height to about 15m (50ft). Flowers
(far left) open in late May. Fruits are orange red,
ripening in September. Leaves (p56) have 11–15
leaflets which are hairless beneath. In late
October they colour (near left) scarlet red then
dark purplish, in opposite sequence to
S. commixta, and remain longer on the tree. Leaf
buds are about 1·2cm (½in) or more long,
pointed deep red.

Hupeh Rowan

Sorbus hupehensis Schneid.
Native to western China, planted in European
parks and gardens. Height to about 15m (50ft).
Flowers (far left) open in May about 0·8cm (⅓in)
across with pinkish purple anthers in rounded
heads 7·5–15cm (3–6in) across. Fruits (near left)
are about 0·6cm (¼in) across, ripening to white
or pink in September and persisting on the tree
late in winter. Leaves (p56) have 11–13 dark
bluish green leaflets, toothed only round their
tips on a red grooved central stem. They turn red
in autumn.

Swedish Whitebeam

Sorbus intermedia (Ehrh.) Pers.
Native to Scandinavia, the U.S.S.R., around the
Baltic Sea, and north-east Germany. Planted in
northern Europe in streets and parks,
particularly useful in cities and towns as it
withstands atmospheric pollution. Height to
about 10m (33ft). Flowers (far left) open in late
May, each about 1·2cm (½in) across with pale
pink anthers in heads 7·5–10cm (3–4in) wide.
Fruits (near left) are about 1·2cm (½in) shiny
green, ripening to orange-red or reddish-brown
in September. Leaves (p47) have 3–7 toothed
lobes on each side, becoming shallower and
reduced to teeth towards the tip. Leaf buds are
green or dark reddish-brown with greyish down.

Sorbus 'Joseph Rock'
An ornamental tree from China, sometimes planted in gardens. Height to about 10m (33ft). Flowers open in May, fruits (far left) ripen to golden yellow and remain on the tree through winter. Leaves (p56) have 15–19 leaflets and colour orange-red and purple in autumn (near left).

Service Tree of Fontainebleau

Sorbus latifolia (Lam.) Pers.
Native to western and central Europe. Thought to be derived from a hybrid between the Wild Service Tree (*S. torminalis*) and one of the whitebeams. Height to 18m (60ft). Flowers (far left) open in May on downy stalks, fruits (near left) ripen brownish with speckles in September. Leaves (p47) are broader than other whitebeams with shallow lobing near the middle. They are dark green above and white felty below with a downy stem. Bark is dark brown, shaggy and peeling.

Pyrenean Whitebeam

Sorbus mougeotii Soy.-Will. & Godr.
Native to the western Alps and Pyrenees, on high mountain slopes where it may be a shrub or a small tree. Flowers (far left) open in May each about 1·2cm (½in) across. Fruits (near left) ripen in September and have a few sparse speckles. Leaves (p47) are narrower than *S. latifolia* but have more deeply cut lobes. They are dark shining above and whitish felty below.

Sargent's Rowan

Sorbus sargentiana Koehne
Native to western China, planted in parks and
gardens, often grafted onto Rowan
(*S. aucuparia*). Height to about 10m (33ft).
Flowers (far left) open in June in clusters up to
15–20cm (6–8in) across (the one shown is much
smaller). The flower stems have white hairs.
Fruits (near left) are 0·6cm (¼in) across
produced in huge clusters. Leaves (p55) are
larger than Rowan (*S. aucuparia*) to 35cm (14in)
with 7–11 leaflets. They colour bright scarlet and
orange in the autumn. Leaf buds are deep red
and shiny covered with drops of resin.

Bastard Service Tree

Sorbus × thuringiaca (Ilse) Fritsch
A hybrid between *S. aria* and *S. aucuparia*,
sometimes planted in gardens and streets.
Height to about 12m (40ft). Flowers (far right)
open in May, each about 1·2cm (½in) across in
flowerheads 6–10cm (2¼–4in) across with downy
stems. Fruits (near left) are about 1·2cm (½in)
across and ripen in September, sometimes with a
few brown speckles. Leaves (p47) reflect the
parent trees, deeply lobed with 1–4 pairs of free
leaflets at the base. They are dark green above
and white felty below. Leaf bud is about 0·8cm
(⅓in) long, dark red-brown. Bark is smooth dull
grey with shallow cracks.

Wild Service Tree

Sorbus torminalis (L.) Crantz
Native to Europe (including Britain), Algeria,
the Caucasus and Middle East. The fruits are
very acid but edible when over-ripe; they used to
be sold in south England under the name of
Chequers and have been used in medicine.
Height to 25m (80ft). Flowers (far left) open in
late May, each about 1·2cm (½in) across in loose
heads about 10cm (4in) across with downy stems.
Fruits (near left) are about 1·2cm (½in) long,
covered with speckles, ripening in September.
Leaves (p47) are unlike other *Sorbus* and this tree
can easily be mistaken for a maple (*Acer*). They
have 3–5 pairs of lobes, shiny bright green on
both sides and colour deep reds in the autumn.
The leaf buds are round and shining green. Bark
is dark brown or grey, cracked into scaly plates.

Sorbus 'Wilfred Fox'

Sorbus 'Wilfred Fox'
A hybrid between Whitebeam (*S. aria*) and the
Himalayan Whitebeam (*S. cuspidata*), named
after the creator of Winkworth Arboretum,
Surrey, and who made a special study of *Sorbus*
species. Height to about 12m (40ft). Flowers (far
left) open in May, about 1·8cm (¾in) across with
deep pink anthers in heads about 7·5cm (3in)
across. Fruits are large, about 1·8cm (¾in)
across, ripening golden brown in September.
Leaves (p34) have shallow lobes and 12–15 pairs
of veins. They become almost hairless, dark
green above, remain light and felty below. Leaf
buds are oval, green and brown. Bark is dark
purplish grey with fine scales.

Japanese Stewartia or Deciduous Stewartia

Stewartia pseudocamellia Maxim., family
Theaceae
Deciduous tree, native to Japan, sometimes
grown in gardens. Height to 20m (65ft), usually
less. Flowers look similar to *S. sinensis*, about
5cm (2in) across with clusters of bright yellow
anthers and broad wavy-edged petals. The flower
buds are set between two red-tipped bracts and
open in late July and August. Leaves (p26) may
be wavy edged and are dull green above and
shiny underneath with downy tufts in the vein
axils. They colour yellow and scarlet in the
autumn (near right). Bark is orange brown and
peels away to leave lighter orange new bark (far
right).

Chinese Stewartia

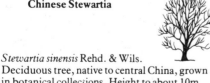

Stewartia sinensis Rehd. & Wils.
Deciduous tree, native to central China, grown
in botanical collections. Height to about 10m
(33ft). Fragrant flowers (near right) open in late
July and are about 3·7–5cm (1½–2in) across and
their buds are surrounded by a 5-lobed bract,
each lobe tinged red at the tip. Leaves (p26) are
larger than *S. pseudocamellia* and are bright green
in both surfaces. They have red hairy stems and
colour red and crimson in the autumn (far right).
Bark (p220) is dark coppery brown and peels
away leaving large areas of smooth light grey,
green or creamy bare stem.

Snowbell Tree

Styrax japonica Sieb. & Zucc., family
Styracaceae
Deciduous tree, native to China and Japan,
grown as an ornamental in gardens. Height to
about 11m (36ft). Flowers (far left) are often
produced in great abundance, the undersides of
each branch densely packed with clusters of 3–4
flowers (only one cluster is shown). They open in
July and are about 2·5cm (1in) across. Fruits
(near left) are about 1·2cm (½in) long. Leaves
(p35) have a few tiny teeth and a short stem.
They are shiny above and less so beneath, with
tufts of down in the vein axils.

Big Leaf Storax

Styrax obassia Sieb. & Zucc.
Deciduous tree, native to Japan, grown in
gardens but less popular than *S. japonica*. Height
to about 14m (45ft). Fragrant flowers (far left)
open in June about 2·5cm (1in) across in
flowerheads up to 20cm (8in) long, hanging from
branch tips. Fruits (near left) are about 1·8cm
(¾in) long covered with soft brown down.
Leaves (p39) are almost round with a pointed tip
on mature trees and rather hairy on the upper
surface. Young trees may have leaves with teeth
near the tips or with flat tips.

Taiwania cryptomerioides Hayata, family
Taxodiaceae
Evergreen conifer, native to Formosa, China and
Burma. Height to about 14m (45ft) in
cultivation. Cones (not shown) look similar to
those of *Cunninghamia lanceolata*. Foliage (p12)
is similar to *Cryptomeria japonica* but needles are
bluer and taper from a broader base to a sharp
spiny point.

Swamp Cypress or
Bald Cypress

Taxodium distichum (L.) Rich.,
family Taxodiaceae
Deciduous conifer, native to swamps of south-
eastern United States. When near water their
roots form 'knees' which stick up above the water
level. Grown in gardens and parks in Europe and
N. America. Height to 45m (150ft) in the wild.
Male flowers appear in late autumn, turn yellow
and shed pollen (near right) in April when the
clusters are 10–30cm (4–12in) long. Female
flowers are tiny green conelets about 0·2cm
(¹/₁₀in) long shown in photograph (near right) at
the base of male catkins. Cones (far right) are
about 2·5cm (1in) across, and ripen from green to
brown. Leaves (p13) are soft and flat, evenly
arranged in two rows. They turn a dull orange in
the autumn and fall with their branchlets.
Branchlets are arranged alternately or not quite
opposite. Bark (p220) is reddish brown and
ridged or peeling and fibrous, often fluted at
buttressed base. Compare with Dawn Redwood
(*Metasequoia glyptostoboides*).

Taxus family Taxaceae, **Yew**
Evergreen trees or shrubs. Male and female flowers on separate plants, and seeds are held in fleshy cups. Leaves are flat and narrow.

Common Yew or English Yew

Taxus baccata L.
Native to Europe, Iran and Algeria. Planted for shelter ornament and topiary. Leaves and seeds are poisonous and the wood is hard and durable. Height to 25m (80ft). Flowers (far left) open in March or April, males yellow, about 0·6cm (¼in), females tiny and green. Fruit (near left) are about 1·2cm (½in). Leaves (p14) are comb-like above and below, pointing well forward. Bark (p220) is dark brown and reddish peeling in thin strips.

Irish Yew

T. baccata cv. 'Fastigiata'
A cultivated yew with upright growth habit. Often planted in churchyards and sometimes called the Churchyard Yew. Most are female.
T. baccata cv. 'Fastigiata Aureomarginata', **Golden Irish Yew** A form of Irish Yew with golden new growth (p14). Only male flowers are produced, no fruit.
T. baccata cv. 'Fructo-luteo', **Yellow-berried Yew** A form with orange yellow fruits (far left).

Taxus brevifolia Nutt., **Pacific Yew or Western Yew** Native to the Pacific coast of N. America. Height to 12m (40ft). Flowers similar to *T. baccata* and fruit has a red fleshy cup with a green seed protruding. Leaves (p14) dark, green above, paler below.

Chinese Yew

Taxus celebica (Warburg) Li
Native to China, sometimes grown in botanical collections. Height to 8m (26ft). Male flowers (near left) are about 0·2cm (¹/₁₀in) across, scattered along the undersides of shoots, and shed pollen in late February and March. Fruit is sparse, about 0·6cm (¼in) across, green with a darker green protruding seed and which rarely ripens to red in cultivation. Leaves (p14) are yellowish green on both sides and are sparse, giving this yew a rather straggly appearance.

Japanese Yew

Taxus cuspidata Sieb. & Zucc.
Native to Japan, grown in botanical collections. A bushy tree or shrub to 15m (50ft). Male flowers (far left) are about 0·2cm (¹/₁₀in) across and shed pollen in late February and March. Females are tiny and greenish, similar to those of *T. baccata*, and develop into distinctive fruits (near left), about 0·8cm (⅓in) across, with dark greyish green seed protruding. Leaves (p14) are curved or stick straight upwards. They are hard, dark shiny green above, yellowish green beneath with a sharp tip.

Spur Leaf

Tetracentron sinense Oliv., family
Tetracentraceae
Deciduous tree, native to China, grown in
botanical collections and some large gardens.
Height to about 15m (50ft). Flowers are in
catkins 9–15cm (3½–6in) long which appear in
the spring and gradually expand and open
through the summer. The photograph near right
shows the catkin in May, far right in August.
Leaves (p42) look similar to *Cercidiphyllum
japonicum* but are arranged alternately. They are
distinctive since they arise singly from spurs of
branches and twigs.

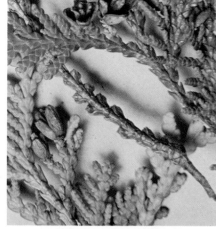

Thuja family Cupressaceae, **Arbor-vitae**
Evergreen coniferous trees and shrubs with
scale-like leaves pressed closely to the stem. Male
and female flowers on the same tree. Cones are
small with few scales and winged seeds.

**White Cedar or
American Arbor-vitae**

Thuja occidentalis L.
Native to eastern N. America, grown in
N. America and Europe for ornament or
hedging. Cultivated dwarf forms are more
common in Europe than the type. Height to
about 15m (50ft). Flowers (far left) open in
March and April, males dark red, females dark
brownish yellow (bottom right of photograph),
both about 0·1cm (¹/₂₀in) across. Cones (near left)
ripen from yellowish-green the following
autumn, about 1·2cm (½in) long with 8–10
scales. Leaves (p10) are dark green above,
yellowish beneath and when crushed give off a
smell of apples.

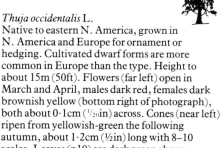

**Chinese Cedar or
Chinese Arbor-vitae**

Thuja orientalis L.
Native to China, Manchuria and Korea, grown,
with its numerous cultivated varieties, in Europe
and N. America. Height to 18m (60ft). Flowers
(far left) open in March, males dark yellow,
females dull bluish-green about 0·1cm (¹/₂₀in).
Cones (near left) about 1·8cm (¾in) across,
usually with 6 hooked scales. They ripen from
bluish-green to brown in the autumn, opening to
release winged seeds. The specimen in cone
photograph is of the cultivar 'Elegantissima'.
Leaves (p10) are dark green on both sides and
have no smell when crushed.
T. orientalis cv. 'Elegantissina'. A small
cultivated variety with upswept branches.
Leaves are golden tipped in the summer, fading
to green in the winter. A good tree for small
gardens or for growing in pots.

Western Red Cedar or Giant Arbor-vitae

Thuja plicata Donn ex D. Don
Native to western N. America where it is an important timber tree. Grown in Europe for timber, shelter, in gardens and often as hedging. Height to 40m (135ft) or more. Flowers (far left) open in March, males dark red, pale yellow when shedding pollen, females yellowish green, both about 0·2cm (¹/₁₀in) long. Cones (near left) are about 1·2cm (½in) long with 10–12 scales, ripening from yellowish green to brown and opening slightly to release winged seeds. Leaves (p10) are dark and glossy above and paler beneath with some light whitish marks. They emit a strong fruity smell even without being crushed.

Japanese Thuja or Japanese Arbor-vitae

Thuja standishii (Gord.) Carr.
Native to central Japan, grown in botanical collections and gardens. Height to about 20m (65ft) in cultivation. Flowers (far left) open in March, males dark reddish turning yellow when shedding pollen, females brownish green, both about 0·1cm (¹/₂₀in) across. Cones (near left) are about 1·2cm (½in) with 10–12 scales, ripening from bright green to dark brown in the autumn. Leaves (p10) are dull yellowish green or greyish above with patches of grey at leaf bases beneath. The shoots are often curved at the tip and have a lemony smell when crushed.

Hiba or Hiba Arbor-vitae

Thujopsis dolabrata (L.f.) Sieb. & Zucc., family Cupressaceae
Evergreen conifer, native to Japan, grown for ornament in large gardens. Height to about 20m (65ft) in cultivation. Flowers open in late April or May, males dark blackish green, females bluish green, both about 0·1cm (¹/₂₀in) long. Cones (far right) are 1·2–1·8cm (½–¾in) long, with 6–10 scales, ripening to dark bluish brown from bluish green, and opening to release seeds. Leaves (p11) are larger than on *Thuja* species, dark green and glossy above with 2 white bands on underside. Bark (near right) is dark reddish brown and peels in strips.

Tilia family Tiliaceae, **Lime, Linden or Basswood**
Deciduous trees with broad toothed leaves, small fragrant clustered flowers, with a long leafy bract attached to the stem, and small round, usually one-seeded fruits.

American Lime, American Linden or Basswood

Tilia americana L.
Native of eastern N. America, cultivated for shade or ornament in north-eastern states and occasionally in Europe. Important in N. America as a source of nectar for honey bees. Height to about 21m (70ft) or more in the wild. Flowers (far left) open in early July, each about 1·2cm (½in) on downy stems, with a rounded bract up to 10cm (4in) long. Fruits are about 0·3cm (⅛in) across, smooth and hairless. Leaves (p41) are large, about 20cm (8in) long, light green on both surfaces, and hairless except for tiny downy tufts in the axils of the veins underneath. Bark (near left) is dark greyish brown and rough, ridged and furrowed.

Small-leaved Lime

Tilia cordata Mill.
Native to Europe (including Britain), the Caucasus and Siberia, planted in parks and gardens and by roads, particularly useful in towns and cities. Height to about 30m (100ft). Flowers (far left) are about 1·2cm (½in) across and open in early July, usually in spreading clusters of 5–10 with a strong sweet fragrance. Fruits (near left) are about 0·6cm (¼in) wide. Leaves (p41) are smaller than most limes, about 3·7–7cm (1½–2¾in) long, dark green above and paler beneath with rust-coloured tufts of down in the vein axils and at leaf base. Bark is smooth and grey ageing to dark grey with large cracks and flakes.

Caucasian Lime or Crimean Lime

Tilia × euchlora K. Koch
Thought to be a hybrid between *T. cordata* and another from the Caucasus. Planted in Europe in parks, streets and some gardens. Height to about 20m (65ft). Flowers (far left) open in late July, larger and more yellow than other limes with 3–7 in a cluster. They have a narcotic effect on bees, which may be found lying on the ground under the trees. Fruits (near left) are elliptic and downy, about 1·2cm (½in) long. Leaves (p41) are dark glossy green above and paler beneath with conspicuous tufts of pale brown hairs in the vein axils. Bark is smooth dull grey with some deep cracks.

Common Lime or European Linden

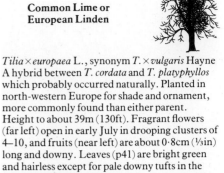

Tilia × europaea L., synonym *T. × vulgaris* Hayne
A hybrid between *T. cordata* and *T. platyphyllos*
which probably occurred naturally. Planted in
north-western Europe for shade and ornament,
more commonly found than either parent.
Height to about 39m (130ft). Fragrant flowers
(far left) open in early July in drooping clusters of
4–10, and fruits (near left) are about 0·8cm (⅓in)
long and downy. Leaves (p41) are bright green
and hairless except for pale downy tufts in the
vein axils beneath. They are often covered with a
shiny resin or honey-dew exuded by aphids
which amass on these trees. A good distinctive
feature are the numerous suckers produced at the
base and forming dense burrs on the trunk.
Leaves on suckers can be large and should not be
confused with larger-leaved species.

Oliver's Lime

Tilia oliveri Szysz.
Native to central China and sometimes grown in
European gardens and collections. Height to
about 24m (80ft). Flowers (far left) open in early
July, with large bright green bracts about 10cm
(4in) long. Fruits (near left) are about 1·2cm
(½in) across, soft downy surfaced. Leaves (p41)
are dull green and smooth above with silvery
undersides. Bark is smooth and grey with thin
dark streaks and triangular folds at old branch
scars.

Weeping Silver Lime or Weeping White Linden

Tilia petiolaris DC.
May be native to the Caucasus or of garden
origin. Grown in gardens, parks and town
streets. Height to about 24m (80ft). Strongly
scented flowers (far left) open in late July, and
have a narcotic effect on bees. Fruits are slightly
ridged, about 1·2cm (½in) long and are rarely
fertile. Leaves (p41) are dark green above, white
and downy beneath with long downy stems, and
are borne on hanging shoots. Bark is dark grey
with narrow ridges and furrows.

Large-leaved Lime

Tilia platyphyllos Scop.
Native to Europe (including Britain), the
Caucasus and Asia Minor, planted in European
streets, parks and avenues. Height to 41m
(135ft). Flowers (near left) open in late June,
each about 1·2cm (½in). Fruits are downy, about
1·2cm (½in) long with 3–5 ridges. Leaves (p41)
are dark above and paler, usually hairy on the
lower surface, especially the midrib, vein axils
and the stem. Bark is dark grey with narrow
cracks or ridges.

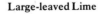

Silver Lime

Tilia tomentosa Moench.
Native to south-eastern Europe and south-west Asia, planted in European parks and gardens. Height to about 24m (80ft) or more. Strongly scented flowers (far left) open in late July, and have a narcotic effect on bees. Fruit (near left) is about 0·6–1·2cm (¼–½in) long, downy with 5 ridges. Leaves (p41) are dark and wrinkled on upper surface and grey underneath and downy underneath and on the stem. Bark of mature trees is dark grey and ridged.

California Nutmeg

Torreya californica Torr.,
family Taxaceae
Evergreen, native to California grown for ornament in western Europe. Height to about 21m (70ft) or more in the wild. Male flowers (near right) are about 0·8cm (⅓in) long, turn yellow and shed pollen in June. Females, on separate plants, are tiny and green at the base of new shoots. Fruits (far right) about 3·7cm (1½in) long, shining green with purple streaks and containing a large brown seed. Those shown in the photograph are preserved specimens. Leaves (p13) are dark yellowish green above with 2 whitish bands underneath and taper to a hard sharp spine.

Torreya nucifera (L.) Sieb. & Zucc. **Japanese Nutmeg**
Native to Japan. Height to 9m (30ft). Male flowers oval, light green, about 0·2cm (¹/₁₀in), females tiny and green. Fruits about 2·5cm (1in) similar to *T. californica*. Leaves (p13) are dark shiny green above with 2 white bands underneath. They emit an strong tangy smell.

Tsuga family Pinaceae, **Hemlock**
Evergreen coniferous trees with small flat leaves and small woody cones.

Eastern Hemlock or Canadian Hemlock

Tsuga canadensis (L.) Carr.
Native to north-eastern United States and Canada, cultivated in northern states and in western Europe in gardens and botanical collections, and occasionally for its timber, although of poor quality. The inner bark has been important in leather tanning. Height to about 30m (100ft). Flowers (far left) open in May, males about 0·3cm (⅛in) across, greenish yellow, females slightly larger and greenish. Cones (near left) are 1·2–2·5cm (½–1in) long, ripening from green to brown in October. Leaves (p14) are in rows on either side of the shoot with an extra row along the top flattened to the shoot and with the white underside uppermost, a useful feature for recognition.

Carolina Hemlock

Tsuga caroliniana Engelm.
Native to south-eastern United States, grown occasionally for ornament in northern states and in western Europe. Height to about 15m (50ft). Flowers (far left) are open in late April, males dark crimson, females pale pinkish lilac, both about 0·6cm (¼in) long. Cones (near left) are about 2·5cm (1in) long, opening when ripe. Leaves (p14) point out irregularly to the sides and above the shoot, narrower than other *Tsuga* species, with bright white bands beneath.

Chinese Hemlock

Tsuga chinensis (Franch.) Pritz.
Native to central and western China, grown in botanical collections. Height to about 12m (40ft) and may be rather bushy. Flowers (far left) open in late April, males yellow tinged purple, females dark pinkish purple, both about 0·6cm (¼in). Cones (near left) are up to about 2·5cm (1in) long, dark purplish ripening to brown. Leaves (p14) are similar to *T. heterophylla* but are lighter green above and greener below.

Northern Japanese Hemlock

Tsuga diversifolia (Max.) Mast.
Native to central and northern Japan, grown in botanical collections and some gardens. Height to about 24m (80ft). Flowers (far left) open in April, males dark crimson, females pink, about 0·3cm (⅛in). Cones (near left) are about 1·8cm (¾in), ripening from green to brown. Leaves (p14) are densely set, dark green above with 2 bright white bands underneath and have notched tips.

Western Hemlock

Tsuga heterophylla (Raf.) Sarg.
Native to north-western N. America, planted for its strong timber in northern and western Europe. Also cultivated for ornament in gardens and estates. Height to about 45m (148ft) and sometimes more, with a distinctively drooping leading shoot. Flowers (far left) open in late April or May, males dark crimson, females reddish purple, both about 0·3cm (⅛in) long. Cones (near left) are about 2·5cm (1in) long, dark bronzy green ripening to brown. Leaves (p14) are in 2 sets but point outwards and upwards. They are of varying lengths, dark green above with 2 bluish bands below and have rounded tips. Foliage has a strong aromatic smell when crushed.

Mountain Hemlock

Tsuga mertensiana (Bong.) Carr.
Native to the mountains of western N. America from Alaska south to California, of little value for timber but occasionally grown in eastern states and western and central Europe as an ornamental in large gardens. Height to about 21m (70ft) but may be much taller in the wild. Flowers (far left) open in late April, males dark rosy purple about 0·3cm (⅛in), female dark violet (though may be yellow green), slightly longer. Cones (near left) may be 5–7·5cm (2–3in), larger than any other *Tsuga* cone. They ripen from purple (or green) to brown when they open to release their seed. Leaves (p14) are set all round the shoot, blue-green on both surfaces.

Southern Japanese Hemlock

Tsuga sieboldii Carr.
Native to southern Japan, cultivated in botanical collections and some large gardens. Height to about 30m (100ft). Flowers (far left) open in April, males dark crimson, about 0·2cm (¹/₁₀in), females pale pink or purple, about 0·4cm (¹/₆in) long, nodding. Cones (near left) are about 2·5cm (1in) long, ripening from green to brown. Leaves (p14) are rather broad with a notched tip and 2 whitish bands below. Their arrangement look more irregular than on Northern Japanese Hemlock (*T. diversifolia*).

Ulmus family Ulmaceae, **Elm**
Deciduous trees with fruit surrounded by a leafy
wing and simple double-toothed lopsided leaves
arranged alternately.

Ulmus americana L. **American Elm or
White Elm**
Native to eastern N. America. Height to 36m
(120ft). Flowers in March on stems 1·2cm (½in)
long. Fruits oval, about 1·2cm (½in) long with a
notched tip. Leaves (p33) rough above with
light downy tufts in the vein axils beneath.

**Wych Elm or
Scotch Elm**

Ulmus glabra Huds.
Native to Europe (including Britain) and western
Asia. Its wood is hard, resistant to splitting and
wetting. Planted for ornament in Europe and
north-eastern N. America. Height to about 41m
(135ft). Flowers (near right) open in early March
in clusters about 1cm (½in) long. Fruits (far
right) are about 2·5cm (1in) across with the seed
in centre, ripen pale brown and fall in July.
Leaves (p34) are rough on the upper surface and
softly hairy beneath with very short stems almost
concealed by a curved base on one side. Bark is
smooth and grey becoming brownish grey with
cracks and furrows on mature trees.

Camperdown Elm

U. glabra 'Camperdown'
Commonly planted in European city and town
streets, parks and gardens and also occasionally
in north-eastern N. America. Height to around
12m (40ft) with distinctive tortuous growth and
mushroom shape. Flowers and fruit (near and far
right) are similar to *U. glabra* but show the zig-
zag hanging twigs. Leaves are larger than
U. glabra leaves, up to 20cm (8in) long and often
more lopsided.

Ulmus × hollandica Mill. 'Hollandica', synonym
U. major Sm. **Dutch Elm**
One of a group of hybrids between *U. glabra* and
U. minor. Height to about 35m (116ft). Flowers
open in late March, fruits about 1·8cm (¾in)
long with the seed touching the edge of the wing.
Leaves (p34) are broad, with dark green rough
upper surface and paler under surface with rough
hairs on the veins. New shoots are hairy. Bark is
dark grey and flaky.

**Huntingdon Elm or
Chichester Elm**

Ulmus × hollandica 'Vegeta',
synonym *U. vegeta* Lindl.
Planted in streets, parks and gardens. Height to
about 35m (116ft) with a dome-shaped crown.
Flowers (near right) open in early April and fruit
(far right) are set by late April, about 1·8cm
(¾in) long with seed in the centre, usually
marked by a reddish or crimson blotch. Leaves
(p34) are longer and narrower than

U. × hollandica 'Hollandica' and have longer
stems, 1·2–1·8cm (½–¾in). They are smooth
and shiny above with tufts of down in the axils
beneath. Young shoots are bright green and only
slightly hairy. Bark is grey or brown, and ridged.

European White Elm or Fluttering Elm

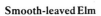

Ulmus laevis Pall.
Native to central Europe and western Asia, grown in botanical collections. Height to about 20m (65ft). Flowers (near right) open in March on unusually long stalks, allowing them to flutter in the wind, hence one of its common names. Fruits (far right) are set by May, about 1·2cm (½in) long with white hairs around their edges. Leaves (p34) are strongly lopsided, one side at the base having 2 or 3 extra veins. They are slightly downy above and paler and downy beneath. Bark is grey or brown with broad ridges and deep furrows and often with clusters of twiggy shoots forming burrs.

Smooth-leaved Elm

Ulmus minor Mill.,
synonym *U. carpinifolia* G. Suckow
Native to Europe (possibly including Britain), northern Africa and south-west Asia. Height to about 30m (100ft) with upright branches forming a dome-shaped crown. Flowers (near right) open in March, fruits (far right) are about 1·8cm (¾in) long with the seed near to the notched tip. Leaves (p34) are variable but always bright shiny green above with tufts of down in the axils beneath on a downy stalk. Bark is greyish brown with long ridges and furrows.
U. minor var. *cornubiensis* (Weston) Rehd., **Cornish Elm** This has a loosely conical crown, with shiny green cup-shaped leaves. To about 35m (116ft).
U. minor var. *sarniensis* (Loud.) Rehd., **Jersey Elm** or **Wheatley Elm** This has a neat conical crown and dark green leaves. To about 38m (126ft).

English Elm

Ulmus procera Salisb.,
synonym *U. campestris* Mill.
Native to Britain, once widespread in fields hedges parks and streets, but now devastated by Dutch Elm disease and being replaced by other species. Also planted in north-eastern United States. Its wood is hard and resists wetting and splitting. Height to about 30m (100ft), suckering freely to form new trees, often along a hedge. Flowers (near right) open in late February and early March and fruits (far right) are set by April and May, smaller than those of *U. glabra* with seed near the tip. Leaves (p29) are variable in shape, dark green and rough above with pale down on the main vein beneath on a short downy stalk. Bark (p220) is dark brown and cracked into small rectangular plates. Many localised forms occur in different parts of Britain.

Rock Elm or Cork Elm

Ulmus thomasii Sarg.
Native to north-eastern N. America, sometimes planted there for shade and ornament and occasionally in botanical collections in Europe. Its wood is hard and strong, once much used in N. America. Height to about 30m (100ft). Flowers (near right) open in March in long slender clusters, each flower stem about 1·2cm (½in) long. Fruits (far right) are about 1·2cm (½in) long and downy, ripening in May. Leaves (p33) are rough at first with downy undersides, becoming smooth, dark green and shiny above, paler and downy underneath. Twigs often have corky wings, though not shown in photographs. Bark is dark brownish grey, with broad flaked ridges and fissures.

California Laurel, California Bay or Headache Tree

Umbellularia californica (Hook. & Arn.) Nutt., family Lauraceae
An evergreen, native to the coastal region of California and Oregon, which has yielded a valuable timber, useful for house interiors. Sometimes grown in collections and gardens in Europe. Its foliage is strongly aromatic when crushed and is said to induce a sharp headache after inhaling it. Height to about 24m (80ft), sometimes shrubby. Flowers (far left) open in January (much later in cool climates) in 2–4 clusters of about 10. Each flower is about 0·6cm (¼in) across. Fruits (near left) are about 2·5cm (1in) long and ripen from yellowish green in August and September. Leaves (p32) are smooth, and uniformly pale green. They fade to yellow or orange before falling in their second season.

Common Prickly Ash or Toothache Tree

Zanthoxylum americanum Mill., family Rutaceae
Deciduous tree, native to eastern N. America, sometimes grown in European gardens. The North American Indians are said to have chewed the twigs and fruit to ease the pain of toothache. Height to about 8m (26ft) as a tree but usually a shrub. Flowers (near right) open in May or June. Fruits (far right) are about 0·6cm (¼in) long and ripen to black in October or November. Leaves (p55) have 5–11 leaflets, with small rounded teeth and branches bear stout sharp prickles.

Zelkova family Ulmaceae
A small group of deciduous trees, in the same family as the elms (*Ulmus*) but differing in having male and female flowers separate on the same tree and fruit in the form of small nutlets.

Caucasian Elm

Zelkova carpinifolia (Pall.) K. Koch
Native to the Caucasus mountains, planted in European parks and large gardens. Height to about 35m (116ft) with a distinctive shape (see silhouette). Flowers (far left) open in April, the males as clusters of anthers about 0·6cm (¼in) long, females smaller in the leaf axils at the tip of new growth. Fruits (near left) are about 0·6cm (¼in) long with 4 ridges. Leaves (p29) have 6–12 pairs of veins, dark green and often roughly hairy on upper surface with hairs on the main vein beneath. Bark (p220) is smooth, splitting into scales, to show exposed orange bark beneath.

**Keaki or
Japanese Zelkova**

Zelkova serrata (Thunb.) Mak.
Native to Japan, sometimes grown in large gardens and parks in Europe. Height to about 20m (65ft) or more. Flowers (far left) open in late April or May, males in leaf axils at base of new growth, about 0·4cm (⅙in) long, females smaller and green towards the tip of the shoot. Fruit is about 0·3cm (⅛in) and green. Leaves (p29) have longer stems than *Z. carpinifolia* and have 8–12 pairs of veins. They have more pointed teeth and colour yellow, orange and red in the autumn. Bark (near left) is smooth when young, becoming brown and orange and flaky when mature.

Bark is the outer layer of a tree trunk and provides protection to the nutrient carrying vessels beneath the surface. It is produced by a one cell thick layer known as the cork cambium. In some trees this lies in overlapping plates so that the bark breaks along the joins as the trunk expands, forming ridges as in Chestnut (*Castanea sativa*), or plates as in many of the pines (*Pinus*). On other trees it is a complete sheath, continually renewing itself and peeling off the surface in thin strips, as on Paper-bark Maple (*Acer griseum*) or Paper Birch (*Betula papyrifera*). Different species, therefore, have bark characteristics which may be useful when identifying a tree. All bark varies with the environment; for example, in cities they may be blackened by exhaust fumes or in very damp places they may be covered by moss or lichen. They may also differ according to age and growth of the specimen, so that a great deal of experience may be needed before making a positive identification. However, some are distinctive and easily recognised. A few photographs and descriptions are included in the text, but the following is a selection of interesting, attractive and/or distinctive barks.

Greek Fir *Abies cephalonica* (p61)

Nikko Fir *Abies homolepis* (p62)

Red Snake-bark Maple *Acer capillipes* (p66)

Paper-bark Maple *Acer griseum* (p69)

Horse Chestnut *Aesculus hippocastanum* (p81)

Common Alder *Alnus glutinosa* (p83)

Monkey Puzzle *Araucaria araucana* (p85)

Blue Birch *Betula coerulea-grandis* (p88)

Downy Birch *Betula pubescens* (p91)   **European Hornbeam** *Carpinus betulus* (p93)   **Sweet Chestnut** *Castanea sativa* (p95)

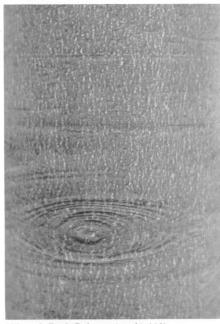

Common Hawthorn *Crataegus monogyna* (p108)   **Winter's Bark** *Drimys winteri* (p113)   **Cider Gum** *Eucalyptus gunnii* (p114)

Maidenhair Tree *Gingko biloba* (p120)   **Honey Locust** *Gleditsia triacanthos* (p121)   **Common Holly** *Ilex aquifolium* (p122)

Japanese Walnut *Juglans ailantifolia* (p125) **Black Walnut** *Juglans nigra* (p125) **European Larch** *Larix decidua* (p129)

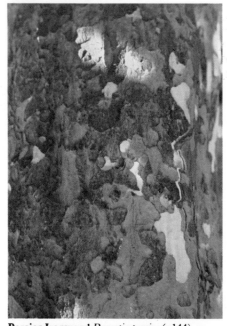

Roblé Beech *Nothofagus obliqua* (p142) **Persian Ironwood** *Parrotia persica* (p144) **Sitka Spruce** *Picea sitchensis* (p150)

Knobcone Pine *Pinus attenuata* (p153) **Lacebark Pine** *Pinus bungeana* (p154) **Corsican Pine** *Pinus nigra* var. *maritima* (p159)

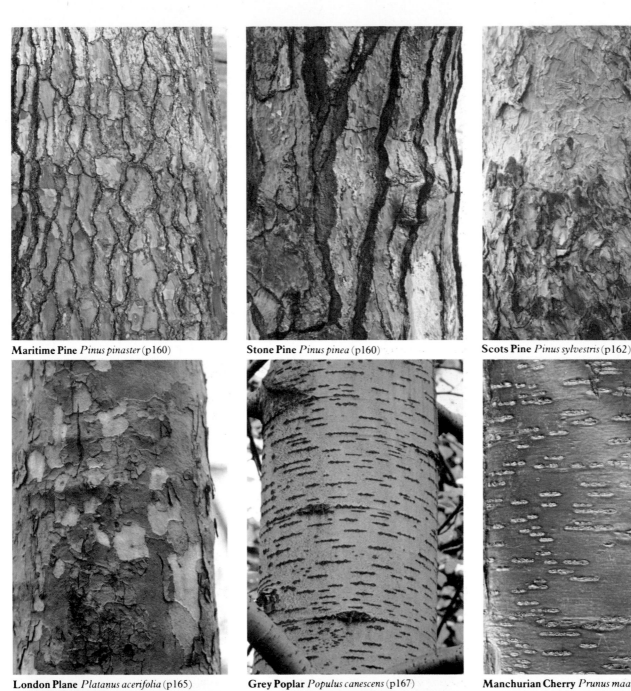

Maritime Pine *Pinus pinaster* (p160)

Stone Pine *Pinus pinea* (p160)

Scots Pine *Pinus sylvestris* (p162)

London Plane *Platanus acerifolia* (p165)

Grey Poplar *Populus canescens* (p167)

Manchurian Cherry *Prunus maackii* (p172)

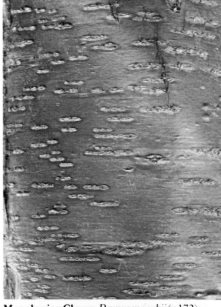

Common Pear *Pyrus communis* (p179)

Turkey Oak *Quercus cerris* (p181)

Holm Oak *Quercus ilex* (p183)

Cork Oak *Quercus suber* (p190)

False Acacia *Robinia pseudoacacia* (p192)

Coast Redwood *Sequoia sempervirens* (p196)

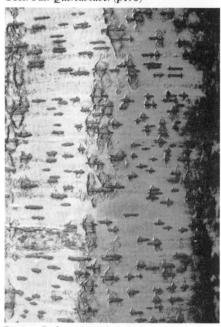
Rowan *Sorbus aucuparia* (p198)

Chinese Stewartia *Stewartia sinensis* (p202)

Swamp Cypress *Taxodium distichum* (p203)

Common Yew *Taxus baccata* (p204)

English Elm *Ulmus procera* (p213)

Caucasian Elm *Zelkova carpinifolia* (p215)

Index of Common Names

(Note – An index of botanical names has not been included, as the text entries are arranged alphabetically. Numbers in bold refer to the main text entry.)